W*i*LD

Knowledge

WiLD
Knowledge

Science,

Language, and

Social Life

in a Fragile

Environment

WILL WRIGHT

University of Minnesota Press • Minneapolis

Published by the University of Minnesota Press
2037 University Avenue Southeast, Minneapolis, MN 55414
Printed in the United States of America on acid-free paper.

Library of Congress Cataloging-in-Publication Data

Wright, Will.
    Wild knowledge : science, language, and social life in a fragile environment /
Will Wright.
      p. cm.
    Includes bibliographical references (p.   ) and index.
    ISBN 0-8166-2050-4 (cloth). — ISBN 0-8166-2051-2 (pbk.)
    1. Human ecology—Philosophy. 2. Knowledge, Sociology of. 3. Language and
languages. 4. Environmental policy. I. Title.
GF21.W75   1992
304.2—dc20   91-37574
                                                               CIP

The University of Minnesota is an
equal-opportunity educator and employer.

to Dhana, Rebecca, and Keith

Contents

Preface

As our environment deteriorates, we hear repeated warnings of impending ecological disasters, warnings that new productive and organizational structures are required—new social and economic commitments. Generally, these warnings remain quite abstract and vague, indicating that fundamental changes are necessary without being very clear about exactly what kinds of fundamental changes are possible. When specific recommendations are made, they tend to be strictly political and economic—more governmental regulation, less profit orientation, more individual responsibility, less private property, and so on. But the ecological problem always seems to be more complicated than this, more a profound issue of social order than a strategic issue of legal controls. In many ways it seems to be a problem with our legitimating idea of rationality. Industrial society is based on a political and organizational commitment to the idea of rationality, but as the planet becomes more committed to rationality, in the Enlightenment sense of science and individualism, it also seems to become more irrational, in the ecological sense of sustainability. Rational society seems to be disrupting itself systematically, and if so, then there is a fundamental problem with our legitimating idea of rationality, because this idea is legitimating ecological disaster in the name of reason. If our "rational" social order is inherently irrational, then we must either give up on it (as, for example, the "deep ecologists" recommend) or articulate a more coherent idea of rationality, an idea that will legitimate a more ecological and sustainable social order. In effect, we must try to retain the social benefits of a commitment to rationality—individuality, technology, democracy, criticism, and so on—without the apparent ecological indifference, and to do this we must be more careful and analytic about our legitimating notions of knowledge and reason.

This is the effort I undertake in this book, where I suggest that we can retain the benefits of rationality only by developing more coherent and ecological conceptions of knowledge and reason. In particular, I argue that our legitimating idea of reason, as we have inherited it from the Enlightenment, is grounded in the idea of scientific knowledge, and that scientific knowledge is both ecologically and conceptually incoherent. In industrial society we have essentially defined our ideas of knowledge and reason in terms of the scientific conception of objective nature, and while this may have made good historical sense (as a legitimating strategy against feudal Christianity), it no longer makes good social or ecological sense. According to science, the ultimate reference for valid knowledge is the external reality of objective nature, where nature is seen as the embodiment of pure explanatory rationality, that is, as mathematical, detached, and indifferent. In contrast, I argue that the legitimating ideas of knowledge and reason must be defined in terms of a social-natural reference, an ecological reference, and that such a reference can be only to the formal structure of language, as the structure that necessarily enables the possibility of social-natural interactions. The reference to nature, as an external mathematical reality, makes the idea of knowledge incoherent, and only a reference to language, as the structure that mediates between humans and their world, can establish a coherent, and thus an ecological, conception of knowledge.

The reference to objective nature has created a remarkable *technical* conception of knowledge, but what we need now is a remarkable *ecological* conception of knowledge, and such a conception requires that knowledge be understood as primarily an issue of language, rather than as primarily an issue of nature. As a formal structure, language is the enabling ground for both social life and knowledge, the structure that makes human social life and human knowledge possible. In this sense all efforts at explanation, including the scientific idea of nature, are first of all aspects of language, and so the idea of knowledge can be made coherent and ecological only through a reference to its own enabling structure, the formal structure of language. And through such a reference, the idea of knowledge must become "wild"—that is, reflexive and critical, as opposed to absolute and authoritative—because the validity of knowledge will become an issue of sustaining social life rather than of mirroring external reality. In particular, the reference to language will generate a *linguistic* approach to social theory, as opposed to a scientific, or *natural*, approach to social theory. In these terms a linguistic social theory will be committed to understanding both natural processes and social life from within a conceptual commitment to sustaining the possibility of language, which means from within a conceptual commitment to sustaining the possibility of social life.

For science, knowledge is primarily an issue of objective nature, not social life, and this has made social theory something like the bastard child of knowledge, a secondary and ambiguous form of knowledge, as opposed to the precise and definitive knowledge of nature. But this is an incoherent idea of knowledge, and it is incoherent because it cannot recognize that knowledge is as much an issue of social life as of natural processes, in the sense that assertions of knowledge are exactly the basis for organizing and legitimating social–natural interactions. If the idea of knowledge is to be coherent, it must recognize its own inherent social–natural dimensions, and this means that the understanding of social life must become as central to the idea of knowledge as the understanding of natural processes. From an ecological perspective, social theory must become linguistic, with a commitment to sustaining social–natural interactions, as opposed to scientific, with a commitment to mirroring objective reality. As an aspect of scientific knowledge, social theory can appear only as a befuddled, value-laden anomaly, but as an aspect of an ecological knowledge, social theory becomes a necessary conceptual complement to the explanation of natural processes.

In the legitimating context of science, both social theory and ecological concerns have been conceptually patronized, as biased and subjective, while technical proficiency has been conceptually honored, as neutral and objective. But in the last two or three decades there have been increasing cracks in the scientific facade of neutrality and objectivity, as well as in our Enlightenment confidence in scientific rationality and technology. The philosophers of science have had to abandon their epistemological claim of theory-neutral observations, leaving them in the position of accepting some kind of social reference within the idea of knowledge. Also, the historians of science have begun to focus on the political and legitimating commitments of the early scientists, including Newton himself, commitments that shaped the scientific conception of nature in accordance with certain economic and class interests. The philosophers and

historians of mathematics have increased their questioning of its ostensi-
ble purity and innocence, recognizing that the epistemology of observations cannot be rescued by the epistemology of mathematics. And the
physicists themselves, far earlier than the last three decades, have had to
incorporate the idea of consciousness into the equations of natural processes, through quantum mechanics, thus admitting a fundamental conceptual incoherence within the scientific idea of objective nature. From
another perspective, the idea of discourse analysis, as an emerging historical strategy, suggests that no specific conceptual issue, such as the
knowledge of nature, can be divorced from its concomitant dimensions
in political and institutional legitimation. Also in linguistics and literary
criticism, as well as in philosophy and artificial intelligence, there is increasing recognition that language is more complicated and encompass-
ing than science has told us, and that a full understanding of language
requires the abandoning of basic scientific assumptions. And finally, in
the schools of business and management there is increasing concern that
technical efficiency does not guarantee organizational efficiency, and that
organizations should become environments of learning and reflexivity
rather than of bureaucratic rigidity and hierarchy.

During the same decades, increasing attention has been focused on our
technological impacts on the environment, impacts that seem to be severely, and perhaps irreversibly, disrupting the ecological conditions that
support human life, including the possibility of language, knowledge,
and technology. We have tended to think of these technological impacts,
from a scientific perspective, as primarily an issue of politics, or of economics, or of technology out of control. I argue, in contrast, that they are
primarily an issue of the incoherence of scientific knowledge, as a form of
knowledge that cannot recognize its own legitimating commitments,
and thus can legitimate only technical, as opposed to ecological, practices. Scientific knowledge legitimates a scientific society, whether capitalist or socialist, and it is in terms of this legitimating conception of
social-natural interactions that we must begin to address our environmental dilemmas.

It is this overarching environmental concern, I suggest, that must begin to bring together and inform all of the various critiques of scientific
knowledge listed above, critiques that otherwise will always appear as
separate and specific concerns of essentially independent disciplines.
From an environmental perspective, all of these critiques—from the collapse of epistemology through quantum mechanics to the analyses of

both language and efficiency—can be seen as reflecting different aspects of the fundamental incoherence of scientific knowledge, as a legitimating, social-natural conception. And from this perspective these various critiques can be explored and combined in an effort to achieve a more coherent and ecological conception of knowledge. This is the effort I am making, an effort to apply a social and ecological perspective to the various conceptual and institutional conundrums of scientific knowledge, with a view toward articulating a *sustainable* notion of rationality, and thus of social order. As the world has become more committed to rationality, it has also become more confused about the idea of rationality, and it is my argument that this is an institutional and environmental confusion about *scientific* rationality, and that a more reflexive and ecological conception of rationality—a more *linguistic* conception—must be developed.

I have been working on this argument for a number of years, and it incorporates my work as a mathematician as well as my work in both the sociology of popular culture and the sociology of health. As a mathematician I was struck by how the appearance of rational coherence can be derived from essentially arbitrary foundations, and by how a formal mathematical structure would always appear as a set of arbitrary assumptions to the mathematician and as a basis for natural explanations to the physicist. My familiarity with mathematics was obviously useful for this argument about knowledge, and an implied aspect of this argument is that social theorists have been generally far too removed from, respectful of, and intimidated by mathematics (as the language of science) to undertake a serious social analysis of the scientific version of itself, as objective knowledge of reality. My work in popular culture is less obviously relevant to this argument, but that work—concerning the structural analysis of western movies—was basically about how humans explain their own social relationships to themselves, suggesting that we will always turn to a narrative structure, as opposed to a scientific (mathematical) structure, to explain our social relationships to ourselves. Narrative explanations always involve a reference to human life, which means they always involve a reference to the inherent goal of sustaining human life, and in this sense there is an apparent correlation between our conceptual dependence, as language users, on narrative explanations and our institutional requirement, as language users, for ecological explanations. In essence, narrative and ecological explanations must have the same formal structure, but I do not explicitly develop this explanatory correlation in this argument about knowledge, for reasons of space and complexity. Nevertheless, this apparent correlation certainly informs my analysis of scientific knowledge, and it shows how the issues of popular culture are not that distinct from the issues of scientific and ecological knowledge.

The analytic work on this explanatory correlation has yet to be done, and when it is, it will almost certainly focus on the conceptual issue of health, as the obvious reference that defines the idea of sustaining human life, the obvious inherent goal of both narrative and ecological explanations. In my previous analysis of the idea of health I argued that medical knowledge, unlike scientific knowledge, involves an explicit social reference, and this is an argument I extend, in this present work, to ecological knowledge, relying heavily on an analogy between the idea of health and the idea of sustainability. In this way all of my previous work—the mathematical analysis of symbols, the structural analysis of narrative, and the conceptual analysis of health—has gone into this argument about a "wild," ecological knowledge, an argument that suggests that the explanatory structure of social life (narrative and health) should begin to take institutional and legitimating precedence over the explanatory structure of scientific nature (mathematics).

This book is the result of a lengthy project, and I am indebted to many people for their encouragement and criticism, including Doug McAdam, Carrie Baldwin, Elliot Layton, Sonny Jerkic, Susan Allen-Mills, Debbie Soule, Grainne Goodwin, Rick Johnstone, James O'Conner, Neil Smelser, Ellen Basso, Steve Wall, Chris Findlayson, Evie Place, Caroline New, Norman Freeman, Keith Lovin, Doug Steeples, Neil Hughes, Pauletta Otis, Will Coe, John Crowder, Norman Linton, Steven Kaplan, Dhana Broser, Alexandra Todd, Boyd Littrell, Brian O'Brien, Rick Gardner, Gary Means, Ron Thorn, Peter Sinclair, Roger Peters, Barbara Neis, Robert Alford, Stanley Aronowitz, Evelyn Fox Keller, and Vine Deloria, Jr. I particularly want to thank Lisa Freeman, at the University of Minnesota Press, for her interest and support, and Micki Markowski and Sharon Pruett for their help in preparing the manuscript.

Introduction: Ecological Incoherence

It is only somewhat comforting to realize that environmental destruction is becoming more of a general social concern than nuclear Armageddon. As the recognition of environmental dangers mounts—the greenhouse effect, the depletion of the ozone, the accumulation of toxic wastes, the pollution of food, the destruction of the forests—we hear increasing calls for the redirecting and restructuring of social and economic priorities: new productive strategies, international commitments, a planetary awareness. In this context new political lines are drawn and alliances formed—environmentalists begin talking with representatives of the nuclear power industry, environmental imperialism becomes a new international topic, environmental concerns begin to take precedence over national autonomy—as the emerging "tragedy of the commons" seems to entail a reexamination of such Enlightenment notions as justice, equality, and progress. A civilization built upon fossil fuels has to replace them; prosperity built upon waste and pollution has to incorporate conservation and cleanliness; and a social order committed to endless economic growth has to accept productive limits. The need for new social directions and new economic perspectives is apparent, and increasingly articulated, but exactly what does this mean? What kind of new directions and perspectives are possible, or available? What would it mean to restructure and reorganize industrial, or even postindustrial, society? How do we get there from here, or how do we even begin to conceptualize the possibility of getting there from here?

1

As it turns out, this is an ambiguous and complicated question, since it is not always clear what issue is being addressed. Do we want a political answer, an economic answer, a technological answer, a moral answer, a religious answer? Generally, at least, we want an answer that tells us we can somehow eliminate the negative aspects of industrial society—rapacious destruction and pollution—without necessarily losing the positive aspects—technology, reason, critical thought, human rights, citizen participation, productivity. With a few exceptions, the guiding image of such environmental concerns is that we should be able, through rational analysis and political attention, to achieve environmental sanity without sacrificing all our modern possibilities and achievements. Put another way, we don't want to throw the baby out with the bathwater. There are, of course, exceptions, commentators who recommend abandoning our modern "benefits" in favor of some more appropriate, biocentric, religious, or traditional social order. But even these commentators appeal to the central values of modern society—the values of reason and criticism—in order to authorize their principled rejection of that society.

The underlying issue, of course, is scientific knowledge, the knowledge that has encouraged and generated much of the problematic technology, as well as the social commitments to reason and criticism. When we are told that we must fundamentally change our social priorities and restructure our institutions, does this include a rejection of scientific knowledge? Is science part of the problem, or is it simply a neutral tool, presenting factual, technical possibilities, with no inherent environmental implications, either positive or negative? If it is the latter, then our environmental dilemmas can potentially be solved by science as easily as they can be generated by science. In this case the social issue is moved to a separate domain, the domain of political will and economic interests, where only the *applications* of scientific knowledge warrant critical attention. But if it is the former, where does that leave us? In what sense can we reject science, as a form of knowledge? And if such a thing were possible, what would it mean? Would it mean that we must simply give up on the possibility of valid, objective knowledge? Or would it mean that we must find another, more environmentally compatible form of valid knowledge? And if it were the latter, would that mean that we were rejecting scientific knowledge simply because of external social problems, or because of internal conceptual problems? Would science have to be seen as socially wrong but conceptually valid, or would it have to be seen as conceptually wrong—wrong about nature, wrong as knowledge?

In this book I will argue that science is indeed the problem and that science is indeed conceptually wrong, wrong about nature and wrong about knowledge. But this is not a book about the environment; rather, it is a book about the conceptual form and the social role of knowledge. More precisely, it is about the need for incorporating an ecological reference in any coherent version of knowledge. Much of the argument will involve a demonstration that scientific knowledge, as our modern version of valid knowledge, does not and cannot include such an ecological reference, and therefore cannot be a coherent form of knowledge. Scientific knowledge is not coherent in the sense that it involves conceptual confusions and conundrums that cannot be resolved, confusions generated by the defining assumption of an external, objective nature. These inherent confusions have been recognized by scientific epistemology (the failure of incorrigible access, of theory-independent observations, and so on) as well as by physics itself (as quantum physics, the equations of consciousness), but none of this has disrupted our acceptance of science as valid knowledge, indeed, as our cultural definition of knowledge. Rather, science has become even more accepted as valid knowledge, not because it is free from confusion and incoherence, but because it has been so successful at technology, and thus at social legitimation. Scientific technology has provided a de facto basis for the credibility of scientific knowledge, so that the intractable conceptual dilemmas of the scientific assumptions about observation and nature have been relegated to the esoteric domain of epistemology. The conceptual confusions are recognized, but they are seen as "merely" epistemological, since the productive technology of scientific knowledge works so well.

It is increasingly less clear, however, that scientific technology does "work so well." Environmental dilemmas and disasters seem to be multiplying, generally resulting from the remarkably productive use of industrial technology, the technology of a scientific society. It is becoming apparent that scientific technology could appear to "work well" only so long as resources could seem to be unlimited and pollution could seem to be trivial. Scientific knowledge has indeed been productive, but it has also been destructive, with the latter impact taking somewhat longer to appear than the former. Generally we have accepted the productive contributions to be a consequence of science itself—its accuracy and validity about nature—while we have attributed the more destructive aspects of scientific technology to social factors—power, class, politics, profit. In this way the de facto basis for the validity of scientific knowledge is difficult to refute: science does "work well," and when it does not, it is not the fault of science, but rather the fault of society.

Social theory has repeatedly attacked the social issues of power, politics, and profit, as well as the social dimensions of technology and the environment. But social theory has not generally focused its attention on scientific knowledge itself, since scientific knowledge is, by definition (scientific definition), about nature, and nature is external to and independent of social concerns. As a result, social theory can be, and has been, quite critical of various forms of industrial institutions, the institutions that have developed with and are based on scientific knowledge. But social theory has not been very critical of scientific knowledge as such, and in particular it has not been very critical of the scientific idea of nature. Through this idea of objective, detached nature, scientific knowledge has claimed to be conceptually detached from the institutional analyses of social theory, so that such things as electrons and the weak force are simply placed in a separate conceptual domain, the domain of nature as opposed to society. And while this idea of nature may appear to be conceptually confused, it has been so culturally successful, both as scientific technology and as scientific knowledge, that social theory has been willing to define itself in terms of these separate conceptual domains. As a consequence, social theory can be critical of only the issues within its legitimate domain, the issues of social relations; it cannot be critical of scientific nature and scientific knowledge.

We live in a scientific society, and science has been accepted as a valid basis for knowledge, reason, and truth, in part because of its epistemology of neutral observations and in part because of its productive technology. But the epistemology is in disarray, and the technology is increasingly suspect, for environmental reasons. We are beginning to recognize that our greatest success with knowledge may also be our greatest failure, that the productive success of science may also entail ecological disaster. Our environmental dilemmas are forcing us, at the level of social theory, to question the basic structure of our productive technology, not simply its various institutional contexts. This structure is derived from scientific knowledge—from physics, with its electrons and weak force—and scientific knowledge has lost its epistemological support, the very support that asserted its conceptual immunity from social theory. The idea of a pure, objective "nature" makes no sense—such a "nature" can never be observed—and without this supporting idea science is no longer conceptually credible, even if it is technically proficient. The idea of objective nature is no longer coherent, and while this incoherence could be culturally ignored in the wake of the technical (productive) successes of science, it cannot be ignored in the wake of the technical (environmental) failures of science.

If the idea of objective nature is incoherent, then the technology, and social actions, derived from that idea will also, very probably, be incoherent, and in particular they will probably be ecologically and socially debilitating. Moreover, the recognition of this incoherence removes the conceptual barrier that has inhibited social theory from analyzing scientific knowledge, since it means that the idea of "objective nature" was never very objective in the first place. As a result, social theory must begin, belatedly, to analyze the conceptual assumptions underlying scientific knowledge, and to show that these assumptions are eminently social and institutional, rather than purely natural and perceptual. This is the analysis I will undertake in this book, an analysis that involves a social (and ecological) critique of the scientific idea of knowledge. More specifically, I will critique science, and particularly physics, from the perspective of a coherent idea of knowledge. For various reasons (generally political and social, as I will argue), our modern society has essentially identified science with the idea of knowledge, but science is a particular form of knowledge, with particular assumptions, and the idea of knowledge is a very powerful evaluative term, like reason and truth, imposing all sorts of legitimacy and credibility on the particular claims associated with it. Part of my argument, then, will be to separate the idea of science from the idea of knowledge, in order to show not only that science is an incoherent form of knowledge, but also that an alternative form of knowledge must and can be developed, a coherent, and therefore ecological and sustainable, form of knowledge.

Scientific knowledge incorporates conceptual confusions and incoherences through its notion of an objective external nature, a notion that has generated such conundrums as the mind/body dilemma, the mysteries of mathematics, and the role of consciousness in physics. I will analyze these various confusions from a social perspective, because in general scientific knowledge has categorically denied the idea that "knowledge" is an inherently *social* concept. For science—and specifically for physics, as the science that underlies all the others—knowledge is exclusively an issue of *nature*, where nature is defined as categorically nonsocial. It was this idea of nature that enabled the new possibility of scientific knowledge, as opposed to the intrinsically social conception of religious (Christian) knowledge from which science emerged. For various political and economic reasons the idea of objective nature could be used successfully to establish an alternative version of knowledge, and thus to legitimate new forms of social institutions and power in the name of (scientific) reason and truth.

Clearly the scientific idea of nature was socially and politically effective, but it was also conceptually incoherent, and this incoherence revolved around the effort to detach the idea of nature from any conceptual involvement with social life. For a while, in the glow of technological achievements, this incoherence could be set aside and ignored, but it is an incoherence about the understanding of natural-social interactions, and now this incoherence is being felt as ecological disruption. Consequently, if the ecological dilemmas of rational, industrial society are to be addressed successfully, they must first be addressed at the level of our fundamental conception of knowledge, the conception of objective nature and scientific observations. More specifically, we must bring the idea of social life back into our idea of valid knowledge, so that all assertions of knowledge involve a reference to both nature and society, and to their interaction, rather than strictly a reference to nature. In this way the demand for a coherent idea of knowledge will also, ultimately, involve a demand for an ecological, social-natural idea of knowledge.

Knowledge and Legitimation

In order to articulate such an alternative, ecological idea of knowledge, we must begin by looking more carefully at the idea of knowledge itself, and at how claims about knowledge always involve claims about social life. In particular, knowledge is always a *legitimating* idea, in the sense that assertions of knowledge always assert what is correct, what is proper, what is legitimate. If an explanatory or causal statement is accepted as knowledge, then it is accepted as an aspect of *truth*, and as a basis for *reason*, for rational action, where knowledge, truth, and reason are all interrelated, legitimating ideas. In this way an assertion of knowledge always legitimates certain kinds of actions and certain kinds of institutions. If something is known, in the sense of known to be true, then we are supposed to act on the basis of it, and if we do not then we are being foolish or irrational or disruptive. Thus an assertion of knowledge is always an assertion about "proper" social actions; religious knowledge has always incorporated and depended upon this legitimating function. Religious knowledge is always as much concerned with telling people what to do as with explaining natural phenomena, and so its explanations are always moral and instructive. Science, however, has always denied this social and legitimating aspect of knowledge, by definition, and so its explanations are always presented as objective and morally neutral. Certainly science has had social and legitimating effects, but these effects, according to science, are irrelevant to the validity of science as knowledge—the knowledge of nature—whereas the social effects of religious knowledge are central to its validity. Scientific knowledge must be validated exclusively on its own terms, within the domain of "pure" nature, so that no social, or social-natural, concerns can possibly affect the evaluation of that knowledge. In this way science disconnects the legitimating aspect of knowledge from the explanatory aspect of knowledge, and thus, I will argue, makes the idea of knowledge incoherent.

In the context of early modern Europe this scientific idea of knowledge was certainly effective and probably necessary, as a conceptual support for an attack on Christian knowledge and feudal relationships, and for the emergence of a new social and political order. Certainly scientific knowledge, as physics, contributed to the legitimation of new individualistic and market institutions. Early physics was most effective at social and political legitimation, not natural explanation, and yet we have continued to accept the scientific version of itself, and thus to believe that this legitimating function was and is irrelevant to science as knowledge. Indeed, this idea of science as socially neutral is more convincing now, in the twentieth century, than it was then, in the seventeenth century, when the political aspects of science were more apparent. In the seventeenth century, in the context of feudal institutions, the new scientific idea of nature was obviously directed at social legitimation, whereas today, in the context of scientific institutions, the same idea of nature can appear as much more austere and detached, and as definitively indifferent to social concerns. But this idea of objective nature has always been inherently legitimating, today as well as then, and thus it has always been an implicit social theory, a social theory that derives its conceptual credibility from the denial of any social concerns. Scientific knowledge, and specifically physics, has always been a disguised social theory, with inherent legitimating commitments to particular institutional structures, but science must categorically deny these inherent social commitments, and so it has been difficult to see physics as a social theory. If we were to see physics that way, then we would have to change our idea of physics, as well as our ideas of knowledge and nature, for it would mean that the scientific knowledge of nature is intrinsically social and political, despite the internal denials of science itself. Indeed, it would mean that the concepts of physics—electron, force, charge, spin, and so on—would all involve inherent legitimating references, references that tell us what kind of social actions are appropriate in a world explained by physics.

In the following chapters I will argue that physics is indeed such a social theory but can never admit it, and thus that scientific knowledge can only be incoherent, both conceptually and environmentally. As the fundamental science of nature, physics contains inherent institutional commitments, and these commitments, I will argue, have provided the basic legitimating support for our modern industrial order, whether capitalist or socialist. Physics has always been as much an issue of social legitimation as of natural explanation, and its historical success at social legitimation has tended to cover up both its inherent social commitments and its inherent conceptual confusions. Science has been remarkably effective at both institutional legitimation and technological production, and so its internal incoherence has been easily set aside (relegated to philosophy) until recently—until, that is, this conceptual incoherence began to appear as ecological incoherence. Now we must begin to take the conceptual confusions of science more seriously, and to recognize that they are essentially *social* confusions, confusions arising from the effort to define a nonsocial, nonlegitimating idea of knowledge. Knowledge is inherently legitimating, and so any coherent idea of knowledge must incorporate a reference to social life. In particular, it must incorporate an ecological reference, a reference to the social-natural conditions that support social life, and it is exactly the possibility of such a conceptual reference that physics has categorically denied. Science has systematically, but effectively, misunderstood the idea of knowledge, and through this misunderstanding physics has essentially legitimated modern social life. Now, however, in the context of our environmental dilemmas, we must begin to correct this misunderstanding, which means we must begin to analyze physics as a social theory, and to articulate a more coherent and more ecological conception of knowledge.

In this discussion I will concentrate on physics, as opposed to chemistry or biology, because physics is the fundamental science, the science that underlies all the rest. Physics is fundamental in the sense that it defines the idea of a mathematical, lawlike nature, the idea that characterizes scientific knowledge, the idea that all efforts at knowledge must refer to if they are to be called science. Thus in order for biology to be accepted fully as science, it was necessary for the processes of life to escape from the mysteries of vitalism and be explained physically, in terms of the mechanisms of the double helix. Sciences such as biology and psychology may have special explanatory concepts (evolution and perception, for example) that cannot be strictly reduced to the concepts of physics, but physics still establishes the basic conceptual ground on which these sciences operate, the ground of objective nature. Physics establishes the fundamental conceptual domain of scientific knowledge, and all the other sciences explore particular explanatory issues from within the basic conceptual assumptions of physics. As physicist Ernest Rutherford once commented, "All science is either physics or stamp collecting."

Physics defines the natural world that scientific knowledge explains, and science fails as coherent knowledge because it fails to recognize, by definition, the relevance of social concerns to the validity of its natural concepts and explanations. If a conception of knowledge is to be coherent, it must incorporate the possibility of evaluating knowledge claims according to social as well as natural criteria. (In this sense the distinction between social and natural phenomena is reasonable but not absolute: social processes are those over which human beings seem to have some direct, conscious control, and natural processes are those over which human beings seem to have little if any direct, conscious control. This distinction is experiential and probably universal, in one form or another, but the experience of a social–natural difference does not entail the categorical conceptual separation demanded by science.) Science refers its validity as knowledge only to natural criteria, which means only to the local and technical issues of predictability and manipulation. For this reason science is remarkably good at very technical and specific concerns, such as electricity and genetics, and remarkably bad at more social and general concerns, such as ecological compatibility and sustainable production. Given its defining idea of nature, science must remain essentially a technical, and nonecological, conception of knowledge.

Religious knowledge, on the other hand, always refers the validity of its explanations to some kind of social criteria, typically criteria involving traditional practices and values. Indeed, in this discussion I will assume that religious knowledge is exclusively an issue of religious, traditional societies, such as feudal and tribal societies, and not an issue of the beliefs and theologies associated with the religious organizations of our modern, scientific societies. In this way I will assume that religious knowledge, like scientific knowledge, is primarily an issue of legitimating its own particular institutions, not of simply offering particular moral codes to individuals in a nonreligious society. In these terms a religious version of knowledge is more concerned with maintaining a particular form of traditional order than with technical achievements, and there is no sense in which the validity of the knowledge is independent of that particular traditional order. Thus religious knowledge tends to maintain particular social practices without much technical incentive, and scientific knowledge tends to encourage technical proficiency without much concern for maintaining particular practices, or even for sustaining the ecological possibility of social life. Religion tends to commit knowledge to a specific tradition and science tends to commit it to unrestrained technology, and they manage to do this by focusing the validity of knowledge primarily on either social or natural criteria, respectively.

In these terms, then, a coherent and ecological form of knowledge must incorporate both social *and* natural criteria for validity, criteria that evaluate knowledge claims in terms of the interactions between social practices and natural processes. Such criteria would enable the validity of knowledge to be determined, in part, by the legitimating effects of natural explanations on the social world, as well as by the ecological effects of legitimated actions on the natural world. Religious knowledge makes it difficult to legitimate social change in terms of valid explanations, and scientific knowledge makes it difficult to legitimate ecological sensitivity in terms of valid explanations. If knowledge is to be made coherent, it must be made social–natural, in an ecological sense, and this means it must be made *reflexive*, where the criteria for the validity of explanations include a critical evaluation of the social-natural effects of those explanations, as legitimated social actions. The idea of knowledge must be understood as necessarily incorporating reflexive criteria, so that the validity of knowledge becomes in part dependent on the social impacts and consequences of that knowledge (as well as on such things as predictability, reliability, and technical success).

This kind of reflexivity will make knowledge absolutely *critical*, in the sense that the possibility of criticism against accepted explanations will be made more legitimate than the explanations themselves. Reflexive knowledge will legitimate the possibility of criticism more fundamentally than it will legitimate the particular explanations themselves, or the particular institutions they support. Put another way, knowledge must become more a reflexive issue of legitimate critical access than an objective issue of some absolute reality, whether external, lawlike nature or all-powerful, controlling gods. In terms of such an absolute reality, knowledge must at some point reject the possibility of legitimate social or ecological criticism, since valid explanations are absolute, regardless of their effects. (This is what makes some scientists say that physics will still be right about nature even if its technology destroys us.) It is this kind of absolute truth, and the associated denial of criticism, that a reflexive knowledge must dismantle, in the name of ecological, social–natural criteria for knowledge. Reflexive knowledge will evaluate the legitimacy of criticism over any postulated reality, and in this way the idea of knowledge can be turned away from some absolute reality and can begin to reflect on its own continued possibility, the possibility of sustaining social life through valid knowledge.

From Health to Sustainability

Thinking of knowledge in this way, as reflexive and sustainable, may seem somewhat complicated and abstract, but in fact it is a rather familiar cultural attitude toward knowledge, or at least toward a certain kind of knowledge. This is the way we generally think about achieving medical knowledge concerning the issues of health, or rather it is the way we must necessarily, as fragile physiological beings, think about the issues of health despite the best *scientific* efforts of medicine. As an aspect of science, medicine tends to approach the issue of health in terms of an image of objective natural (physiological) processes, processes that are physically and universally manipulable. As human beings, however, we tend to think about health reflexively, not objectively, as an issue more of trial and error than of natural truths. Thus, although we are respectful of scientific medicine, because of its apparent successes, we are also willing, culturally, to reject certain medical claims, despite their scientific legitimacy, if we find them to be illegitimate with respect to the achievement of health. We have done this often, around such issues as thalidomide, DES, the swine flu vaccine, the intrauterine device, acupuncture, nutrition, and holistic medicine. And in general, medicine, after some (or much) "scientific" resistance, has tended to adjust its version of legitimate medical knowledge to include these nonscientific approaches to health, rather than maintain its "scientific" position of absolute explanatory authority.

Consider a possible situation. Suppose you were concerned about your heart, and a doctor, upon examination, told you that without medical intervention it would soon fail, but that she could intervene in such a way as to guarantee its continued functioning. She could cut it out, encase it in plastic, hook it up to some tubes, pumps, and machines, and it would work for many more years. Such an offer would probably make you want to change doctors, and perhaps report your doctor to the authorities, because she had misunderstood your concern, and indeed had misunderstood the very idea of the heart, as an issue of medicine and health and human beings. But you would also feel that this would be technically possible, that this was not a failure of technical knowledge but rather a failure of valid or coherent knowledge, of medical knowledge. You would not feel that her knowledge of the heart was technically wrong so much as that she had *missed the point* of such knowledge, that the heart has to be understood in the context of the body and of social activity, not just as a separate, independent organ. Even as nonspecialists we intuitively understand that legitimate medical knowledge must ultimately refer to a context of social participation, and this understanding gives us effective critical leverage over medical science, leverage that has been used in debates over women's health issues, in exposing routine recommendations for unnecessary surgery, and in discussions of alternative practices such as acupuncture, nutrition therapy, and holistic strategies.

This means that the idea of health is a more fundamental reference for medical knowledge than the idea of objective nature, despite the obvious contributions that a scientific approach has made to the understanding of health. Medical practice is more fundamentally legitimated in terms of the social–natural idea of health than in terms of the biological idea of the body, even to the degree that scientific medicine can be legitimately criticized *as valid knowledge* in the name of health. In this sense, *health* is a reflexive term, and as the fundamental reference for medical knowledge it legitimates continued critical access more than it legitimates specific kinds of explanations and practices. The idea of health is certainly compatible with a scientific approach to knowledge, but only to the degree that health maintains its critical legitimacy over the scientific idea of biological "truth." And *health* is an intrinsically social term, so that the cultural criteria for health in any society are as much about the possibility of social interaction as they are about the proper functioning of physiological processes. This is why we tend to call people "vegetables" whose physiological functioning has become absolutely separated from the possibility of social interaction. And this is why such social issues as stress, midwifery, and nutrition (with regard to food additives, chemicals, and so on) can often redirect, through cultural pressure, the more strictly physiological and nonsocial focus of scientific medicine.

In general we tend to think of medical practice as an art as much as a science, because the objective detachment of science cannot be directly applied to a domain dominated by the inherently social and essentially normative notion of health. But this has not meant a complete social resistance to all scientific efforts to develop effective medical technology. Rather, it has meant that such scientific technology can be legitimated only in terms of the nonscientific, reflexive notion of health. Thus we can legitimate certain kinds of surgery and drugs and genetic intervention, but we cannot legitimate Nazi or Tuskegee experiments or certain other kinds of genetic intervention, at least not for very long and not in public. Because of the dominating notion of health, we cannot seek physiological knowledge strictly for its own sake, but only for the sake of achieving individual health, even though we may not be, and may not be able to be, absolutely clear on what that means. Clearly the idea of health includes different definitions, both in our culture and across cultures, but it cannot be defined independently of some image of ordinary social participation, an image that necessarily includes both social and natural criteria. It is for this reason that medicine has not been able to define health in strictly scientific and physiological terms, even though it has tried with dedication. In essence, people tend to know when they are not healthy even though they may not be able to define the term exactly, and they can use this experiential knowledge as a legitimate critical reference against scientific medicine even when they are willing to accept, for the same reasons, the general principles of scientific medicine.

The idea of health provides this general critical reference, against all medical practice, because we are all, as human beings, necessarily familiar with our own social and physical fragility. We all experience, as part of daily life, the need for a notion of health as a basis for judgments of social-natural interactions, a notion that legitimates both certain medical practices and the possibility of criticizing those practices. It is the necessity of this experience that requires a reflexive, social-natural reference for medical knowledge, despite intense institutional efforts to incorporate health into the domain of objective science. At the level of individual experience the idea of health legitimates the possibility of criticizing established knowledge, through a reflexive concern with sustaining the possibility of individual life. Thus the relationship of health to medical knowledge, as a limited domain of knowledge, provides a familiar model for a reflexive image of knowledge in general, for knowledge in its most fundamental, legitimating sense. In the case of medicine, the necessity of reflexive knowledge is often in conflict with the more general scientific idea of objective knowledge, where scientific knowledge is understood as incorporating all legitimate forms of knowledge, including medicine. And in this case, because of our cultural confidence in science, we have tended to try to force medicine to become more scientific (strictly physiological, more human experiments, and so on), rather than using the model of health to try to make all knowledge (the idea of knowledge) more reflexive.

If we try to do the latter, however, which is the argument of this book, then we will begin to make more sense of the idea of knowledge as well as legitimate more sustainable social practices. In general, we will be able to use the legitimating relationship of *health* to *medicine* as a conceptual model for articulating a similar legitimating relationship between the idea of *ecological sustainability* and the idea of *knowledge*. The analogy will not be exact, because we have historically been willing to consider medicine as an art, that is, as a special case that somehow escapes the rigor of real knowledge. And we have done the same kind of thing with our understanding of the relationship of social science to natural science. For this reason medicine and social science have been something like the black sheep of real scientific knowledge. But now we should try to reverse the legitimating pressure, in the sense of requiring all knowledge to be modeled on the reflexive idea of health, rather than requiring medical knowledge to be modeled on the objective idea of scientific nature. This would mean that science, rather than medicine, would appear as odd and incoherent, and it would mean that we would have to change fundamentally our cultural image of valid knowledge, the image given to us by science. We would have to rethink our explanations of natural processes, and to understand that these explanations, like the explanations of physiological health, are always conceptually intertwined with the explanations and legitimations of social practices. In general, we would have to recognize that nature can be coherently conceptualized only in terms of a reflexive and ecological reference, a reference that enables natural explanations to incorporate a validating consideration of their own social-natural effects, as legitimating explanations.

The idea of health has necessarily resisted the scientific pressure to become objective because we are all so directly familiar with the fragility of our bodies. We simply cannot accept, as an issue of ordinary experience, an absolute, nonreflexive reference for legitimate medical knowledge. We do not have the same kind of ordinary familiarity with the fragility of our environment, however; indeed, we are most familiar with the notion that our environment, our planet, is far too indifferent and immense for our mundane social actions to affect it seriously. We have normally experienced our natural environment as ordered by forces that are absolute, and thus well beyond our meager human capacity to disrupt or subvert, as opposed to influence or annoy or manipulate. Moreover, in scientific knowledge we have codified this normal experience into a conception of an absolute, indifferent reality, the reality of objective, immune nature. It is through this conception of objective nature that we have generated the technological achievements and legitimated the institutional practices of science. But now we must begin to recognize that our natural environment is not absolute and immune, and that we must begin to conceptualize it as fragile, consciously, in the same way we have always understood our bodies to be fragile, intuitively. Unlike in the case of our routine experience of our bodies, we have not had millennia to experience the increasing fragility of our environment. As a result, we must begin a conscious conceptual effort to incorporate this modern experience into our legitimating idea of knowledge, just as we have always, of necessity, incorporated our experience of bodily fragility into our legitimating idea of health. We must begin to think of natural knowledge, and to legitimate social practices, in terms of a reflexive conception of sustainability, just as we have generally thought of medical knowledge, and legitimated medical practices, in terms of a reflexive conception of health. And when we do, we will have to recognize that scientific knowledge, and specifically physics, is fundamentally incoherent and mistaken, not because it cannot be productive and technical and legitimating, but because it is fundamentally wrong about nature.

Language and Reflexivity

This is the general argument of the book, a critique of science from an ecological perspective, a critique that depends upon the articulation of a more coherent and reflexive idea of knowledge. If the idea of knowledge is to become more coherent, it must be understood as inherently social-natural, rather than as categorically natural. In particular, social theory must become as central to the idea of knowledge as natural theory, rather than relegated to a second-class, derivative status, as it has been in the context of scientific knowledge. Knowledge is as much about legitimating social actions as it is about explaining natural processes, and thus it is as much about social institutions as it is about effective technology. But science, as physics, has distorted this social aspect of knowledge, with debilitating ecological consequences. This distortion is contained in the image of objective nature as the fundamental reference for knowledge, and so we must articulate another, a more coherent and reflexive, reference for knowledge, a reference that will absolutely enable ecological criticism rather than only technical proficiency. And the articulation of such a reference must be modeled upon our conceptual familiarity with the reflexive idea of health, so that the idea of knowledge can be referred to the reflexive idea of sustainability, the idea of understanding and legitimating sustainable social-natural interactions.

This reference, I will argue, will turn out to be the formal, enabling structure of *language*, in the sense that language underlies and constitutes the very possibility of *human* social life, including knowledge, institutions, and social-natural interactions. Indeed, language constitutes the possibility of conceptualizing "nature" and "human beings" as things that are in some sense independent but yet have to interact effectively. In this sense language enables effective and reliable human actions in a world that is both independent and inherently amenable to language, and it does so through a formal structure of necessary conceptual commitments, commitments that formally constrain all particular cultural efforts at knowledge. These commitments are *formal* in the sense that they are not substantive: they are inherent in the formal structure of language and therefore they necessarily shape the abstract *form*, not the particular substance, of all efforts at knowledge. This is a formal and *active* idea of language, where language is seen as formally organizing human social life, and it is intended to contrast with our more standard scientific idea of language, where language is seen as a formal and *passive* structure — syntax, semantics, phonetics — a structure that is passively available to, but does not define or organize, the human beings who use it. The central issue here, as I will develop it later, is whether human beings can be defined independently of language or whether they cannot. If they can, then the idea of being human is logically prior to the idea of language, and language must be understood as something that is available to, but does not enable and constitute, human beings. But if language characterizes and constitutes human beings, then the idea of language must be logically prior to the idea of being human, and both human beings and human society must be understood in terms of the active and organizing structure of language. I will argue for the latter view of language, and in this sense suggest that the idea of language, not the idea of nature, can provide the only coherent reference for knowledge, a reference that is both ecological and reflexive.

Language enables social (human) actions on the world, and that means that the world must be understood (conceptualized) as something that is both independent and knowable: independent of linguistic control but amenable and responsive to linguistic knowledge. Thus the world must be understood as a certain kind of thing if language is to be possible, the kind of thing that supports the effective use of language (organized actions based on valid knowledge). And what it means for language to be effective is that it can sustain its own possibility, that the organized use of language will sustain the possibility of human actions and social life, and thus the possibility of language. If language is understood in this sense, then a reference to language will include a reference to the formal conceptual conditions that are necessary for the idea of valid knowledge to legitimate sustainable social–natural interactions. Language would be understood as reflexive, in the sense of formally striving to sustain its own possibility, through ecological efforts at valid knowledge. Also, the reference to language would be understood as including a reference to both social life and natural processes, since both of these are first of all *concepts*, and they have to be formulated linguistically in order to achieve valid knowledge of how they can be made to interact effectively. Knowledge is an issue of language before it is an issue of nature or experiments or observation or sacred texts, so if we can begin to refer the idea of knowledge to the idea of language, as an active, formal structure, then we can achieve a more coherent and reflexive idea of knowledge, an idea of knowledge that legitimates ecological sustainability rather than technical proficiency.

This is the argument I will make, that scientific knowledge is conceptually incoherent, technically proficient, and ecologically debilitating because of its fundamental reference to objective nature, and that the idea of knowledge can be made coherent and ecological only through the articulation of an even more fundamental reference, a reference to the formal structure of language. In many ways this will seem an odd argument, since science has essentially defined our idea of knowledge, and for science valid knowledge is strictly an issue of objective nature. Even for those sciences that are somewhat conceptually removed from nature, such as the scientific social theories of economics, sociology, and political science, the final reference is still objective nature, since these sciences tend to revolve around some version of "natural" individual motivations — "natural" desires, needs, interests, and the like. The social sciences essentially define themselves in terms of natural science — that is, in terms of the idea of objective nature — since their general idea of good science is physics. In this sense they are essentially residual disciplines: they accept what is left over (social life) after physics has defined nature, knowledge, and reason. In particular, social theory has not mounted a systematic, critical investigation of physics from the perspective of social legitimation, and it has not done so because social theory defines itself in terms of the scientific model of physics, including the idea that the fundamental reference for knowledge is objective nature.

As a result, we have tended to approach language from a scientific perspective in such disciplines as social theory, linguistics, and philosophy. The idea of language involves an inherent social reference, a reference to language users communicating and acting on the basis of the social organizations that language enables and mediates. As a consequence, scientific knowledge is based on the assumption that language can only be another object of knowledge, like atoms or neurons or inflation. From the scientific perspective, language cannot be a reference for knowledge, because then the idea of knowledge would involve a social reference, and scientific knowledge is definitively natural and nonsocial. This means that scientific knowledge must assume that language imposes no formal or structural conditions on the achievement of knowledge, because knowledge is strictly an issue of objective nature, not of language. For science, language can be only a neutral communicative tool, a useful symbolic mechanism that can be used passively by logically prior human beings in their efforts to gain knowledge, organize socially, and act effectively. These efforts can be more or less accurate, in accordance with the objective reality of natural processes, but their accuracy owes nothing to their basis in language, because language contributes nothing to the conditions for valid knowledge. Knowledge is strictly an issue of a direct observational connection, using the correct rational methods, between the mind and nature, and although language mediates that connection, it does so only passively, with no significant explanatory involvement.

In contrast, I will argue that language does add something significant to the achievement of knowledge, and that we can conceptualize nature (or social life, or human beings, or whatever) coherently only if we first understand the necessary conceptual constraints imposed on these ideas by the formal structure of language. Language enables social life, including the possibility of knowledge, and any coherent conception of knowledge must begin with an analysis of linguistic structure, not with some linguistic idea (such as "objective nature") that is then postulated as an absolute reality and thus presumed to be the basis for all valid ideas. For science, nature is objective and *external*, in the sense that it can be known by the rational observer from the outside, from a detached, uninvolved perspective. As a consequence, scientific knowledge presumes that all objects of study can be observed and known from the outside, including language. Thus science must presume that scientific language can somehow be used to study the structure of language *from the outside*, as though scientific language is detached from and external to language. This is one of the incoherences that results from the idea of objective nature, and in contrast I will argue that language must be studied *from the inside*, as though language-using beings are involved in and acting through the formal and enabling structure of language. From the inside, language can be seen as the only coherent reference for knowledge, because language enables knowledge and enables it only under certain formal conceptual conditions. From the inside, then, we must begin to articulate these formal conceptual conditions, and to construct an idea of knowledge on the basis of these linguistic conditions, the conditions that make both knowledge and social-natural interactions possible.

This is the task I am undertaking, to demonstrate the conceptual and ecological incoherence of "objective nature" and to articulate an alternative and linguistic idea of valid knowledge. I will begin, in chapter 1, with a discussion of the epistemological incoherence of science, arguing that this incoherence must be recognized as the basis for analyzing science as a social belief system, rather than as only the basis for more epistemological scrambling. In chapter 2 I will compare science and religion as legitimating belief systems, arguing that scientific knowledge must begin to be approached anthropologically, in terms of its inherent legitimating commitments, just as we have routinely approached religious knowledge. I will also argue, however, that science and religion have quite different legitimating commitments, and in chapter 3 I will show how scientific explanations were originally formulated as much for political and class legitimation against the feudal order as for the explanation of natural processes. In chapter 4 I will continue the anthropological argument by showing how the scientific idea of objective nature, as it appears in physics, incorporates inherent legitimating commitments within its basic explanatory framework, the framework of a detached mind directly observing mathematical nature. These legitimating commitments pervade such scientific terms as *electron* and *force* because these terms are defined mathematically, as part of a mathematical reality, and it is through mathematics that scientific knowledge establishes its basic legitimating image, the image of the "natural," a priori individual.

This is the foundational individual of scientific knowledge, the individual that legitimates all scientific social practices, and so in chapter 5 I will show how this legitimating individual arises out of the conceptual structure of physics. In this way physics will be shown to contain inherent but hidden legitimating commitments, just like religion, only in the case of physics the legitimating commitments point in a different institutional direction. In chapter 6 I will conclude the anthropological argument by showing how this scientific individual has legitimated only certain kinds of scientific social institutions and only certain kinds of scientific social theories. Then, in the last three chapters, I will use the anthropological analysis of science as a basis for developing an alternative and more coherent conception of knowledge, a conception that recognizes and incorporates its own legitimating dimensions, as an issue of reflexivity. Such a conception would make knowledge an issue of sustainability, in the same sense that medicine should be an issue of health, and it would refer the idea of knowledge to the formal structure of language, as an active structure that strives to sustain its own formal possibility. The crucial issue, as I will argue in chapter 9, is to articulate an idea of knowledge that legitimates absolute critical access for all individuals in the name of sustainability, even if the criticism is directed at the institutions legitimated by that idea of knowledge. A reflexive idea of knowledge involves an absolute commitment to reflexive criticism, and this is the only idea of knowledge that can be made coherent, and thus ecological.

A reflexive knowledge is committed to the legitimacy of critical access more than it is to any particular version of absolute "reality," and in this sense knowledge becomes "wild." "Wild" knowledge is knowledge that always legitimates criticism against established institutions in the name of the formal conditions for ecological sustainability, because these conditions are indeed *formal* and therefore cannot be identified with any particular, substantive set of social practices. If knowledge is an issue of formal, reflexive conditions, then it cannot be an issue of some absolute, categorical "reality." As a result, the idea of knowledge must remain critically "wild" in the sense that it cannot be "captured" and "tamed" by some particular set of social institutions, the institutions that are uniquely compatible with the "true" knowledge of absolute "reality." "Wild" knowledge legitimates criticism absolutely because no substantive, cultural set of institutions can be uniquely identified with the formal, linguistic conditions for sustainability. "Wild" knowledge is thus ecological knowledge, and it legitimates a social order based on individual critical access rather than "natural" individual motivations. As such, it contrasts with both religious and scientific knowledge, since both are "tamed" by their respective versions of "true reality" and so can legitimate only the specific institutional arrangements—either traditional or technical—that are compatible with that "reality." The mathematical "reality" of science is far more formal than the sacred "reality" of religion, and so science has legitimated a far greater commitment to criticism than has religion. But scientific knowledge can never become truly "wild" because it can never legitimate an ecological, reflexive criticism of its defining idea of absolute "reality," the idea of objective nature.

The formality of mathematical nature enables science to legitimate criticism *within its own explanatory framework,* in the sense of criticizing one mathematical version of physical laws in the name of another mathematical version of physical laws. In this way scientific knowledge becomes "semi-wild," in the sense that science legitimates the possibility of limited disruptive criticism but not the possibility of science disrupting and replacing its own explanatory framework, in the name of social sustainability. Nevertheless, scientific knowledge has legitimated a far greater *social* commitment to the idea of criticism than did religious knowledge, and it is this social commitment to criticism, in the midst of scientific institutions, that I am using to criticize science fundamentally, in the name of a more coherent and "wild" version of knowledge. Science has made the idea of criticism acceptable, but now we are beginning to see that science is not "wild" enough, for it tends to inhibit criticism at exactly the place we need it, the criticism of scientific knowledge and technology, the criticism of scientific society. In the midst of mounting environmental disasters, we must decide to complete the critical direction that science has begun, and so articulate an idea of knowledge that will legitimate criticism even against its own particular assertions of "truth" and "reality." Only through such criticism can we systematically evaluate and redirect our institutional practices in the context of their environmental effects, and such criticism can be legitimated only through an ecological and reflexive idea of knowledge, a "wild" knowledge.

ONE

The Desperate Privilege of Science

In our modern technological society, issues of knowledge and truth are generally understood as properly belonging to the domain of science. The scientific method of observation and experiment has convincingly demonstrated its ability to define, analyze, and answer the perennial questions of how the world works and how events are connected with actions. As a result, our culture has virtually identified the achievement of knowledge with the procedures of science. Science is understood as giving us valid knowledge, or as close to valid knowledge as we are ever likely to get. It can increase production, cure disease, transmit images, take us to the moon, obliterate cities, create and reorder life itself, and, perhaps most important, legitimate certain forms of social hierarchy and authority. Technological culture has developed a new and stunningly effective way of understanding natural phenomena, and concomitantly we have accepted scientists as the modern high priests of knowledge, as the men and women who can effectively control fundamental and unseen processes through the mastery of rather mysterious languages and rituals.

In particular, we have been willing to accept science as giving us definitive access to objective knowledge, including the knowledge of social life. Our philosophers and social theorists have generally assumed that science—specifically natural science—provides us with the only legitimate version of knowledge, so not only do the natural sciences provide valid explanations, they also provide the legitimating model for explanation in general, for the very idea of valid knowledge. Thus the social sci-

ences, even if requiring different methods and strategies, are still understood as needing to emulate the physical sciences, as much as possible.
The scientific study of society should be modeled on the scientific study
of nature, with physics as the ultimate reference, the paradigm of valid
knowledge.

Scientific knowledge, then, rests on the idea of objective nature, that
is, the idea that external, detached knowers can directly observe lawlike
and indifferent natural processes through the use of mathematical concepts and experiments. The term *science* is used with various meanings in
various contexts, and these meanings are not always fully compatible. I
am assuming, however, that the underlying reference for scientific
knowledge is always the image of objective nature, as that image is defined by physics. Underneath all its various uses, the notion of science
depends on the assumption that the mathematical order of objective
nature can be directly known through scientific observations, an epistemological assumption that has generated the familiar scientific conundrums: mind versus body, fact versus value, theory versus observation,
and so on. This is the epistemology of incorrigible perceptual access, of
theory-independent observations, and in the seventeenth century it began to support a new, scientific version of truth and reason, where truth
and reason became strictly issues of nature, observation, and mathematics. By definition, then, this new scientific version of knowledge contained no inherent moral and social commitments, unlike the inherently
moral knowledge of Christianity, the version of knowledge that science
began to replace.

From its beginning the scientific epistemology of privileged observations
has provided the conceptual foundation for our explanatory confidence in
science, because this epistemology has defined the idea of objective nature as
well as the appropriate methodology for privileged observational access to
nature. But as science began to replace feudal authority and to legitimate its
own institutional context, we also began to achieve a more immediate cultural confidence in science, a confidence based more directly in its technological achievements, as opposed to its epistemological purity. Originally,
scientific credibility depended primarily on its epistemology of incorrigible
access, but more recently this credibility can be derived directly from scientific technology, since now the epistemology can be seen as having obvious
technological payoffs, despite its many conceptual problems. And these
conceptual problems have been extensive, beginning with Descartes's problem of the mind and continuing with Berkeley's problem of perception,

Hume's problem of certainty, and the modern problem of observation. In effect, the epistemology of incorrigible access has collapsed, having been recognized as incoherent, and at the same time we are beginning to recognize that scientific technology may be equally incoherent, as the environmental dilemmas and disasters of this technology continue to appear.

From a social perspective it has been important to distinguish between scientific knowledge and scientific technology, because the latter can be seen as a proper subject for social analysis whereas the former cannot. Scientific technology is clearly involved in the legitimate domain of social theory, since it is directly a factor in such social issues as power, production, class, and organization. But while scientific technology can be analyzed socially, scientific knowledge cannot, since it is purely objective and natural, and therefore independent of any social involvement. This separation makes use of the epistemological distinction between facts and values, a distinction that protects the objective neutrality of scientific knowledge. As physicist Richard Feynman (1964) comments, "Scientific knowledge is an enabling power to do either good or bad—but it does not carry instructions on how to use it" (p. 4).

This distinction means that scientific technology can be analyzed only in terms of its strictly *social* dimensions—power, class, interests, and so on—not in terms of its conceptual foundations and assumptions—nature, mathematics, observation, and the like. This technology is properly subject to social analysis, but only as a factor in social relations, not as a problematic issue of valid knowledge. In general, scientific technology has been analyzed from two distinct social perspectives: the perspective of dominant institutional interests and the perspective of an inherent technological logic. According to the first, particular technologies are developed to serve the particular economic and political interests of powerful groups, such as owners of property and controllers of government. According to the second, particular technologies have their own inherent social logics, logics that require social relations and social organization to adapt to the technology, rather than the other way around. The first perspective sees technology as under institutional control, either of market rationality or of class domination; the second sees technology as essentially independent of institutional control, so that social relations are more an issue of technological logic than of individual or class interests. These are quite different social interpretations of technology, and both have generated interesting and revealing analyses, but they share a common conceptual assumption, the assumption that scientific knowledge, as such, is innocent of any social involvement and thus can remain completely immune from any such social analysis. In both cases the analysis always stops at the level of scientific technology, with no further social analysis or criticism of scientific knowledge itself, as physics or chemistry, as the knowledge of objective nature. In this way social theory is always quite respectful of the epistemological claims of scientific knowledge, the claims of objective detachment and social neutrality.

However, while scientific epistemology has been successfully holding social theory at bay, this epistemology has also been conceptually collapsing, or rather its inherent conceptual flaws have become increasingly difficult to ignore. At the conceptual level, this collapse revolves around the recognized incoherence of the idea of theory-neutral observations, the bedrock idea of scientific privilege. But it is important to remember that this was never simply a claim about perception, observation, and nature, a claim that could have seemed quite acceptable within the feudal context of Christian knowledge. Rather, it was always, and even primarily, a claim about reason, truth, and reality, which means it was always a claim about social authority and legitimation, a claim that inevitably began to discredit the feudal version of legitimation. The image of objective nature grounded the new ideas of reason and equality against the old ideas of tradition and authority, and thus scientific epistemology has always carried a kind of double weight. It has directly supported the idea of objective natural facts, and at the same time it has indirectly supported the idea of social and technological progress, where the latter can be achieved only through an institutional commitment to scientific reason and knowledge. Now, however, the idea of technological progress seems far less credible, owing to increasing environmental problems, and at the same time the idea of epistemological certainty seems far less convincing because of intractable conceptual problems. As the social confidence in scientific institutions begins to decline, so also, it would seem, does the conceptual confidence in scientific epistemology.

In essence, the epistemological argument asserted that the rational human mind could have direct perceptual access to the external and objective laws of nature. Through these neutral and untainted observations the individual mind could achieve true knowledge of objective reality, the reality of independent natural processes. At its origins the central point of this argument was that knowledge and reason could be achieved directly, without any necessary dependence on the traditional texts and authorities of feudal Christianity. But as reason and the market triumphed over feudalism, the conceptual details of this argument became more significant, as they contained the defining assumptions about such central scientific notions as nature, the mind, reason, reality, observation, and mathematics. The essence of the argument was developed in the work of the early natural philosophers, including Galileo, Descartes, and Locke, and even then its conceptual flaws were apparent—in Descartes's disconnected mind, in Hume's rejection of causality, in Berkeley's critique of perception, and in Kant's unperceived reality. But these conceptual problems were increasingly separated from scientific knowledge itself and relegated to the esoteric domain of philosophy, as scientific knowledge began to achieve ever greater cultural and institutional legitimacy in the new market society. From time to time, generally in response to persistent incoherences, efforts have been made to shift the certifying ground for this epistemology, from perception, to the mind, to language. But the basic epistemological argument, as Richard Rorty (1979) has shown, has remained essentially the same: an effort to guarantee pure, untainted access to objective nature, to achieve a mirror of nature, and thus to provide a privileged observational foundation for valid knowledge.

However, over the last quarter century, led prominently by the work of Thomas Kuhn, the concept of the possibility of theory-neutral observation has been systematically criticized, with the result that the idea of a privileged foundation for knowledge now appears incoherent. It has become clear that observations, for conceptual reasons, are never pure and direct. Rather, they are always necessarily constrained and directed by the conceptual structure of what we expect to see, of what we are looking for. This is the dilemma of knowledge: we can observe and conceptualize the world only by imposing some general explanatory structure on our experience of the world, thus enabling that experience to be organized into observations and concepts. We can see only what in some sense we already expect to see, and so observations can never be truly pristine, never fully independent of prior theoretical commitments and expectations. For this reason scientific epistemology must fail, since we can never have direct and innocent knowledge of an independent and objective world. This is the failure of a privileged foundation for knowledge, and it arises from the idea of an external and detached observer, from the idea of achieving objective knowledge of a world from somewhere outside of the world to be known. Thus it is a fundamental problem for scientific knowledge, and it cannot be simply displaced and resolved through philosophical efforts to shift the conceptual attention from observation and perception to such things as language, or mathematics, or cognitive processes. Many such philosophical efforts have been made, but the conceptual problem is in scientific knowledge itself, not in the particular epistemological grounds for certainty, and so the hope for a privileged, incorrigible foundation for scientific knowledge cannot be fulfilled.

This leaves the philosophers in something of a quandary. In the scientific context the basic point of epistemology has been to provide conceptual support for scientific knowledge, and so now the philosophers must find another kind of epistemological support, or, perhaps, begin to argue that scientific knowledge can do without epistemological support. In his book *Philosophy and the Mirror of Nature*, Richard Rorty (1979) takes the latter path, and he also suggests why the philosophers are having such a difficult and even desperate time:

> The conviction that science differed from softer discourse in having "objective reference" to things "out there" was bolstered . . . by the thought that . . . there certainly were points of contact with the world in the presentations of sense. This contact . . . seemed to give science what was lacking in religion and politics, the ability to use contact with the real as the touchstone of truth. The horror which greeted Quine's overthrow of the dogmas, and Kuhn's and Feyerabend's examples of the "theory-ladenness" of observation, was a result of the fear that there might be no such touchstone. For if we once admitted that Newton was better than Aristotle not because his words better corresponded to reality but simply because Newton made us better able to cope, there would be nothing to distinguish science from religion or politics. It was as if the ability to tell the . . . observational from the theoretical, was all that stood between us and "irrationalism." (p. 269)

Theory dependence threatened the very possibility of truth, knowledge, and even perhaps stability, and somehow science had to be rescued from this reversion to the explanatory jungle.

The philosophers have responded to this epistemological morass in various ways. Rorty (1979) embraces relativism, arguing that the loss of certainty is absolute and that there can be no objective foundation for knowledge. He sees all versions of knowledge as essentially cultural, and recommends that "we think of incorrigible knowledge simply as a matter of social practice" (p. 96). In his view, however, this social relativism is not a great catastrophe. "Irrationalism" does not result, and science can remain essentially unaffected. Science can simply stand on its own, without objective foundations, as simply our society's particular and effective way to get things done, or, as he puts it, science makes us "better able to cope." For him, "epistemology is the attempt to see the patterns of justification within normal discourse . . . as hooked on to something which demands moral commitment—Reality, Truth, Objectivity, Reason" (p. 385). Rather than worry about it, we should "look at the normal scientific discourse of our day . . . as patterns adopted for various historical reasons and as the achievement of objective truth, where 'objective truth' is no more and no less than the best idea we currently have about how to explain what is going on" (p. 385).

Similarly, Hilary Putnam (1981) argues that the familiar epistemology of incorrigible access has really been a disguised effort to assert particular social values and commitments:

> One cannot choose a scheme which simply "copies" the facts, because *no* conceptual scheme is a mere "copy" of the world. The notion of truth itself depends for its content on our standards of rationality, and these in turn rest on and presuppose our values. (p. 215)

Thus the standard epistemology has rested on a serious mistake, and philosophy has been "hypnotized" into accepting this mistake, despite its conceptual incoherence, by "the enormous instrumental success of science" (p. 185).

Both Rorty and Putnam argue, as I do, that scientific knowledge has always contained, and always hidden, specific cultural values and commitments. However, for them this recognition—the fact that scientific knowledge is inherently legitimating—does not seem to imply the necessity of a thorough social analysis of scientific knowledge, an analysis of physics. Rather, they are willing to accept an epistemological relativism, where the impossibility of objective certainty simply suggests that every society will have its own particular conception of knowledge, and that no external criteria for the validity of that conception can exist. From this perspective physics is simply one such relativistic conception, and so its epistemological incoherence becomes irrelevant, since physics is only a cultural effort to cope, and as such is quite successful. As a result, scientific knowledge, including physics, can effectively retain its conceptual immunity from social analysis and criticism, even though the epistemological grounds for that immunity have been dissolved. In relativistic terms the conceptual privilege becomes more ad hominem than objective, but still scientific knowledge is protected from social criticism. Such criticism can be based only on relativistic cultural values, not on objective reality and truth, and so we might as well simply keep what we have, since it has had such "enormous instrumental success" and it makes us "better able to cope."

In essence, relativism suggests that scientific knowledge cannot be criticized from the perspective of a more coherent idea of knowledge, even though scientific knowledge is recognized as conceptually incoherent. Science retains its explanatory privilege because relativism disconnects the pragmatic idea of technical ability from such legitimating ideas as reason, truth, and social progress. In this way relativism manages to disavow the Enlightenment promise of science while still validating the technical authority of science. Science has lost its connection with truth and reality, but it can still be accepted as simply another way to get things done, a way that is as good as any other, better than most, and uniquely *ours*. Science may fail as objective knowledge but it does not fail as legitimate, practical knowledge, and so it retains its effective immunity from social criticism. This is a sort of backdoor, bite-the-bullet version of scientific privilege, and it seems to reveal its own level of defiant desperation. It is a version utilized by various theorists of scientific knowledge, both in philosophy and social theory, and it has the effect of hiding the increasing *ecological* incoherence of science behind the acceptance of relativism — that is, behind the acceptance of *conceptual* incoherence.

Most philosophers resist the plunge into relativism, however, believing instead that some kind of credible scientific epistemology can be reestablished. Arthur Fine (1984) is one of these, and he argues that science can be rescued from the loss of realism, that is, from the loss of direct observational knowledge of a real, external world. For him we can trust the truths of science in the same way we trust the everyday truths of our own senses, the truths we live by in daily social life:

> I certainly trust the evidence of my senses, on the whole, with regard to
> the existence and features of everyday objects. And I have similar
> confidence in the system of . . . scientific investigation. . . . So, if the
> scientists tell me that there really are molecules, and atoms, and . . .
> maybe even quarks, then so be it. I trust them and, thus, must accept
> that there really are such things. (p. 95)

Fine argues that scientific "truths" (presumably in contrast with religious or traditional or cultural "truths") should be given "equal status" with "everyday truths," and that valid knowledge will then result from "our accepting both as *truths*" (p. 101). In this way science can be returned to the status of privileged credibility, if not privileged objectivity. Indeed, this would enable us "to answer the question of what, then, does it *mean* to say that something is true . . . by focusing . . . on the concrete historical circumstances that ground that particular judgment of truth. For, after all, there *is* nothing more to say" (p. 101). Objectivity is lost, but we can retain scientific credibility simply by deciding that the reliability of science is uniquely comparable to the reliability of everyday experience, even though this involves the necessity of a reference to the social criteria of "concrete historical circumstances," whatever that may mean. For Fine, as for me, the loss of realism forces science to recognize its dependence on a social reference, but for Fine this reference seems absolutely nonproblematic, somehow transcending any particular values, politics, or interests. The basic point of scientific objectivity was to deny any social reference, but now, for Fine, a vague social reference can reestablish scientific credibility without the need for any social analysis or criticism. Social life has been discovered at the base of scientific knowledge and simply finessed.

Another approach is taken by C. Bas van Fraassen (1984), who recognizes that "there cannot be a 'theoretical/observable distinction' " (p. 255). His solution is simply to decide that science does not depend upon the prior legitimacy of observations, but rather that observations depend upon the prior legitimacy of science, a legitimacy that is not problematic. The philosophical mistake has been to think that the possibility of pure observation was a conceptual problem, involving issues of language and definitions of terms. Rather, it is strictly an empirical problem, and must be decided by science:

> If there are limits to observation, these are empirical and must be described by empirical science. The classification marked by "observable" must be of entities in the world of science. And science, in giving content to the distinction, will reveal how much we believe when we accept it as empirically adequate. (p. 256)

Thus science does not need an epistemology but is simply announced to be the ultimate definition of reality and knowledge. Whereas Fine thinks that our trust in everyday experience, with its inherent social involvement, can make science credible, van Fraassen thinks that we can trust only science, because everyday experience, with its confusion about what is observable, is not credible. Both find that science can retain its privilege, but while Fine still feels a need to defend science as knowledge, van

Fraassen is willing simply to define science as knowledge. Science may not be objective truth, but it can be accepted as "empirically adequate," meaning that scientific theories must meet scientific criteria for observation and prediction. Science defends itself internally, by becoming the only legitimate basis for any critical experience, and no external judgments of social or ecological adequacy can be leveled against it.

Fine and van Fraassen represent two of the various epistemological strategies for rejecting relativism, and thus for resurrecting the conceptual privilege and credibility of science after its loss of objective certainty. In effect, they argue that we can still accept science as "true" — that is, as still uniquely connected with the legitimating terms *truth* and *reason* — even though the scientific ideas of "truth" and "reality" can no longer be made coherent. For them scientific knowledge must still be defended as uniquely valid, and thus as deserving its privileged immunity from social criticism. For the relativists, on the other hand, scientific knowledge cannot be defended as uniquely valid, and yet it can also retain its privileged immunity because science is "good enough" and there are only arbitrary and relativistic grounds for criticism. In these ways, and others, the philosophers have been trying to reestablish the unique credibility of scientific knowledge in the context of epistemological failure. And all of these strategies tend to reestablish the problem of valid knowledge at the strictly philosophical level, where this problem can continue to be discussed with esoteric disregard for the messier issues of social legitimation, political interests, institutional structures, and environmental degradation. Indeed, maintaining this philosophical detachment is the central point, since otherwise the loss of neutral, nonsocial objectivity might imply that scientific knowledge must be analyzed in social terms, and that physics must be recognized as having always been as much a theory of social relations as a theory of natural processes. Ostensibly these philosophers are carefully discussing the conceptual problems of knowledge, but more fundamentally they are apologists for science, conceptual lobbyists trying to maintain a "rational" defense of scientific knowledge in order to maintain the "rational" legitimacy of scientific social institutions.

The Appeal to Technology

All observations have now been recognized as theory dependent, and thus these new epistemological strategies must somehow confront and then set aside the fact that all scientific "facts" have inevitably been defined in terms of particular cultural values and beliefs. This means that these strategies must somehow recognize a social dimension—a social reference—within the structure of scientific knowledge, and then attempt to incorporate that reference into the continued credibility of science. The most obvious way to do this is to refer to the "success" of scientific technology, a justifying reference that is commonplace today but was unavailable for the origins of scientific knowledge in the seventeenth century. On the basis of its technological achievements, the scientific idea of objective nature can seem obviously "adequate," or even "correct," especially when all other supports for objective certainty have failed. Thus Rorty accepts science for making us "better able to cope," and Putnam remarks on "the enormous instrumental success of science." Fine "trusts the evidence of [his] senses," and so grounds science on the direct experience of what seems to work, while van Fraassen builds scientific credibility on the basis of "empirical adequacy." Underneath all of these scramblings for scientific privilege is the idea that science is technically "successful," and that this judgment of "success" is apparent and nonproblematic. Indeed, the assumption seems to be that the evidence for technological "success" is as clear and direct as the evidence for incorrigible, theory-neutral observations was once thought to be.

For many philosophers this reference to technological "success" is not something to be hidden behind more sophisticated conceptual arguments, but is rather the only argument necessary to rescue science from the apparent quagmire of theory dependence. Richard Boyd (1984), for example, accepts that "the actual methods of science are profoundly theory-dependent" (p. 67) and then shrugs it off:

> The fact remains that the [theory-dependent] methodology of science gives evidence of being instrumentally reliable. Let *that* constitute the justification for the inferences which scientists make. . . . It is . . . well confirmed by the observational evidence presented by the recent history of science and technology. (p. 68)

Likewise, W. H. Newton-Smith (1981) recognizes that theory and observation statements cannot be distinguished and then decides that this is not epistemologically relevant, since "a rough pragmatic distinction of degree can be established" based on "our success in coping with the world" (pp. 24, 28). "The impressive technological spin-off of contemporary physics is just one measure of this increased predictive and manipulative power" (p. 196). Also, Ian Hacking (1983) believes that irrationalism is not the necessary consequence of theory-dependent observations because "engineering, not theorizing, is the best proof of scientific realism about entities" (p. 274).

This is the kind of argument that seems most convincing about the acceptability, if not the objectivity, of scientific knowledge. The technology of science is remarkable, and its "success" is so obvious that we must be doing something right. It is an argument that seems convincing both to the philosophers and to the general public, and it seems capable of justifying at least a weak cultural legitimacy, if not a strong objective validity. But it depends upon the idea of technical "success," and in particular upon taking this idea to be as direct and nonproblematic as the idea of "pure" observation was once thought to be. On the face of it, the idea of technical "success" seems fairly obvious and straightforward, but under closer scrutiny it begins to appear much more complicated and, indeed, as deeply involved with social and legitimating judgments, as opposed to only simple and obvious "technical" judgments. Under closer scrutiny, the idea of a judgment being *only* "technical," in the sense of involving no social values, begins to appear as unconvincing as the idea of theory-independent observation. Generally, the philosophers who have appealed to the idea of technical "success" have simply taken it for granted, as though it were obvious and nonproblematic, as though it could be easily, if only pragmatically, substituted for the loss of "pure" observation. But this conceptual inattention can only be another aspect of epistemological desperation, because usually philosophers are more careful than this. And if they were more careful, they would have to see that the idea of technical "success" must always involve a deeply *social* judgment, a judgment about the quality and sustainability of social life, not simply about a technical adjustment of specific means to specific ends.

When scientific knowledge is said to be objective—or valid, or credible, or acceptable—because of its technological "success," a claim is being made that this technology is at least compatible with the continued possibility of social life. In this context the judgment of "success" includes an assumption that the social use of this technology will not fundamentally disrupt or destroy the possibility of achieving valued social goals, including the goal of maintaining the prospects of social order and social life. We would not call something "successful," and use it to authorize a conception of knowledge, if we thought it was "successfully" undermining the basis of our social life, including the basis of individual life—if we thought it was "successfully" generating war, illness, and death. This is the point of the medical analogy developed in the introduction, the point that cutting out the heart cannot be a "successful" approach to repairing or maintaining it. This analogy suggests that the idea of valid or acceptable knowledge always incorporates an implicit dependence on the reflexive idea of social sustainability, in the same sense that the idea of valid medical knowledge always incorporates an implicit dependence on the reflexive idea of health. When we say that knowledge is technically "successful," we always include the idea that it can be used to achieve our *human* goals, or at least that its use does not inevitably work against those goals. Sometimes, of course, we may be mistaken about the goal our technology is serving, and when we are we must reject the technology, not the human goal. This is the point of the medical analogy, and it was also the case, for example, when DES seemed to have local technical "success" (preventing miscarriages) but then was found to be in conflict with more fundamental human goals (preventing cancer). Thus if scientific technology is systematically destroying the ecological basis for social life, then we will not continue to call that technology "successful." The judgment of technical "success" always implies social sustainability, and so if the conceptual incoherence of scientific knowledge entails the ecological incoherence of scientific technology, then it can only be a desperate epistemological mistake to call that technology "successful."

Generally, however, we want our technology to do more than simply *not* be destructive. When we judge it to be "successful" we also tend to imply that it is a good thing, that it is socially beneficial and supports the achievement of desired goals. In this sense the judgment of technical "success" is a comparative one: our knowledge is adequate and acceptable because its technology is so much more "successful" than other, alternative versions of knowledge. The judgment of technical "success" is not just the idea that our technology is not inherently debilitating, it is also the idea that our technology is better than other forms of technology at achieving our social and human goals. And it is as a comparative judgment that the idea of technical "success" needs to be analyzed further for its inherent social assumptions. On the face of it the comparison seems to be quite straightforward; for example, our fertilizer is better at making crops grow than are their rituals, and so on. But the judgment of "success" is not about crops, or transportation, or other technical specifics. Rather, it is about the validity and acceptability of a conception of knowledge, so the judgment is about whether one version of knowledge is better than another, based on technical criteria. In this context the first point to remember is that local technical "success," as specific means achieving a specific end, does not necessarily validate the knowledge on which that technical effort is based. If it did, we would have to believe, for example, that rain dances can indeed influence the forces that bring rain since rain dances typically precede the rainy season, or that the sun must indeed orbit the earth since the navigational devices based on a Ptolemaic universe have been so "successful." Technologies may "work" for the wrong reasons, and so the "success" of a technology cannot provide a direct and authorizing epistemology for its version of knowledge. Thus in the absence of such an epistemology the judgment of technical "success," as evidence for the validity of knowledge, can be only a comparative judgment about the general *social* "success" of different versions of knowledge, where this knowledge is more valid because it is more capable of technically achieving the desired social goals.

In the scientific context such comparisons of technical ability are always to religious knowledge, the knowledge of religious, traditional societies. These are the only versions of knowledge available for comparison, the knowledge of societies that are committed to tradition rather than reason. These societies legitimate their respective traditions through an appeal to sacred truths, that is, through an appeal to concepts that explain social-natural interactions in terms of attentive and powerful beings, such as gods and spirits. In general, religious knowledge identifies these powerful beings as committed to maintaining the traditional order, so that valid knowledge will always direct social action toward maintaining the tradition in order to appease those beings, rather than toward developing new technology in order to increase efficiency. Certainly all religious societies utilize their own specific technologies in order to accomplish their specific social goals, and so particular comparisons with scientific technologies are always available, in terms of success at agriculture, communication, war, and so on. But the epistemological judgment must be about the validity of knowledge, not about specific technical achievements, and the philosophers simply assume superior technical "success," as though the comparative results would be so obvious that they need not be further developed. Thus the comparison is always implicit—scientific technology is remarkably "successful," meaning "better"—but the implied reference is always to the technology of religious knowledge, the technology of traditional societies, including feudalism and tribalism.

In this context the judgment of technological "success" always seems obvious because scientific technology is obviously superior to religious technology, as technology. Clearly science has excelled at technology, and it is also clear that the reason for this superiority is the scientific idea of an objective natural order, as opposed to the religious idea of a sacred traditional order. Science has certainly made us more technically proficient, in the sense of specific technical achievements, but whether it has made us more technically "successful," in the sense of validating scientific knowledge over religious knowledge, is less clear. If scientific knowledge is more valid than religious knowledge because of its technology, then it must follow that religious knowledge has always been trying to achieve greater technical "success" but has failed because of its explanatory mistakes. This is what the epistemological appeal to technology really asserts, that religious societies have been less "successful" at technology than we have because their version of knowledge has been less valid than ours. If technology can be used as a legitimate reference for validity, then religious knowledge must have been trying to do the same thing as scientific knowledge, only doing it worse. From this perspective all versions of knowledge are inherently directed toward technical proficiency, and those that are less "successful" are those that are more fundamentally mistaken in their explanations of the world.

In the realm of epistemology this assumption is generally taken for granted, along with the certainty of our technical superiority. But if it were made explicit and analyzed, then it would be far less obvious, since it is almost certainly mistaken about religion. Virtually all the studies of religious societies tell us that the explanations of religion are not directed toward achieving technical ability, but are rather directed toward achieving social stability, toward maintaining the traditional order. Religious explanations tend to be far more concerned with ordering and maintaining traditional social relations than with experimenting on and manipulating natural processes. In fact, religious societies tend to inhibit the introduction of new technical approaches, and they do this exactly in order to maintain the traditional patterns as much as possible. In traditional societies new technology can severely disrupt the social order, such as when missionaries introduced the steel ax into the Yir Yoront tribe of Australia. As a result, efforts at new technology would often be feared and rejected by the religious authorities, such as when the priests refused to look through Galileo's telescope and the Church imprisoned him. Religious societies are generally well satisfied with their technology, and

have little interest in improving it. Their technology is not about technical efficiency, as Mary Douglas (1966) has commented about tribal life:

> In a primitive culture the technical problems have been more or less
> settled for generations past. The live issue is how to organize other
> people and oneself in relation to them. . . . To serve these practical
> social ends all kinds of beliefs in the omniscience and omnipotence of
> the environment are called into play. (pp. 90-91)

So the technological assumption about the inherent goals of religious
knowledge would seem to be factually wrong. This is not surprising,
however, since it is really a *scientific* assumption, an assumption about the
inherent goals of scientific knowledge. Science is fundamentally oriented
toward technical proficiency, and, in comparison with religious versions
of knowledge, science does technology much better. In other words, the
epistemological appeal to technology involves judging between scientific
and religious knowledge on the basis of criteria for validity that are
uniquely and specifically scientific, the criteria of technical proficiency
for its own sake. In these terms science can be judged as more "valid"
and objective nature as more "realistic" because scientific knowledge is
better at doing what only scientific knowledge is trying to do—that is,
generate "successful" technology. The technological argument evaluates
scientific knowledge in strictly scientific terms and then announces that
the issues of theory dependence and objectivity are resolved. Science can
retain its analytic privilege, and its immunity from social criticism, primarily because it is so good at being science.

The Social Goals of Technology

If a comparison between scientific knowledge and religious knowledge is
to make any sense, it would have to involve a comparison of the scientific
ability to accomplish scientific goals with the religious ability to accomplish religious goals. The goals of science are to predict and manipulate
nature, to generate effective technology. The idea of objective nature was
an effort to detach the explanation of natural processes from any traditional or moral constraints, such as the constraints imposed by religious
explanations. This effort has been quite successful, and it has enabled the
members of scientific society to experiment and innovate with technology, and change social relations, without transgressing against the sacred
rituals of the traditional order. But the goals of religious knowledge have

always been to protect and maintain a traditional order by imposing moral and ritual restraints on technical innovation and social change. Religious explanations always suggest, through the idea of attentive gods, that a supportive natural environment can be maintained only through a moral adherence to traditional values, so that the goal of a viable social order can be achieved only by inhibiting new technology, rather than by encouraging it. Thus a serious comparison of scientific and religious knowledge would have to weigh the ability of science to generate technology with the ability of religion to maintain the tradition, and in this case both would have to be seen as quite "successful." Scientific knowledge is clearly good at generating technology, and religious knowledge, it would seem, has been equally good, in various forms, at maintaining specific traditions for thousands of years.

The comparison would have to go further, however. Religion, it would also seem, has been fairly ineffective at maintaining the tradition when confronted with science or, more accurately, when confronted with scientific societies and scientific technology. Generally in this confrontation science has been more "successful" at continuing to generate technology than religion has been at continuing to maintain the tradition. Scientific explanations always seem to dominate and disrupt religious explanations, primarily because scientific explanations demand a certain skepticism toward received social authority, while religious explanations tend to lose their coherence in the face of such skepticism. In this sense science certainly seems to be more "successful" than religion at achieving its inherent social goals. Science is better at incorporating criticism and at adjusting to social change, and so in most historical encounters science has succeeded better than religion at maintaining its social legitimacy, and thus at maintaining its commitment to technical proficiency.

On the other hand, science has been good at technical proficiency for only a hundred years or so, whereas religions have been good at maintaining traditions for much longer. In many cases religious knowledge has "successfully" maintained traditional stability for thousands of years; a similar "success" for scientific knowledge seems unlikely, at least at the present. Scientific technology, it would seem, can be "successful" only by constantly disrupting its environmental base, while religious technology is always committed to stabilizing its environmental base absolutely, through ritualized social-natural interactions. Of course, religious knowledge can always misunderstand its environmental base, and thus ritualize potentially destructive social-natural interactions, resulting in overpopulation, soil exhaustion, lack of game, and so on. But for religion the tradition is ritualized exactly because it appears to be environmentally stable—it appeases the gods—and when it does not appear to be environmentally stable the tradition can often be adjusted slightly in the name of the tradition. Religious knowledge can certainly incorporate social change, but only gradually, and so these societies seem most vulnerable to relatively abrupt social changes, such as conquest or cultural confrontation, particularly when confronted with scientific technology. In any case, religious technology, unlike scientific technology, seems capable of only limited and localized environmental damage, since religious actions, unlike scientific actions, can remain legitimate only to the degree the natural environment remains supportive. In trying to maintain the tradition, religious knowledge tends also to maintain the supportive environment, and so this knowledge would have to be characterized as quite "successful" at achieving its goals over the long term, at least in the absence of science.

In contrast, science seems increasingly bad at protecting its environment. Indeed, it seems bad at this in almost exact proportion to its ability to generate technology. Of course, it could be argued that this is not the fault of science, but rather the fault of politics, interests, values, and so on. In any case it seems apparent that the society characterized by scientific "success" is doing a particularly poor job of maintaining its supportive environment. And unfortunately, this environment is the environment of the entire planet, not just a localized valley, or drainage system, or coastline. If scientific society is bad for the environment, then it is bad for everyone, whether or not they have accepted the privileged credibility of scientific knowledge. Indeed, it may well be bad for the continued possibility of social life, the possibility of having knowledge and of developing technology and of worrying about objectivity. In this sense the social practices legitimated by science, including its technology, do not seem quite so "successful." More precisely, from the perspective of the environment the comparison with religion may begin to turn decisively in the favor of religion, since religion will appear to be far more "successful" at maintaining the tradition than science will appear to be at sustaining the ecological possibility of generating technology.

This is the issue that is overlooked by the epistemological appeal to technology, the issue of what it really means to say that scientific technology is so remarkably "successful." The idea of technical "success" can appear to be obvious and straightforward, but it always includes the assumption that the productive use of this technology will allow social life to continue, that scientific technology will not systematically undermine the possibility of having technology and of being productive. In the epistemological argument, the localized, technical judgment of means-ends "success" is surreptitiously elided with the social, legitimating judgment of valid knowledge, and in these terms scientific knowledge can once again begin to appear as obviously coherent and valid. When the ecological issues are added, however, the judgment of "success" must be seen as involving hidden social criteria, criteria that are implied but not admitted, particularly the criteria of sustainability. The idea of "successful" technology includes the assumption that social life can continue in the context of that technology, and indeed it generally includes the assumption that social life will be better because of that technology.

Some scientific technologies, however, unlike any religious technologies, can have devastating environmental as well as social consequences, such as the technologies of nuclear weapons, genetic engineering, chlorofluorocarbons, and information control. Of course, we may be able to establish sustainable political control over such technologies, or indeed science may yet save us from them by creating even better, counteractive technologies. But scientific technology, unlike religious technology, is not about social or ecological sustainability. Rather, it is about localized technical proficiency, for its own sake, and so these technologies have no built-in legitimating constraints. Indeed, these technologies could destroy the world and still be judged technically "successful," in scientific terms. Given this potential, our theorists and philosophers should probably stop granting scientific knowledge a kind of de facto immunity from social analysis and criticism, an immunity they derive from their scrambling epistemological efforts to base scientific privilege on technological "success." Rather, they should probably begin to investigate scientific knowledge as a legitimating belief system, a belief system that is inherently legitimating and thus the validity of which, as knowledge, is an issue of social life, not strictly of esoteric epistemological issues. From this perspective scientific knowledge could be coherently and legitimately criticized in terms of its social and ecological effects, and the idea of knowledge would be recognized as containing a necessary reference to the idea of sustainability, on the model of medical knowledge.

Scientific knowledge has lost its objective privilege and its epistemology has collapsed into incoherence, and yet our social theorists continue to grant it analytic privilege, presumably on the basis of the philosophers' efforts to resurrect a scrambling and desperate epistemology. More likely, however, this analytic privilege has continued because scientific knowledge has become deeply integrated into our fundamental institutional structures, the structures that scientific knowledge has legitimated. These structures include our productive and political systems, and they also include our colleges and universities, our centers of academic research, where the separate disciplinary domains of social knowledge and natural knowledge are strictly observed. It is probably through this institutional and disciplinary structure, more than any convincing epistemology, that scientific knowledge, and particularly physics, has been accepted as conceptually self-contained, and thus as conceptually unavailable to legitimate critical evaluation from a social perspective.

It is this image of critical immunity, of the absolute critical detachment of scientific nature from all social concerns, that must be made problematic, despite its embedded institutional credibility. We must begin to recognize that physics has always been a social theory, and that we have been willing to ignore this aspect of physics, with the help of epistemology, because we have been so generally satisfied, as a culture, with the institutions and technology physics has legitimated. But the party may be over, which means that the social and ecological implications of physics must begin to be investigated, as an issue of the explanatory validity of physics. It seems clear that science is better at technology and criticism than is religion, and it also seems clear that religion is better at stability and ecology than is science. So we must begin the social investigation of science with the idea of developing a conception of knowledge that can incorporate and legitimate both criticism and ecology, both technology and sustainability. We must recognize that both science and religion are based on fundamental incoherences about the idea of knowledge, incoherences that make religious practices absolutely vulnerable to scientific practices and that make scientific practices absolutely vulnerable to ecological disaster. From this perspective, then—from a critical, ecological analysis of science and religion—we can begin to articulate a coherent and sustainable conception of knowledge, a conception that recognizes the legitimating as well as the technical requirements for valid knowledge.

TWO

Belief Systems

Science and religion have often been compared, but not often as legiti-mating belief systems, where both are seen as committed to legitimating specific kinds of social practices. Generally they are compared as differing efforts at prediction and explanation, functions at which science tends to excel, or as differing efforts at providing cultural meanings and values, functions at which religion tends to excel. In these cases the comparison typically rests on the differing definitions of what each does (provide technical control, provide social integration), and then demonstrates that each is better at doing its particular thing than the other. But if science and religion are compared as legitimating belief systems, they can be compared on the basis of their similarities as accepted systems of knowl-edge, where each system legitimates certain social practices in the name of truth, reason, and reality.

A comparison of this kind can put the idea of knowledge into analytic relief, by exposing what religious knowledge and scientific knowledge have in common as legitimating belief systems. Generally we have sim-ply accepted scientific knowledge as real knowledge and then compared science with religion, a strategy that has tended to privilege science and to make religion appear as a somewhat confused effort at knowledge. But if we compare the two as belief systems, without assuming one or the other to be especially privileged, we can learn more about each of them, as well as about the idea of knowledge. We can see that they are similar in some ways, as systems of knowledge, and that they have quite different social and institutional implications. This means that we can analyze their similarities and differences in terms of their respective social involvements, rather than in terms of the unique truth, and social detachment, of science. From such an analysis we can discover how to define both science and religion in *social* terms, rather than in "scientific" terms. Also, we can discover how it is that each legitimates, in the name of knowledge, such different institutions and practices.

In this way we can begin to articulate a more coherent conception of knowledge, a social-natural conception, in which knowledge is understood as having inherent social as well as natural references. As belief systems, science and religion differ exactly in their respective assumptions about the "true" relationships between social and natural references, and this difference has important implications for the legitimation of social actions. A more coherent, social-natural conception of knowledge would explicitly recognize the necessity for both social and natural references, as well as the necessity of assuming sustainable social-natural interactions, rather than assuming sacred institutions or indifferent nature. This would mean that knowledge would begin to be understood in terms of the analogy with health, in terms of reflexive, ecological criticism. The idea of knowledge would be referred to its own continued possibility, through the legitimation of sustainable social practices, rather than to some absolute ("sacred," "objective") reality. In this way both science and religion could be analyzed and criticized in terms of the sustainability, or lack of it, of the institutions they legitimate. Both science and religion have functioned effectively as legitimating belief systems, but both, it would seem, have tended to make their respective societies remarkably vulnerable, if not untenable. By analyzing them as belief systems we can understand better how both have worked as well as how the idea of knowledge must work if we are to organize a sustainable social life.

The idea of analyzing both science and religion as belief systems raises some interesting issues. On the one hand, we are certainly familiar with the idea of analyzing religion as a belief system, since we tend to think of religion in terms of "shared beliefs" rather than "objective truths," and since our historians and anthropologists have routinely approached religions as legitimating belief systems. According to these scholars, it makes little sense to think that religious knowledge—with its gods, spirits, magic, ritual, rain dances, and so on—offers valid explanations of natural phenomena. Consequently, these explanations tend to be interpreted, for analytic purposes, as though they were not "really" about natural phenomena, even though they offer explicit explanatory accounts of such things as rain, fertility, death, and illness. Rather, these accounts are interpreted as more fundamentally about social legitimation, that is, about the maintenance of tradition, the authority of ritual, the necessity of proper behavior, the sacred moral order. This has been a productive and insightful analytic approach, and indeed few people today would argue with the assumption that religious beliefs are decisively committed to social legitimation. But it should be remembered that this is a *scientific* interpretation of religious explanations, an interpretation from the perspective of the presumed credibility of scientific explanations. Religious believers tend to take religious explanations straight, as though they were about exactly what they say they are about (rain, illness, and so on), just as scientific believers tend to take scientific explanations straight. It is only from a scientific perspective that we have been able to see what religious knowledge is "really" about.

On the other hand, we are not very familiar with analyzing science as a legitimating belief system. We tend to look at the world from a scientific perspective, and science tells us that its explanations are perfectly indifferent to social concerns. Scientific knowledge presents itself as strictly about objective nature, and as having no inherent relationship, as knowledge, to the social institutions surrounding it. In our society scientific explanations tend to be accepted at face value, as directly about independent natural processes, which means that they do not have to be "explained," as do religious explanations, by analytic insights into their social role, insights that only detached anthropologists, not scientific believers, can have. Indeed, the only way that such social accounts of scientific beliefs can make any sense is if science is internally mistaken about itself—that is, if science is mistaken about its pristine detachment, as objective knowledge, from any social involvement. Thus if we begin to analyze science as a legitimating belief system, as we have routinely analyzed religion, then we are assuming, in effect, that scientific knowledge must be mistaken in some way, mistaken about itself and about nature, just as we have routinely assumed that religious knowledge must be mistaken.

Generally, our anthropologists have assumed that scientific explanations are essentially correct and should be taken at face value, while also assuming that religious explanations are essentially incorrect and should not be taken at face value. In this way they have granted scientific knowledge a privileged immunity from social analysis, while at the same time focusing considerable analytic attention on the inherent social content of religious knowledge. As a consequence, they have found fundamental legitimating commitments within religious knowledge, commitments that could not be seen from within the explanations themselves, not if they are accepted (believed in) at face value. Our anthropologists have used this analytic approach to achieve a better understanding of the social role of religious beliefs, and they have been able to do this because they have been willing to deny, for analytic purposes, the face validity of those beliefs. So now, I am suggesting, we should begin to approach scientific knowledge in the same way. We should begin to analyze scientific knowledge anthropologically, just as we have routinely approached religious knowledge, as a legitimating belief system. When we do we will find that science has always been full of legitimating social content, just like religion, content that cannot be seen if its explanations are accepted at face value. Anthropology has routinely analyzed such explanatory terms as *gods* and *spirits* as though they were more about legitimating social relationships than about explaining natural phenomena, and I am suggesting that we begin to analyze such explanatory terms as *electrons* and *atoms* in the same way, as though they too were more about legitimating social relationships than about explaining natural phenomena.

In order to approach science anthropologically, it must first be distinguished from religion as a belief system. Typically, science has been distinguished from religion as correct versus incorrect knowledge, but as belief systems they must be distinguished as legitimating quite different kinds of social practices, according to quite different versions of truth and reality. Such a distinction requires that the idea of religious knowledge be more clearly defined, since we usually think of religious *beliefs*, as opposed to scientific *knowledge*. In this context I will take religious knowledge to be the knowledge of religious societies, the explanations and beliefs that characterize a thoroughly religious world, and that legitimate thoroughly religious institutions. Thus the idea of religious knowledge will not include the religious beliefs held by individuals in a scientific society, in a society organized around scientific knowledge and technology. I am interested only in comparing scientific and religious societies, where the different versions of knowledge legitimate different kinds of values and institutions. This means that I will exclude the institutionalized religions of industrial society—Catholicism, Judaism, and so on—from this discussion. I am interested in the ways specific belief systems generate and legitimate specific social practices, and from this perspective it seems almost a misnomer to suggest that both religious societies and scientific societies have religious beliefs. To do so is essentially to presume that religious beliefs have some kind of universal social function, a function that can be articulated independent of social context. It is just such a presumption, I believe, that has often led scholars to misunderstand the full social role of science, since the implication seems to be that science serves only instrumental, technical goals, while religion, even in the midst of science and industry, simply continues to serve its special goals of morality, spirituality, meaning, and the like. Rather, I would argue, in the context of scientific institutions religious beliefs become much more personal and moral and much less institutional and legitimating. They may still be religious in some sense, but they no longer define the basic cultural notions of truth and reality, and they no longer organize and direct the social relationships of daily life. For this reason I will discuss religious knowledge as though it were the basic explanatory reference for the institutions and practices of a religious society, in the context of a fully religious "reality."

In this sense of religion, then, we will explore its difference from science as a belief system, beginning with how anthropologists have typically approached and interpreted religious knowledge. Primarily, they have approached it from a scientific perspective, which means they have simply assumed that religious knowledge is mistaken about nature: it is wrong about nature because science is right about nature. As in many things, Durkheim (1967) took the anthropological lead in this, arguing that religion's "primary object" "is not to give men a representation of the physical world; for if that were its essential task, we could not understand how it has been able to survive, for, on this side, it is scarcely more than a fabric of errors" (p. 225). Similarly, E. E. Evans-Pritchard (1970) tells us that among the Zande, "there was little knowledge as to the real causes of disease" (p. 32); Raymond Firth (1970) comments that "magic [is] . . . as far as we can see based on false premises" (p. 38); Philip Meyer (1970) asserts that "witchcraft power is surely imaginary" (p. 49); and John Beattie (1967) suggests that magic and divination "no doubt . . . fills in gaps in people's knowledge of cause and effects" (p. 230).

If this knowledge is so mistaken and yet still so acceptable, the anthropologists conclude, it must be because religious explanations are not really about nature at all. Rather, these explanations—involving such things as gods, magic, witchcraft—must be primarily about legitimating and maintaining social life. These explanations must be primarily directed toward social interactions, and they must be disguised as natural explanations in order to give them more authority, a disguise that anthropologists can see through because they can question that authority, from the perspective of science. Thus Durkheim continues, in the same passage quoted above: "Before all, [religion] is a *system of ideas* with which the individuals represent to themselves the society of which they are members, and the obscure but intimate relations they have with it" (p. 225). Similarly, for Evans-Pritchard (1967a), speaking of the Azande, "the role of magic is to enable . . . social and economic processes to be carried out" (p. 22); for S. F. Nadel (1970), "witchcraft beliefs enable a society to go on functioning in a given manner" (p. 279); for Melford Spiro (1966), "religion, then, is to be explained in terms of society and personality" (p. 122); and for Clifford Geertz (1966), "the anthropological study of religion is therefore a two stage operation: first, an analysis of the system of meanings embodied in the symbols which make up religion proper, and, second, the relating of these systems to social-structural and psychological processes" (p. 42).

In a typical analytic approach, Spiro (1966) distinguishes between "apparent" and "real" functions of religion, with the "real functions" being "those which, in principle at least, can be discovered by the anthropologist, whether or not they are recognized by the actors," and the "apparent functions" being "those which the actors attribute to the [belief] but which cannot be confirmed by scientific investigation" (p. 109). Not surprisingly, then, he finds that genuine belief in religious beings or in the effectiveness of magic and rituals is only the apparent, not the real, function of religion, even though he also finds that such belief is definitive of a viable religion. "Ritual cannot effect rainfall, prayer cannot cure organic diseases, nirvana is a figment of the imagination, etc." (p. 113). Thus, although belief in the reality and efficacy of such things as gods and witches "is certainly false," "the religious actor . . . clings tenaciously to his religious beliefs and practices—however irrational they may seem" (p. 113), because they serve important social, political, economic, and psychological functions of which the religious actor, but not the anthropologist, is unaware.

Clearly, then, the anthropologists have tended to assume that science is right and religion is wrong, and they have therefore tended to discount the more explicitly *natural* assertions of religious knowledge in favor of the more hidden and implicit *social* assertions of that knowledge. In one sense this approach is an apparent effort to maintain the explanatory privilege of science and to assert a kind of cultural superiority of science over religion. But in another sense this is a perfectly reasonable analytic approach, and it is important to understand the difference between these two senses. On the one hand, the anthropologists could certainly be less cavalier about the unquestioned validity of science. They refuse to take religion on its own terms while casually taking science on its own terms, and the only apparent reason for this difference in approach is that they believe in one and not in the other. On the other hand, this biased analytic approach proves to be remarkably insightful and convincing, at least with respect to religion. One reason the anthropologists can remain so cavalier about science is that the resulting analyses of religion seem so valid. Clearly religious knowledge does include hidden social prescriptions and commitments, and clearly this legitimating dimension of religion could not be articulated and analyzed from within those same religious beliefs. By assuming religion to be wrong, the anthropologists have made it possible to understand religion better, even though they have hidden science from a similar analysis in the process.

Thus there are two basic lessons to be learned from the anthropological approach to religion. First, this approach has been quite productive. It has demonstrated that religious knowledge cannot produce a full social understanding of its own implications as knowledge, that is, that the legitimating dimensions of religion can be fully understood only from outside the concepts and explanations of religion itself. Second, the same approach should be applied to science. There is no particular reason to believe that science is any better at understanding itself than religion, except that we are still involved in the beliefs and institutions of science, whereas we have achieved quite some distance from the beliefs and institutions of religion. This involvement may make it more difficult to question science, but it is does not make science any more capable of understanding itself, as a legitimating belief system. Just like religion, science claims to explain natural phenomena, and we already know that the religious idea of nature is inherently social and that the scientific idea of nature is inherently incoherent. Thus we should take the same anthropological approach to science. We should doubt its concepts and explanations—electrons, force, spin, mathematics—in the same way we have doubted the concepts and explanations of religion—gods, spirits, magic, witchcraft. If we do this then we will begin to understand science better, and we will also begin to understand the idea of knowledge better, insofar as knowledge must begin to be understood as an issue of both social legitimation and natural explanation.

If we approach science in this way, then we will have to change somewhat the perspective from which science has typically been compared with religion. Typically, science and religion have been compared on the basis of their respective efforts at *explanation*, meaning their efforts at prediction and control. Stewart Guthrie (1980), for instance, tell us that "religion and science both are concerned to explain and control experience coherently and economically" (p. 186), and Robin Horton (1982) finds that the "traditionalistic" syndrome involves "a determined pursuit of the goals of explanation, prediction, and control" (p. 243). In these terms religious explanations are always found to be, by comparison, somewhat lacking. For Guthrie, "the characteristic religious assertion is, I think, false" (p. 192), and for Horton the "traditionalistic" syndrome contains "little if any explicit critical monitoring of [explanatory] theory in terms of general criteria of empirical adequacy or consistency" (p. 243).

Generally, both science and religion are seen as being equally concerned with explanation, in the sense of prediction and control, with one simply doing it better than the other. But there is an inherent bias here, since the idea of explanation, as prediction and control, is defined in terms of scientific, rather than religious, criteria. Because of its idea of objective nature, science is good at *technical* prediction and control, whereas religion, because of its idea of a sacred tradition, is good at *social* prediction and control. But in these anthropological comparisons it is typically the technical idea of explanation that is assumed, without much argument, to be the definition of genuine or valid explanation. Thus the comparison is always something of a setup from the start: science is better at explanation than religion because science is better at being science than religion. In effect, scientific explanations are defined as real explanations, and then religious explanations are compared with them and found lacking. Ernest Gellner (1974) makes this assumption explicit while arguing that genuine knowledge is inherently indifferent and dehumanizing, that is, inherently scientific:

> Genuine explanation . . . means subsumption under a structure or
> schema made up of neutral, impersonal elements. In this sense,
> explanation is always "dehumanising," and inescapably so. . . . There is a
> reason *why* the world is made up of machines, and that reason lies not
> in the world but in our *practices* of explanation. (pp. 106–7)

Thus genuine explanation is the impersonal, indifferent explanation of science, and so religion must be doing something else well, because it is doing explanation badly.

From this the anthropologists look for what religion must be doing well, since it has been so acceptable and effective, and what they find is social motivation, social reassurance, and social legitimation. In general they suggest that religious explanations themselves need to be "explained," in social, legitimating terms, since they cannot really be what they purport to be. This social dimension, then, turns out to be the defining difference between science and religion, since science is really about explanation, defined in scientific terms, and religion is really about social legitimation, despite its internal claims to be about explanation. Thus the anthropological issue becomes, How does religion achieve its primary social goals while passing itself off as explanation? How does it manage to do what it really does while appearing to do something else? It is through their answers to these questions that these analysts have defined and characterized religious knowledge, and what they have found is that religion tries to make the world more responsive and meaningful, more socially interdependent, than as scientists we know it to be. Thus for Durkheim and Geertz religious beliefs provide meaningful motivations in a way that scientific beliefs do not. For Durkheim (1967), "faith is before all else an impetus to action," so that "religions . . . though having the same subjects as science itself, cannot be really scientific" (p. 479). And for Geertz (1966), religion is "a system of symbols which acts to establish powerful, pervasive, and long-lasting moods and motivations in men," whereas science is concerned with "the suspension of the pragmatic motive in favor of disinterested observation" (pp. 4, 27). For Clyde Kluckhohn (1970), as for Guthrie, religion provides a needed sense of meaning and purpose by falsely anthropomorphizing nature. As Kluckhohn puts it, most people need "some form of personification" in their explanatory beliefs, since "only a small minority among highly sophisticated peoples can fairly face impersonal forces and the phenomena of chance" (p. 227). Or, as sociologist Peter Berger (1969) comments, "The sacred cosmos . . . provides man's ultimate shield against the terror of . . . meaninglessness" (pp. 26–27). And for Robin Horton (1967), "there is a limitation of scope" (p. 243) in religion, and only the "non-personal theoretical idiom" of science can achieve "the progressive acquisition of knowledge" (p. 70).

For these theorists, then, religion provides (social) meaning and purpose while science provides (natural) knowledge and explanation. They assume science to be right, and then they look at what religion does differently. What they find is the explanatory intertwining of social and natural concepts, the idea that social actions can influence natural phenomena and that social values and rituals are integral to any understanding of the universe. Since science is right, they know that this must be wrong, that nature is detached and objective, and that social references have no place in any valid explanations of natural processes. Thus they conclude that while these social references prevent religion from being explanatory, they provide something that science, because it is explanatory, cannot provide—meaning, purpose, motivation, a personal and attentive universe, and the like. This, then, defines the difference between religion and science: one offers false beliefs that are comfortable and the other offers correct explanations that are uncomfortable. The social commitments of religion are definitive but mistaken, and we know they are mistaken because science, as genuine explanation, has no social commitments. The presence of social references undermines explanatory validity, and while both science and religion claim to be explanatory, only science claims to be nonsocial. It is this claim of objective social detachment that makes the difference, and this claim is never seriously questioned, even though its supporting epistemology has collapsed and all scientific observations and concepts are now recognized as theory dependent—that is, as socially dependent.

Comparing Science and Religion as Belief Systems

In order to distinguish between science and religion, the anthropologists are willing to take the claims of science at face value, but not the claims of religion. Suppose, however, we decide to take the claims of neither science nor religion at face value, and then we try to distinguish between them. Suppose we approach them as simply different versions of knowledge, each providing an authoritative basis for explanation and legitimation, but each doing so from different conceptual assumptions and with different social results. From this perspective we can set aside the issue of right and wrong and look more directly at the differences of science and religion as versions of knowledge, as legitimating belief systems. In these terms their difference seems to be apparent: science asserts an absolutely nonsocial version of knowledge, while religion embraces an intertwining social-natural version of knowledge. This is the difference that the anthropologists have pointed to and relied upon, but they have not identified this as the crucial difference because they have taken scientific explanations to be valid, thus making that the crucial difference. But without this scientific bias, and associated scientific privilege, what these analysts have shown is that for religious knowledge social actions and natural phenomena are always conceptually interdependent, whereas for scientific knowledge they are always categorically separate. This is the crucial difference that distinguishes religious and scientific knowledge, and by focusing on it—as a difference only between legitimating strategies, not between truth and falsity—we can begin to get a more critical, and more anthropological, view of science.

In these terms, then, scientific knowledge is characterized by its effort to conceptualize nature as an independent explanatory domain, so that natural processes are properly understood as fundamentally separate from and indifferent to all social actions and concerns. Religious knowledge, on the other hand, is characterized by its effort to conceptualize both nature and the traditional social order as part of the same explanatory domain, so that natural regularities are properly understood as connected with and responsive to the values and actions of ritualized relationships. Science envisions an amoral world, where social actions can have no possible conceptual involvement with natural explanations. And religion envisions not simply a moral world but a *traditional* world, where traditional, ritualized actions have a necessary conceptual involvement with natural explanations. Thus the difference between science and religion is not the difference between an amoral world and a moral world, but rather the difference between an amoral world and a traditional world. Scientific knowledge disconnects social actions and natural processes formally, as a matter of principle, but religious knowledge does not connect them formally, as a matter of principle. Rather specific religions connect them in specific, substantive ways, and only in terms of particular, traditional values.

Put another way, religious knowledge does not connect the abstract *idea* of social actions with the abstract *idea* of natural processes, so that different particular versions of that connection can be proposed and, possibly, rejected on the basis of experience, values, elegance, and so on. Rather, religious knowledge allows only a very specific, cultural image of social actions—particular traditions, rituals—to be conceptually interconnected with certain specific concerns about natural phenomena—rain, game, harvests, fertility—so that no formal revision or criticism of the specific conceptual connection is possible. In religion it is the substantive, traditional relationship that counts—ritualized dances and rain—not the formal, mathematical relationship, as in science. As a result, science can permit critical revisions, within a mathematical framework, of conceptual explanations — such as of how matter formally relates to energy — but a religion cannot permit similar critical revisions of its explanations — such as how dances formally relate to rain. In this way religious knowledge is committed to the necessity of social-natural explanations, but only in the sense of *traditional*-natural explanations, thus making those explanations unavailable to conceptual criticism in the name of reason or experience. It is because the scientific separation of nature and society is formal and abstract that science can legitimate a *critical* idea of reason, and it is because the religious connection between nature and society is substantive and traditional that religion can legitimate only a *sacred* idea of reason.

This argument, then, has two parts. First, religious knowledge is fundamentally social-natural, in the sense that social actions and natural processes are conceptually interconnected. Second, this interconnection is always traditionally specific, in the sense of sacred, ritualized behavior. Both of these points are commonly made by the anthropologists of religion. With respect to the first, for example, Victor Turner (1968) finds that in Ndembu ritual "the natural order, represented by wild species of trees, is identified with the moral order, sanctioned by the ancestor spirits" (p. 21). More generally, according to John Skorupski (1976), throughout the anthropology of religion "the claim that traditional thought does not make the distinction which we make between the 'natural' and the 'social' is a central assumption" (p. 168). Similarly, for Claude Lévi-Strauss (1966), "religion consists in a *humanization of natural laws* and magic in a *naturalization of human actions* — the treatment of certain human actions *as if* they were an integral part of physical determinism" (p. 221).

The second point is also amply documented. Among the Netsilik Eskimos, according to Asen Balikci (1967), "the taboo system is involved in most of the situations endangering social life (lack of game, sickness, bad weather, evil spirit attacks, incest) and apparently controlled by the shaman. The people break taboos; this angers the spirits, who strike and bring misfortune" (p. 208). And for Evans-Pritchard (1967b), "God the creative spirit is the final Nuer explanation of everything. . . . The heavens and the earth and the waters on the earth, and the beasts and birds and reptiles and fish were made by him, and he is the author of custom and tradition" (pp. 140–41). According to H. Ian Hogbin (1967), for the Busama of New Guinea the accepted standards of behavior . . . had been ordained not by men such as we are but by superhuman creatures who were above and beyond criticism. Custom, that is to say, acquired a mystical value which made the slightest murmur of complaint an act of the grossest blasphemy. The man who followed established traditions must have felt that he was playing his allotted part in the divine purpose of the universe. (p. 74)

All of these studies stress the intricate religious connection of traditional customs with natural explanations, and Mary Douglas (1966) sums up the general point about a religious universe:

In such a universe the elemental forces are seen as linked so closely to individual human beings that we can hardly speak of an external, physical environment. . . . The distinctive point here is not whether the working of the universe is thought to be governed by spiritual beings or by impersonal powers. That is hardly relevant. Even powers which are taken to be thoroughly impersonal are held to be reacting directly to the behavior of individual humans. . . . In this sense the universe is apparently able to make judgments on the moral value of human relations and to act accordingly. . . . The universe responds to speech and mime. It discerns the social order and intervenes to uphold it. (pp. 81, 87-88)

As these comments show, religions typically interconnect society and nature through an idea of the gods, an idea of superior beings who can exercise control over natural processes and events and who protect and support the traditional social customs. This is the anthropomorphism of nature, the conceptual strategy that Lévi-Strauss calls "the humanization of natural laws," that Spiro calls the "culturally patterned interaction with culturally postulated superhuman beings," and that Guthrie calls "the systematic application of human-like models to non-human in ad-dition to human phenomena." Guthrie and Spiro define religion in this way, and Guthrie makes the issue quite clear: "Some gods are less like humans than others, but all, in contrast to philosophical or scientific con-cepts, retain some human character," and "All 'religions', by any useful definition, include gods" (p. 184). It is through this idea of the gods that religious knowledge intertwines the conceptualization of social actions and natural processes, and these are always particular, traditional gods, gods who are committed to specific rituals and behaviors. Through this idea of the gods the social–natural connection is understood as one of communication and influence, not one of causality and manipulation. As

Evans-Pritchard (1967b) writes of the Nuer, "God can be communicated with through prayer and sacrifice, and a certain kind of contact with him is maintained through the moral order of society which he is said to have instituted and of which he is the guardian" (p. 114). From this perspective the gods can be addressed and appeased, but they cannot be directly controlled, which means that religion can never become strictly an issue of technical manipulation. Interacting with nature is always a matter of communication, not of causality, and successful communication depends upon the proper moral attitudes, not simply upon a technical repetition of ritualized behaviors. The gods are attentive to the actions of individuals, and individuals can influence and affect the responses of the gods, but only as committed participants in the tradition, not as individualized manipulators of techniques.

Religious knowledge interconnects natural and social explanations, but only in terms of a sacred and absolute tradition, not in terms of a formal conceptual possibility. This means that religions can never legitimate the internal criticism and revision of their own particular versions of social-natural explanations, they can only accept that version absolutely or lose it absolutely. From a religious perspective moral obligations cannot be strictly formal, and the world cannot be abstractly meaningful. Either there is a sacred social-natural connection or there is none at all, which means that the gods have stopped paying attention and nature can no longer be expected to respond to moral, social efforts. It is this latter possibility, the prospect of a meaningless, impersonal world, that is always implicit in the religious conception, not the prospect of a formal and critical conception of social-natural interactions. For religion the world is either traditional or meaningless, and it was decisively in the direction of meaninglessness that scientific knowledge defined its vision of the world, as it arose in the context of, but as an alternative to, the traditional authority of religious knowledge. Science envisioned a natural world that was fully independent of social actions, so that natural explanations involved no moral dimensions, and this was both understandable and disturbing from within a religious context. Some early scientists tried to maintain a sense of religious meaning through the idea of an originating but nonintervening God, but this was not very convincing because nature itself had become meaningless and impersonal, in the sense of conceptually disconnected from human or social influence. From within a religious context science presented the only possible explanatory alternative to religious knowledge, the alternative that was always the implied threat behind religious requirements, the alternative of an inattentive, indifferent nature. Religion could not conceptualize a formal connection between nature and society, a connection that would allow social-natural relations to be understood critically and ecologically. But religion could conceptualize the absolute disconnection of nature and society, and from this conceptual beginning science could create a formal and critical idea of nature, an idea of nature as rational and technical rather than sacred and traditional.

This is the idea of objective nature, where the world is made up of uniform, lifeless components (atoms, electrons, and so on) and where natural processes are governed by indifferent, lawlike forces (gravity, the strong force, and the like). By definition, these particles and forces of nature have their own inherent, mathematical order, and while we may discover and utilize this order through rational investigation, we can never communicate with or influence this order through moral actions or attitudes. Science defines a universe that we just happen to be in, as natural, biological beings, a universe we can know but not affect, a universe that has no need of human beings or their knowledge. This is a universe of regular but meaningless processes, and it is this lack of meaning that is definitive of scientific knowledge. As we have seen, the "mistakes" of religion are often "explained" in terms of its efforts to impose a sense of meaning on the world, as opposed to the valid meaninglessness of science. And indeed it is a bleak and purposeless world that science presents to us, a world that can be faced and accepted only by the truly tough-minded, with their scientific confidence and objectivity. Thus Bertrand Russell (1957), as a philosopher and mathematician, finds that "the kernel of the scientific outlook is the refusal to regard our own desires, tastes, and interests as affording a key to the understanding of the world. . . . Only on the scaffolding of these truths, only on the firm foundation of unyielding despair, can the soul's habitation henceforth be safely built" (pp. 40, 45-46). Also, Jacques Monod (1971), from the perspective of biology, finds science to be "cold and austere, proposing no explanation but imposing an ascetic renunciation of all other spiritual fare . . . , leaving nothing in place . . . but a frozen universe of solitude" (p. 170). And Stephen Weinberg (1977), from the perspective of physics, agrees:

> It is almost impossible for humans to believe . . . that human life is not just a more-or-less farcical outcome of a chain of accidents reaching back to the first three minutes. . . . It is very hard to realize that this is all just a tiny part of an overwhelmingly hostile universe. . . . The more

the universe seems comprehensible, the more it also seems pointless. (p. 155)

In these terms, then, the distinction between religious knowledge and scientific knowledge is the distinction between conceptualizing a sacred social-natural connection and conceptualizing an absolute social-natural disconnection. If we assume that science is uniquely correct about the universe, then we can do an anthropological analysis of religion, based on the assumption that religion, but not science, is an inherently legitimating effort at knowledge. But if we assume that all versions of knowledge are inherently legitimating, then we can also do an anthropological analysis of science, and we can analyze the differences between science and religion in terms of their different legitimating strategies and their different institutional consequences. From this perspective the scientific separation of the social from the natural would not be seen as the conceptual condition for achieving objective truth, but rather as the conceptual condition for legitimating certain kinds of social practices, social practices that could not be legitimated by religion. For scientific knowledge the legitimating reference would be objective nature, rather than the sacred tradition, and so the idea of objective nature would be seen, anthropologically, as an inherently social and legitimating idea. By claiming to be nonsocial, this idea would be seen simply as mistaken about itself, in the same way that religious concepts have been interpreted as mistaken about themselves, since all versions of knowledge are now assumed to be as inherently concerned with social legitimation as with natural explanation. But this mistake would be seen as central and informative, since it would be where scientific knowledge both projected and disguised its inherent legitimating commitments. For science the idea of objective nature defines the legitimating notions of truth and reality, but these notions get their legitimating authority exactly from the scientific denial that they have any legitimating authority, the denial that they have any social content. Thus scientific knowledge legitimates social practices in the name of a social reference that cannot be recognized as social, and this means that no social criteria can be used to evaluate the validity of scientific knowledge, despite its institutional effects. This is the definitive social commitment of scientific knowledge, a commitment to denying any possibility of recognizing its own inherent social commitments, and it is this quality that gives scientific institutions both their technical proficiency and their ecological indifference.

In essence, science defines itself in opposition to religion, and so its institutional recommendations are essentially opposed to those of religion. Religious knowledge recommends an absolute moral commitment to the tradition, since the attentive gods will then continue to provide the necessary natural support for the social order. In contrast, scientific knowledge can only recommend an amoral commitment to technical proficiency, since objective nature is indifferent to human concerns and thus can only be technically manipulated for social support. Religion builds in an absolute and sacred reference to the ecological conditions for social life, and so science builds in no such reference at all. In order to break the traditional authority of religious knowledge, science referred the idea of knowledge to a completely inattentive nature, a reference that could only legitimate unrestrained technical efforts, with no possibility of legitimating some set of uniquely supportive, and thus sacred, social practices. Thus the scientific project was inherently political and social, a scientific quality that was understood better by the Church than by many of the early scientists, and it achieved these social and disruptive goals by denying that it had any such goals, which is exactly what a legitimating alternative to religion would have to do. From this perspective the epistemology of privileged observational access was always a conceptual effort to establish a new legitimating reference for knowledge, a reference that could be established only through the assertion that it was categorically nonlegitimating. And this would explain, of course, why the epistemological incoherence can seem so esoteric and irrelevant to scientific knowledge, to physics, because physics was always about social legitimation, not about the reality of objective nature.

In its fundamental opposition to religion, science categorically excludes any conceptual possibility of explaining natural phenomena in social terms, that is, of incorporating a necessary social reference into any valid explanations of natural processes. This means that science excludes not only all religious conceptions of *sacred* social-natural interactions (*traditional*-natural), but also any possibility of articulating a *formal* conception of social-natural interactions. In this way science excludes not only the possibility of religious knowledge but also the possibility of a "wild," ecological knowledge, a knowledge that legitimates reflexive ecological criticism as opposed to sacred rituals or technical proficiency. Such a "wild" knowledge would define an explanatory position between science and religion, in an effort to combine the scientific support for criticism and technique with the religious attention to social and ecological concerns. Through its reference to an abstract idea of mathematical nature, scientific knowledge becomes *formally natural*, and through its reference to a specific idea of the sacred tradition, religious knowledge becomes *substantively social-natural*. Accordingly, through its reference to the formal idea of sustainability, "wild" knowledge would become *formally social-natural*. This reference would be formal in the sense that it could never be finally embodied in some particular version of social-natural truth, just as objective nature can never be substantively embodied in some particular version of natural truth, such as Newton's theory of mechanics or Einstein's theory of relativity. But this reference would also be social-natural, so that "wild" knowledge would always legitimate reflexive ecological criticism against its own social-natural effects, as organized social actions, in the name of a formal commitment to sustainability.

But what are the formal conditions for sustainability, and how can they be identified, as a coherent reference for a "wild" knowledge? Science projects its reference as objective nature, and then it defines objective nature in terms of mathematics, as the formal structure of rationality, the language of nature. Religion projects its reference as the controlling gods, and then it defines these gods in terms of the sacred tradition, the tradition of daily life and ordinary language, as ritual appeal and magical access. In both of these cases the ultimate reference for knowledge is some version of language, where language in a special form is seen as providing privileged explanatory access to true reality, and valid knowledge is the result. Thus I will argue that the abstract, formal structure of language must be recognized as the only coherent reference for knowledge, and that both science and religion are mistaken as knowledge because they are both mistaken about their inherent reference to language. Science mistakes language as strictly technical manipulation, and religion mistakes language as strictly social legitimation, but language must be recognized as both and as more than both. In particular, language must be recognized as a reflexive, enabling structure, as the structure that enables the formal possibility of social life and social-natural interactions. As such a structure, language is both formal and social-natural, and so it is as such a structure that language must be recognized as the necessary reference for a coherent idea of knowledge, a "wild," sustainable knowledge.

THREE

Nature as Politics

Today physics is generally understood as strictly an issue of nature, and not of social theory or politics, but in the seventeenth century physics was recognized as inherently social and political, as an effort to define new and legitimating ideas of truth and reality. Today we tend to take physics at face value, revelling in its natural discoveries and technical abilities, but we also live within industrial and technological institutions, and we tend to forget that these institutions were legitimated through the idea of objective nature, as that idea was defined by physics. Moreover, we tend to forget, or never have been told, that the basic point of early physics was to legitimate a new version of social and political institutions, institutions derived from the ideas of reason and nature rather than from the ideas of tradition and God. At its inception the scientific idea of nature was blatantly political, and indeed the various competing efforts to define scientific nature, including the effort of Newton, were at the center of an emerging debate about class, authority, and property, a debate about the legitimacy of the feudal-Christian order. In the context of this debate these new ideas of nature, including the one that became the basis of physics, were explicitly shaped and molded in accordance with specific political interests, so that the new ideas of objective truth and reality would have the desired political authority. Political strategy, not pure observation, determined the conceptual structure of scientific nature, but the legitimating success of that strategy—as modern industrial society—has tended to make us forget this politicized history, in honor of the scientific version of its own neutral innocence. As this history is re-membered, however, scientific knowledge begins to appear as somewhat less neutral, and the anthropological argument is strengthened, the argu-ment that physics is a legitimating social theory, with its own politicized versions of objective truth and reality.

Our most familiar story about the rise of science generally includes images of certain heroic figures, such as Galileo and Descartes, striving to achieve objective natural truths against the systematic resistance and per-secution of the religious and political authorities. In a sense, this story can stand as modern society's myth of origin, a myth that legitimates scien-tific knowledge through such contrasts as reason versus faith, light ver-sus darkness, progress versus stagnation, and reality versus mysticism. One of the central analytic consequences of this story is that science be-gins to appear as having its own separate history, the apolitical history of neutral efforts at objective knowledge. In this history the scientists are seen as strictly responding to objective nature, with no political interests, so that they have their own independent historical development, the his-tory of science. In this way science is simply assumed to have "gotten it right," so that its history is strictly the history of increasing insights into nature. This means, of course, that the explanatory concepts of science—atoms, electrons, and so on—are self-explanatory, so that they require no further anthropological analysis, as do the mistaken concepts of religion. In particular, it means that the concepts of science are strictly derived from increasingly accurate observations, so that no political analysis of these concepts is necessary, or even possible.

This is the story science tells about itself, but a closer historical exam-ination suggests another, more politicized story about the development of science. According to this story, the new idea of nature did not so much oppose reason to faith as it opposed a faith in reason and nature to a faith in tradition and God. As Carl Becker (1932) tells it, Galileo as-serted the authority of facts over scholastic authority, and

> this subtle shift in the point of view was perhaps the most important
> event in the intellectual history of modern times. . . . The laws of
> nature and nature's God appeared henceforth to be one and the same
> thing, and since every part of God's handiwork could all in good time
> be reasonably demonstrated, the intelligent man could very well do with
> a minimum of faith—except, of course (the exception was tremendous
> but scarcely noticed at the time), faith in the uniform behavior of nature
> and in the capacity of reason to discover its *modus operandi*. (pp. 21-22)

This new scientific faith substituted the rational image of an objective nature for the biblical image of a revealed God. "Obviously the disciples of the Newtonian philosophy had not ceased to worship. They had only given another form and a new name to the object of worship: having denatured God, they defied nature" (Becker 1932, 63). Then in the name of this nature they began to legitimate a new, exciting, and disruptive set of ideas and commitments, including new social practices. "In the eighteenth century climate of opinion, whatever question you seek to answer, nature is the test, the standard: the ideas, the customs, the institutions of men, if ever they are to attain perfection, must obviously be in accord with [nature's] laws" (pp. 51-53).

This new idea of nature, as formulated in Newtonian physics, began to legitimate a new kind of social order, an order based on private property, individualism, and the market. Ostensibly the new physics was about the objective laws of nature, but more practically it was about the political and economic realignments of Europe, as has been pointed out by J. D. Bernal (1971):

> Paradoxically, for all his desire to limit philosophy to its mathematical expression, the most immediate effect of Newton's ideas was in the economic and political field. As they passed through the medium of the philosophy of his friend Locke and his successor Hume, they were to create the general skepticism of authority and belief in *laisser-faire* that were to lower the prestige of religion and respect for a divinely-constituted order of society. Directly through Voltaire, who first introduced his work to the French, they were to contribute to the "Enlightenment" and thus to the ideas of the French Revolution. To this day they remain the philosophical basis of bourgeois liberalism. (p. 489)

All of this is fairly familiar, at least to intellectual historians. It is generally understood that Thomas Hobbes, explicitly following the corpuscular ideas and method of his contemporary Galileo, created a revolutionary new approach to both politics and social theory; that John Locke, explicitly following Newton, advanced the ideas of property and democracy that were used to organize the American republic; that Adam Smith utilized Newtonian principles of corpuscular matter and natural providence to support his analysis of market principles; that the Utilitarianism of Adam Smith, David Hume, Jeremy Bentham, and John Stuart Mill "can be defined as nothing but an attempt to apply the principles of Newton to the affairs of politics and morals" (Halévy, 1955, 6); and that Rousseau, the physiocrats, and the philosophes based their Enlightenment vision, and thus the impetus to the French Revolution, squarely in the Newtonian idea of nature.

Clearly physics was socially influential, but this influence has generally been interpreted as an external social consequence of neutral and objective knowledge, not as an internal legitimating commitment of a politicized conception of nature. If scientific knowledge is neutral, then this knowledge is available for political uses, but it does not entail specific political commitments. From this perspective the scientific idea of reason might be *applied* for political legitimation but it is not *defined* in order to serve particular political interests. Thus scientific knowledge can be seen as having legitimate effects on politics and social life, but politics and social life cannot be seen as having any legitimate effects on scientific knowledge. This is why our historians can generally see only one direction of influence between scientific knowledge and social life. Scientific knowledge can legitimately influence social life, through its technology and its idea of reason, but social life cannot legitimately influence scientific knowledge, since this knowledge is strictly an issue of objective nature. This is the assumption that has characterized most of our social histories of science, as Margaret Jacob (1976) observes in her study of the early, seventeenth-century interactions between science and politics: "Almost without exception the Newtonianism of this early period has been analyzed as an intellectual phenomenon, devoid of social and political content, transcendent of ideology" (p. 173). She herself, however, comes to a different conclusion, at least concerning the initial acceptance of and enthusiasm for Newton's ideas:

> Historians of science have often presumed that the new mechanical philosophy triumphed in England simply because it offered the most plausible explanation of nature. It just may do that, but in my understanding of the historical process that made it acceptable the supposed correspondence of the new mechanical philosophy with the actual behavior of the natural order is not the primary reason for its early success. (p. 17)

Jacob argues that politics played a crucial role in determining the "physical" assumptions underlying the Newtonian conception of nature, an argument supported in the work of Brian Easlea, Jan Golinski, and David Kubrin. These historians suggest not only that science arose in an intensely political context but also that the basic concepts of Newtonian physics were directly shaped by particular political concerns, and that this political content was recognized and included by the scientists themselves. This is a version of scientific history that runs counter to our standard historical story, the story of scientific objectivity and privilege. The idea that the concepts and explanations of physics were determined more by political interests than by observational evidence seems bizarre to us, even though it seems reasonable to suggest, anthropologically, that religious concepts and explanations have been determined in this way. We are generally willing to recognize that the scientific conception has profoundly influenced modern politics and social practices, but we have been generally unwilling to consider that these politics and practices may have built into that conception from the start, in the basic assumptions and concepts of physics. However, it can be argued that this has indeed been the case, specifically in the early efforts to define and characterize objective nature.

In the middle of the seventeenth century, turmoil and unrest in England disrupted confidence in the established social order, as well as in the established Aristotelian cosmology. It was a time of conceptual confusion, with intense public debates that were simultaneously religious and political, debates over the proper perspective toward God, authority, and the world. In this period, Jacob (1976) remarks, "every conceivable theory about religion, society, nature and God could be read by the literate population or preached to the nonliterate," and furthermore, "particular natural philosophies came to be associated with particular political and social theories, or occasionally with political behavior" (pp. 23-24). There were basically four contending natural philosophies, four politicized versions of nature. One was the Hermetic tradition of alchemy and natural magic, a tradition that included Christian visions of demons and witches. This view of nature was utilized to attack inequality and aristocratic privilege, generally in the name of the peasants. A second version of nature suggested a vision of atheistic pantheism, a vision that supported the freethinkers in their attacks on clerical influence and religious intolerance. And then there were two other conceptions of nature, both grounded in the new mechanical philosophy, but with one derived from the severe mechanism of Descartes and Hobbes and the other from the associated subdued mechanism of Newton. The mechanistic nature of Descartes and Hobbes was seen as supporting a world governed by pure individual self-interest, a world in which religion would have no moral authority. And the mechanism of Newton was seen as supporting a Christianized version of market commitments, a world in which the emerging interests of property would be protected by the moral authority of God. This Newtonian perspective was the position defended by the latitudinarians, the well-off, progressive members of the English Church who saw future opportunities in the world of trade, rather than in trying to maintain the rigid constraints of traditional aristocratic privilege. These were the supporters of Newton, the men who adapted, shaped, and directed Newton's theories of nature into a sanctified natural philosophy. Through this scientific conception of nature and the universe, God could be seen as supporting their particular political arguments and economic interests. "In short, the new mechanical philosophy from its very inception possessed social and political significance" (Jacob 1976, 23).

This was the natural philosophy that carried the day, the nature of Newton and the low churchmen, a nature in which God still had some authority, as the guarantor of the rational mechanical order. Through this idea of nature the new authority of rationality (as in trade and profit) could be asserted against the traditional authority of faith (as in aristocratic class privilege), but the moral authority of God was still available to maintain a *traditional* kind of class respect for the *new* authority of class and property (as in private, alienable property, the new rational idea of property). This was a carefully crafted position, a position that could use the idea of reason against the aristocratic claim of sacred property rights and that could use the idea of God against the peasants' rejection of any legitimate property rights. The Newtonian conception of nature was the centerpiece of this political strategy, and this conception was shaped and molded by the latitudinarians for exactly this purpose. These Newtonians attacked the rival cosmological conceptions "not simply because they disagreed with these explanations of how the universe worked, but because they also and primarily saw these philosophies as profound threats to the social, political, and religious order" (Jacob 1976, 178-79). And Newton himself seems to have participated in this political/natural strategy. He wrote extensively in, and was clearly influenced by, the Hermetic tradition, the tradition of alchemy and natural magic. But he very carefully and selectively did not publish this material, choosing instead to publish only mechanical explanations of the natural order. In some cases he changed or withdrew letters solely for the purpose of tempering the implicitly occult flavor he had given to certain physical formulations, such as gravitational force. Indeed, the idea of gravity seems to demand some kind of regulating God, since it has no mechanical explanation. This failure of mechanism was always a problem for the Newtonian philosophy, as it was commonly used as a basis for attacks on Newton, particularly by Leibniz, his political opponent. As Jan Golinski (1988) suggests:

> Leibniz's charge that Newton resorted to occult qualities had the effect
> of weakening the credibility of his opponent as a public figure. It was
> therefore impossible, politically and philosophically, for Newton to
> admit his indebtedness to a secret tradition of alchemical texts. Newton
> and his followers had to emphasize the observable status of his forces of
> attraction, and to conceal their origins in his private alchemical work.
> (p. 166)

The reliance on occult forces had to be hidden from sight, for political reasons, and yet they supported an idea of mechanical nature in which God was still necessary, as an explanatory reference. It was exactly this combination of rational explanations with Godly authority that served the political interests of Newton and his supporters, and it was this combination that Newton carefully articulated in all his published, public work.

The ways in which these early physical concepts and explanations became subject to political requirements are interesting and unexpected — unexpected because we are not used to thinking of physics in this way. Arguments ostensibly about nature but fundamentally about politics sprang up over such issues as whether matter has inherent motion or can be moved only by external forces, whether space is absolute or relative, whether gravity is an occult or a mechanical principle, whether space is void or full, and whether matter is permanent or transformable. Each of these issues hides a political position; each involves an effort to appeal to nature for the "objective" legitimation of particular political interests. For example, if matter has inherent motion, then God has no effective place in the universe and thus there is no support for a God-ordained natural and social order. On the other hand, if matter is dead and subject only to external forces, then these forces must reveal the presence of God behind the mechanistic order, so that God is still available as a legitimating reference. The central tenet of Newtonian philosophy was that nature could be explained only in terms of God's constant intervention in a lifeless, material, mechanical universe. In this way a natural harmony of mechanical matter was envisioned, a harmony that demanded the opening of rational (natural) opportunities for the merchant class and a continuation of traditional (moral) respect from the lower classes. With too little God — the pure mechanism of Hobbes or Descartes — self-interest would run rampant and determinism would destroy the social order, but with too much God—a magical or pantheistic nature—human beings would lose their Godlike position of control over lifeless matter, meaning that the dominant class would lose its justification for profit and property.

> The Newtonian definition of the relationship between man and matter gives a philosophical sanction to the pursuit of material ends, to using the things of this world to one's advantage, in effect, to bargain, to sell, to engage in worldly affairs with the knowledge that this activity is a God-given right. (Jacob 1976, 189)

Among other things, this attitude legitimates the willful appropriation and technological control of the natural environment for human purposes, as Brian Easlea (1980) observes: "There can be no admiration for a de-mothered nature of brute inert matter. . . . Man can clearly make use of such matter as he pleases; such matter has no rights" (p. 139).

In accordance with these legitimating requirements, space must be seen as a void, so that God's active principles can move matter, and space must be seen as absolute so that the void is absolute. Also, gravity must work in a void so that the atoms can be moved in accordance with God's harmony, and matter must be eternal and impenetrable so that it cannot be subject to spontaneous transformation. These are some of the basic explanatory assumptions of physics, and they were originally formulated as part of a politicized effort to conceptualize objective nature, an effort to legitimate market rationality and market practices in the name of knowledge and truth.

> Science acted as an anchor for social theories and provided an underpinning that synchronized the operation of nature with an economic and social order increasingly determined by capitalistic forms of production. To my mind, the most historically significant contribution of the latitudinarians lies in their ability to synthesize the operations of a market society and the workings of nature in such a way as to render the market society natural. . . . Their synthesis survived . . . because it gratified the beneficiaries of that new order. Natural religion made the actions of the prosperous compatible with Christian virtue and with the very mechanism of the universe. (Jacob 1976, 51)

The Politics of Gravity

Perhaps the clearest example of this political-scientific intermingling was the Leibniz-Clarke debates of 1715 and 1716, in which Gottfried Wilhelm

Leibniz, German philosopher and mathematician, corresponded with Samuel Clarke, English minister and Newtonian. The subject of this debate was Newton's explanation of gravity, but the deeper issue concerned the possible role of God in a rational universe. Following Newton, Clarke wanted to maintain a formal, but not truly explanatory, role for God, a position Leibniz found to be incompatible with the idea of rational explanation. In effect, the Newtonians wanted only a certain kind of rational universe, one in which rational market activities could be legitimated from within some degree of traditional, God-ordained class privilege. Leibniz, on the other hand, found this formal possibility of Godly intervention to be incompatible with rational explanation. In general, the Newtonians were trying to deny the abstract possibility of natural-social interaction, in the name of reason, while trying to maintain the idea of a legitimating God, for the sake of traditional privileges. Leibniz was more consistent, however, and the notion of a legitimating God would fall to the notion of rational nature.

The debate centered on Newton's rather notorious idea of gravitational attraction as some kind of mysterious action-at-a-distance. Clarke argued that this idea made sense on the ground that God was constantly attentive and ready to intervene to keep the universe working properly. Leibniz ridiculed this position, suggesting that it denigrated God (since it implied that He could not make the universe perfect in the first place) and that in any case only an understanding of the universe in terms of rational necessity, rather than miraculous intervention, would be truly explanatory. Clarke and the theological Newtonians tried to resist the mechanism that was explicit in Descartes and Hobbes and implicit in Leibniz, and tried to defend the image of a scientifically explained universe actively maintained by a powerful, attentive, and moral God. In contrast, Leibniz argued that the idea of God might be useful to get the whole thing started, but that apart from its origins the universe could be understood quite adequately in terms of pure and necessary rationality, without a need for the constant miracles of a repairing God, with all the attendant requirements for faith and religious mysticism. Conceptually Leibniz was more consistent, and the Newtonian appeal to God would disappear. Nevertheless, it was the Newtonian image of inert objective nature, not the more vital nature of Leibniz, that would prevail as physics, an image explicitly formulated to serve political interests, not observational evidence.

The English Newtonians found these apparently esoteric issues of physical reality to be saturated with political implications; indeed, these issues were seen as explicit efforts to confiscate the notions of truth and knowledge as legitimating weapons in a social struggle over class position. Similarly, the French philosophes began to combine English empiricism with Continental rationalism in order to arrange Newton's idea of nature into the social and political program of the Enlightenment, a program of progress and rationality, a program without the need for a moral or attentive God. And in turn this French variation on Newtonian themes returned to England to combine with the mechanistic psychology of Locke and Hume and provide the philosophical basis for Jeremy Bentham's idea of a utilitarian social order and John Stuart Mill's idea of liberty. Thus it appears that the scientific displacement of religion in the sixteenth and seventeenth centuries was more a political issue of power than an objective issue of nature, and that the scholars of that time understood the political implications of scientific explanations far better than we do today.

As I will argue in the next chapter, the conceptual impetus for the emergence of scientific knowledge was not so much an increased observational attention to nature as an increased explanatory interest in mathematics, an interest generated by the Renaissance revival of Platonic ideas. Mathematics formed the basis of the mechanistic philosophy, with its ideas of inert matter and external, lawlike forces. In this sense the political debates were concerned with the relative explanatory (legitimating) power of magic, pantheism, and mathematics, with mathematics finally prevailing, in the less extreme, more compromising version of Newton. Mathematics made this new mechanistic system explanatory. In effect, mathematics legitimated scientific knowledge, as Copernicus proposed it, Galileo formulated it, and Newton completed it. And mathematics could do this only because it had its own sacred, scholastic authority, an authority that could be used, uniquely, to build an explanatory bridge from a Christian to a scientific world. Mathematics was the necessary explanatory glue that held together and authorized the ideas of inert, uniform corpuscles and lawlike, universal forces, the ideas of absolute space and time, the idea of objective nature. In this chapter I have suggested that these ideas were shaped as much by politics as by observation, and in these terms mathematics was the political key, in the sense that only the authority of mathematics could make the new idea of objective nature seem coherent and rational. Mathematics is still the underlying explanatory reference for scientific knowledge, and the explanatory credibility of science is still dependent upon a somewhat sacred and

mysterious conception of mathematics. Thus my next task will be to analyze the mathematical structure of scientific knowledge, and then to
show how a mathematical idea of knowledge imposes certain necessary
institutional commitments on social life. In this way scientific knowledge, just like religious knowledge, can be analyzed anthropologically, in
terms of its inherent legitimating commitments.

The anthropologists have demonstrated that religious knowledge can
be more effectively analyzed in terms of its legitimating strategies than in
terms of its natural explanations. In modern society we have generally
accepted that scientific knowledge cannot be so analyzed, because it has
no legitimating interests or strategies. In this chapter I have suggested
that, on the contrary, scientific knowledge grew up full of legitimating
strategies, and that indeed its birth and growth may have been fully dependent upon its success as a legitimating strategy. This is the argument
made in the historical work of Jacob and others, work that serves to raise
some historical doubts about the self-professed political innocence of science. It seems fairly obvious to us, anthropologically, that religious explanations contain hidden social instructions, since we no longer live in a
religious society and since religious explanations always contain social
and moral dimensions. It seems somewhat less obvious to us, anthropologically, that scientific explanations contain hidden social instructions,
since we are embedded in scientific institutions and science, as our legitimating idea of knowledge, denies any such social involvement absolutely. The anthropological argument, then, has two basic parts, one
historical and one conceptual. The historical argument suggests not only
that science has a history of social legitimation but that it has a history of
defining its concepts expressly for the purpose of social legitimation. The
conceptual argument involves a demonstration that the scientific idea of
nature contains inherent legitimating commitments, as a matter of conceptual analysis. Thus the two arguments can be mutually reinforcing,
but I believe the conceptual argument is more central and I will spend
more time on it. For my purposes, the historical argument should soften
the ground for the conceptual argument, by indicating that science
clearly works as a legitimating belief system and that this dimension of
science was far more explicit and apparent at its origins than it is now.

Science and religion are both legitimating, but religions base their legitimating efforts on the explicit assertion of specific social commitments, while science bases its legitimating efforts on the explicit denial of
any such social commitments. From our scientific perspective, we have

tended to see religious knowledge as conceptually confused, and thus as primarily legitimating, rather than explanatory. The religious reliance on magic and ritual fundamentally contradicts our scientific reliance on mathematics, as the definition of genuine explanation. From a different perspective, the perspective of ecological knowledge, I have argued that at least one aspect of religious incoherence stems from the inability of religion to legitimate the possibility of criticism, due to its very traditional, concrete vision of a sacred cosmos. In these terms scientific knowledge can indeed legitimate the possibility of criticism, due to its very abstract, formal vision of objective nature. Thus science avoids the religious form of critical incoherence, but then manages to introduce its own form of ecological incoherence, since it excludes any possibility of a social-natural reference for a sustainable idea of knowledge. In the next chapter I will argue that this ecological incoherence stems from a fundamental explanatory incoherence, the incoherence of the scientific idea of mathematics, as the language of nature and the structure of reason. Indeed, I will argue that reliance on mathematics makes science incoherent in the same way that the reliance on magic makes religion incoherent, and that in fact mathematics is the scientific version of magic.

FOUR

The Mathematics of Knowledge

Science claims to have separated the idea of knowledge from necessary involvement with human interests and social life. As philosopher Michael Dummett (1979) puts it:

> The attempt to say what things are like in themselves is an attempt to find a means of characterizing them that is independent, not only of the particular position and circumstances of an individual observer, but also, more generally, of the situation of human beings, located on the surface of a certain planet at a particular stage in its history, being of a certain size and having a particular range of sensory faculties. . . . One of the things that a scientific theory aims to do is to attain an accurate description of things as they are in themselves, or as they really are, in this sense. (pp. 15-16)

This separation of valid knowledge from all things human is supposed to have been achieved through the idea of objective nature, with the associated idea that this nature can be directly and neutrally observed. But if science is analyzed as a social belief system, then the idea of objective nature is not seen as a uniquely objective version of reality, but rather as an interesting and unique way of defining the legitimating notions of truth and knowledge. From this perspective what is interesting about scientific knowledge is not that it has so successfully separated valid knowledge from social life, but that it has so successfully *claimed* to have separated them. If science is a belief system, then it must legitimate specific social actions exactly by claiming not to legitimate them, in the name of objective nature. This is the claim that connects knowledge and truth, as legitimating terms, with the scientific conception of nature, and so it is through an analysis of this claim that we can discover the necessary social commitments of scientific knowledge.

Science relies on an epistemology of direct and neutral observations, observations that can objectively connect valid knowledge with natural reality. Nature must be observed to be known, and so it is this idea of privileged, viridical observations that carries the conceptual weight of scientific knowledge. This notion of observation defines the famous scientific method, the method that validly connects knowledge with reality, the method of hypothesis, experiment, and pure perception. This would seem to suggest that scientific credibility depends upon the possibility of neutral observations, and yet, as we have seen, science remains quite credible despite the accepted impossibility of such observations. So it would seem that the implication of credibility must go the other direction: we accept scientific observations as objective because we accept scientific knowledge as valid, and we accept scientific knowledge as valid because of its remarkable institutional success. This means that the credibility of the scientific method is really dependent on the cultural credibility of science, not the other way around. Science has institutional rather than observational credibility, and as long as we accept science as right about nature, we must also accept the objectivity of scientific observations, despite their loss of epistemological coherence. The epistemology can be rethought and changed—made relativistic, referred to technical success, and so on—as an issue of esoteric philosophical concerns, but the scientific conception of knowledge, with its notion of observation, must remain credible, as the defining reference for truth, reality, and reason.

In this way we can begin to analyze science as a belief system, where the scientific idea of observation can remain credible despite its conceptual incoherence because of its inherent legitimating commitments. To scientific believers this idea of observation can seem quite simple and straightforward, but in fact it is quite complicated and convoluted, and full of hidden assumptions. All versions of knowledge must contain some image of human beings—as knowers, the subjects of knowledge—and the scientific image of human beings is contained in this notion of observation, as neutral, rational observers. As long as scientific knowledge is accepted as institutionally legitimate, this image of human beings is accepted as institutionally legitimate, as the basis on which to build rational institutions. So it is here, in this notion of privileged observation, that all the specific social commitments of scientific knowledge are hidden. These are the commitments imposed by the scientific assumption about human beings, and in particular by the scientific image of the rational and detached mind, the mind of the objective scientific observer.

For science knowledge is an issue of the observing human mind, and yet the human mind is typically influenced by social and cultural ideas, ideas that involve values and beliefs and that are not strictly and neutrally derived from objective nature. Thus scientific observations must establish a neutral and objective connection between the mind and nature, a connection systematically purged of all such contaminating social influences. The mind must become effectively nonhuman for purposes of knowledge, so that the human mind can achieve knowledge that is not *human* knowledge, as Dummett has remarked, not the kind of knowledge that is referred to human values and concerns. Such an objective connection can be made through observation, but only through a special kind of observation, a kind that is uniquely focused on nature and without social content. This is mathematical observation, the only kind of observation that can directly connect the rational mind with objective nature. Mathematics is found to be the special, necessary lens through which nature must be observed, since nature is defined as being exactly a structure of mathematical entities and relations. Objective nature is exclusively a mathematical order, and so mathematical observations can uniquely present objective knowledge to the mind. For scientific knowledge, then, the idea of the *mind* is connected with the idea of *nature* through the idea of *mathematics*. This is the structure of the claim made by scientific knowledge, and it imposes a corresponding structure on the world that scientific knowledge explains, the world of scientific nature and scientific society. This is the structure that contains the legitimating commitments of scientific knowledge, as a belief system, and scientific knowledge has hidden these legitimating commitments behind an appeal to mathematics, as the characterizing structure of both nature and the mind. The mind must become mathematical if it is to achieve valid knowledge, and so the idea of objective nature imposes a mathematical structure on the scientific image of human beings, as the detached, receptive subjects of scientific knowledge. It is this image of human beings, as characterized by the detached, rational mind of mathematical knowledge, that has remained essentially immune from social analysis, since this image is incorporated into the privileged ideas of pristine observations and objective nature. And it is this image that I will begin to analyze, anthropologically, in this chapter and the next, focusing first on the idea of mathematical nature and second on the idea of the mathematical mind.

The Residue of Necessity

As science emerged from the scholastic tradition, this new idea of observation involved the presumption of a *necessary* connection between the rational mind and the natural order, a connection that could guarantee the *certainty* of scientific knowledge. Such a guarantee could be given, it was argued, because the mind had been given the same rational, a priori structure as the universe, so that the appropriate observations could establish a necessary connection and the mind could achieve certain knowledge. Descartes (1965), for example, presumed the existence of "certain laws which God has so established in nature and of which he has imprinted notions in our souls, such that after having reflected sufficiently upon them, we could not doubt that they are exactly observed in everything which is or which occurs in the world" (p. 34). This idea of a necessary, *rational* correspondence between the knower and the known served to sanctify the early conception of scientific knowledge, in the Christian scholastic context. But it also served to disrupt the Christian conception of the world, since if rational knowledge could achieve necessity, then human knowledge would be comparable to God's knowledge, with no sacred mysteries and no need for faith. Many early scientists, including Bacon and Descartes, embraced this implication of scientific knowledge, with Galileo (1967) observing:

> The Divine intellect indeed knows infinitely more propositions, since it knows all. But with regard to the few which the human intellect does understand, I believe that its knowledge equals the Divine in objective certainty, for here it succeeds in understanding necessity, beyond which there can be no greater sureness. (p. 103)

But if individual reason and observation could achieve Godlike knowledge, then individuals could challenge the sacred tradition in the name of rational truth, which is what Galileo did and why the Church imprisoned him and burned his books. The idea that scientific knowledge was *necessary* allowed Galileo and others to challenge the Church directly, on its own terms, in the name of God as the guarantor of knowledge. This was a more rational and less mysterious God, and His support for the new knowledge increasingly disturbed the Church, apparently for good reason. But this God was still Christian enough to be able to guarantee the necessity, and thus the scholastic credibility, of scientific knowledge, a guarantee that certified a necessary correspondence between the rational structure of the mind and the rational structure of nature.

This necessary correspondence was provided by mathematics, as the common rational structure. God had established a mathematical, a priori harmony between the mind and nature, and mathematical observations could reveal this harmony to the mind, thus providing certain knowledge. This idea of mathematical harmony removed a reference to God, as mysterious power, from the methods for achieving knowledge, while still requiring a reference to God, as rational architect, for guaranteeing the necessity of knowledge. And this was an important conceptual trick, because the idea of observation, by itself, could not be the basis of necessary or even credible knowledge in the scholastic world. If certain knowledge was to be achieved through observation, then the idea of observation had to be redefined, and this redefinition was achieved through a reliance on the necessity of mathematics, a necessity that could be guaranteed only by God. Thus the necessity of mathematics enabled knowledge to be based on rational observation, rather than on faith and tradition, and this idea of necessity was part of a scholastic, not a scientific, world. In his book *Mathematics and the Loss of Certainty*, Morris Kline (1980) comments on this emerging view of mathematics: "These [early] mathematicians were sure of the existence of mathematical laws underlying natural phenomena and persisted in the search for them because they were convinced a priori that God had incorporated them into the construction of the universe" (p. 35).

The scientific idea of necessity followed directly from the Aristotelian-Christian idea of necessity, where God had arranged the essential forms of the mind in a necessary correspondence with the essential forms of the universe, and this correspondence was guaranteed by faith, as the only path to certain knowledge. But objective nature was defined in terms of reason, not faith, and so scientific knowledge could not easily depend on the authority of God. Knowledge still required a necessary correspondence between the structure of the mind and the structure of the universe, but now this correspondence had to be fully accessible to human rationality, which meant that this common structure had to be fully rational, not mysterious. Mathematics made such a correspondence possible, because mathematics was understood as having a necessary, a priori rationality. This idea of mathematics derived from Plato, through the Platonic revival in Renaissance Italy. Mathematics was seen as constituting the essential, underlying form of reality, a form that could not be found in the immediate appearance of things but could be found only through careful rational investigation.

The early scientists turned this scholastic view of mathematics into the idea of mathematical observations, the special kind of observations that could establish a necessary correspondence between the mind and nature. These were not the observations of ordinary experience, and indeed ordinary experience could only be false and misleading. These were the kind of observations that could see beneath ordinary experience to the true structure of reality, a reality that was now absolutely rational and mathematical. Only through these special scientific observations could the mathematical structure of the mind be connected with the mathematical structure of the universe, and so only through mathematical observations could certain knowledge be achieved, the knowledge of mathematical necessity.

> What Descartes, Kepler, Galileo, Newton, Leibniz, and many other
> founders of modern mathematics believed can be expressed thus: there is
> inherent in nature a hidden harmony that reflects itself in our minds in
> the form of simple mathematical laws. This harmony is the reason that
> events in nature are predictable by a combination of observation and
> mathematical analysis. (Kline 1985, 213)

The idea that scientific knowledge was *necessary* had at least four important implications: it allowed science to achieve conceptual credibility in a scholastic world, it enabled objective nature to be defined mathematically, it enabled the knowing mind to be defined mathematically, and it enabled scientific observation to be defined mathematically, so that the true observations of science could be distinguished from the deceptive observations of ordinary human experience. The necessity of scientific knowledge required an a priori observational harmony between the mind and nature, a harmony established by mathematics. And for a while, at least, the rational necessity of mathematics could fill in for the mysterious necessity of God's sacred harmony, the preestablished harmony of first principles and final causes.

> Thus the Catholic doctrine postulating the supreme importance of
> seeking to understand God's will and His creations took the form of a
> search for God's mathematical design of nature. . . . Mathematical
> knowledge, the truth about God's design of universe, was as sacrosanct
> as any line of scripture. (Kline 1980, 34-35)

As the scholastic world declined, however, the idea of necessary knowledge became both less important and less convincing. As science became embedded in its own institutions, it gradually replaced the reference to God, even a mechanistic God, with a reference to nature, and so scientific knowledge lost its privileged, scholastic guarantor of a priori necessity. More important, however, science was supposed to be based on empirical observations, not a priori assumptions, so that the idea of a necessary harmony had to be abandoned (Hume) and replaced by some idea of an empirical harmony, such as an empirical a priori (Kant) or an empirical definition of truth (logical positivism). This meant that we could have only an empirical, not a necessary, confidence in scientific knowledge, so that the presumed mathematical connection between the mind and nature became far more problematic, at least in theory.

So how did this loss of necessity affect scientific knowledge, especially with respect to the four important implications of necessity mentioned above—scholastic credibility, objective nature, the rational mind, and privileged observation? Primarily, scientific knowledge lost its scholastic, demonstrative credibility, but then it no longer needed this credibility, since it had begun to establish its own cultural and institutional credibility. Otherwise, the loss of necessity had little effect, and in particular it did not change the scientific ideas of the rational mind, objective nature, or mathematical observations. Indeed, these ideas have become increasingly embedded in scientific knowledge, as this knowledge has become increasingly mathematical. The requirement that knowledge be *necessary* led to the mathematical definitions of mind, nature, and observation, but these definitions easily survived the loss of necessity and still characterize the essence of the scientific conception. It is still assumed that mathematical observations can directly connect the rational mind with objective nature, only now the possibility of such a connection is not derived from an a priori, preestablished harmony.

This means we can no longer be *certain* of such a connection, as a sacrosanct basis for achieving knowledge; we can only have *empirical evidence* for such a connection, meaning technical success, engineering, the best we can get, and so on. This is why scientific epistemology has been scrambling—to find another justification for assuming such a connection—but the assumption itself has not been seriously challenged, neither by science nor philosophy nor social theory. Scientific knowledge is defined by this assumption—that mathematical observations can directly connect the rational mind with objective nature—and this assumption must remain intact as long as science remains culturally credible. As a consequence, the constituting ideas of mind, nature, and observation remain thoroughly mathematical, despite the loss of the justifying image of mathematics. Science remains credible but mathematics has lost its necessity, and this means that the mediating role of mathematics must become puzzling and amazing, even magical. The commitment to necessity justified the explanatory reliance on mathematics, but without this scholastic commitment the mathematical structure of scientific knowledge must appear puzzling, as Albert Einstein (1983) has commented:

> At this point an enigma presents itself which in all ages has agitated inquiring minds. How can it be that mathematics, being after all a product of human thought which is independent of experience, is so admirably appropriate to the objects of reality? . . . In my opinion the answer to this question is, briefly, this: As far as the laws of mathematics refer to reality, they are not certain; and as far as they are certain, they do not refer to reality. (p. 28)

This answer, of course, is not altogether clear, and the question is difficult. So later, when Richard Feynman (1967) considers the same question, he is willing simply to acknowledge the mystery of mathematics, without trying to solve the puzzle:

> Every one of our laws is a purely mathematical statement in rather complex and abstruse mathematics. . . . It gets more and more abstruse and more and more difficult as we go on. Why? I have not the slightest idea. It is only my purpose here to tell you about this fact. (p. 93)

It is here that mathematics becomes magical, as the privileged path to nature's laws that no one can explain. Like magic, the mathematical connection must be accepted on faith, and if it is then science can continue and valid knowledge can be achieved. Unlike in religion, however, the magic must be hidden, since science is supposed to be rational. So we simply continue to honor the certainty of mathematics, as the model of rationality, despite its loss of necessity—that is, despite its magical quality. This is what Einstein and Feynman and others do, as adherents of science—casually recognize the magic, because necessity is dead, and then discount it because science is so obviously right. And this is what philosophy and social theory have done as well—grant mathematics continued immunity from social analysis because it is so convincing in its mystery.

Certainly it is not unusual to base the legitimating ideas of knowledge and reality upon faith and magic, but it is unusual to claim rationality and hide behind faith. Such a legitimating strategy means, among other things, that the scientific idea of reason can be criticized in the name of reason, since science both legitimates the idea of reason and fails to achieve it. Scientific knowledge depends upon a generally tacit appeal to faith, a faith in the explanatory magic of mathematics, and yet science claims that this faith is rational, not absolute, which means that this appeal to faith can be criticized in the name of reason. Science does not make this easy, since it tends to identify reason with mathematics, but it also tends to admit that mathematical explanations cannot be explained rationally, so that the reliance on mathematics must either be accepted on faith or criticized in the name of another, more coherent idea of reason. And this is the argument I am making, where the idea of reason is directed against the scientific idea of mathematics, in the sense that any coherent idea of reason must be both more social and less magical. For this effort I must appeal to an ecological idea of reason, where reason is understood in terms of social-natural sustainability rather than in terms of technical, mathematical achievements. Presumably, scientific society could continue to legitimate its institutions on the unacknowledged magic of mathematics were it not for the tendency of those institutions to disrupt the environment, in the name of valid knowledge. But scientific magic is also environmental disruption, and so a more coherent idea of knowledge must be found, an idea committed to sustainability rather than mathematics.

It is my argument, then, that science is mistaken about nature in the same sense that the doctor would be mistaken to cut out your heart as a strategy for curing it. Science is mistaken because it is incoherent, and it is incoherent because it continues to treat mathematical magic as though it were mathematical rationality. The reliance on mathematics entails tacit social commitments, commitments that take the institutional form of environmental disruption. Thus these commitments must be exposed and mathematics must be recognized as simply an effective, technical form of language rather than as a privileged source of truth. This will involve a social analysis of mathematics, an analysis directed toward articulating a more coherent, sustainable idea of knowledge, an ecological knowledge. Such an analysis must look at mathematics in terms of its inherent relationship to *language*, as a social activity, and see what is hiding behind the identification of mathematics with objective rational necessity. The scientific privilege of mathematics was initially derived from the scholastic reverence for language, as the mystical basis for necessary knowledge. So I will show how this mathematical privilege/reverence was used to define a necessary mathematical connection between the mind and nature, a connection requiring a new, mathematical notion of observation—the scientific *experiment*.

From Sacred Language to Mathematical Observation

For the scholastics the necessary, mediating connection between the mind and the universe was language, language as sacred signs. Theirs was a sacred, Christian universe, a universe that included necessary feudal values and authority, and the principles of this universe could be *revealed* to the mind through the proper interpretation of language, interpretation informed by absolute faith. Language enabled human beings to know God's universe and therefore it had a sacred and revealed quality, where ordinary words could be found, through sacred interpretation (hermeneutics), to contain divine meanings and revelations. These were the words of ordinary language (Latin), particularly as they appeared in the sacred texts (the Bible), and they were the ultimate source of knowledge concerning God's universal principles. These words-as-signs could be interpreted rationally in the sense of reason based on faith, and in this way they could reveal necessary knowledge to the knowing mind, a mind fully incorporated into the moral and class commitments of the feudal-natural order. Language contained the secrets of certain knowledge, and it was the language of faith and authority, where both reason and the mind were defined in terms of the sacred social tradition.

For the early scientists, on the other hand, the necessary connection between the mind and the universe had to be rational and nonmoral, a connection based on the observation of objective nature rather than on the interpretation of social-natural signs. This connection was found in the necessary rationality of mathematics, where mathematics was understood as a special kind of language, the "language of nature." For Galileo (1957), "the universe . . . is written in the mathematical language" (p. 238), and this was the early scientific view of mathematics, as a language containing the secrets of natural, objective revelation. Today some scientists also sometimes call mathematics "the language of nature," but in the modern context this is more of a suggestive metaphor than an analytic insight, because modern science no longer has this scholastic sense of language, the sense of necessity and revelation. For modern science mathematics has its own independent, analytic status, as an issue of reason and nature, and the idea of language is not particularly useful or relevant. Mathematics is seen as directly explanatory, as a way of connecting the mind with nature, and although language may be understood as enabling the possibility of knowledge, it is only as a neutral communicative tool, not as an active, involved contributor. Today language is not the focus of knowledge, since nature can now be defined, in terms of mathematics, without any necessary reference to the idea of language. But it is important to remember that mathematics established its explanatory role in scientific knowledge under a quite different conception of language, a conception in which language, not mathematics, was the authorizing reference for knowledge. It was as a *language* that mathematics achieved credibility, and thus it was through the idea of language that the idea of mathematical, objective nature achieved credibility. Today we have essentially forgotten this original mathematical reference to language, because we now derive our confidence in mathematics directly from science, and scientific nature. But our idea of scientific nature has always depended upon this fundamental reference to language, as the authorizing source of valid knowledge.

As a language in the scholastic sense, mathematics could claim to be both necessary and nonsocial, both revealing of hidden truths and supremely rational. This is what gave mathematics its special, scientific quality. As a language it could ground a necessary connection between the mind and nature, but as a nonsocial, nonmoral language it could ground a necessary connection between the rational mind and objective nature. Mathematics made rational, objective knowledge possible, the knowledge of a mathematical universe, knowledge that had scholastic necessity without Christian commitments. This kind of knowledge required a new kind of mind, a mind that could achieve knowledge without social involvement, the mind of the rational, detached individual. Both Christian knowledge and scientific knowledge were based on an appeal to language, as providing access to hidden, revealed truths, and both involved specific social commitments, commitments incorporated into the idea of the knowing mind. But scientific knowledge denied its social-market commitments through its idea of a perfectly neutral and rational language, the language of mathematics. And Christian knowledge embraced its social-feudal commitments through its idea of a sacred, traditional language, the language of ordinary experience.

In the Christian conception God had created a universe focused on human beings, so that all of that universe—natural processes, social relations, and so on—must be seen as a text of sacred signs, with ordinary language, as sacred words and texts, mediating between revealed knowledge and the mysteries of that universe. This idea of signs implied that language was both divine and human, both universal and mundane, where certain words could be interpreted as the names of the real principles and essences that structured the events and things of the world, and where God guaranteed the linguistic connection between divine truth and the concepts and practices of social life. In this world, according to Timothy J. Reiss (1982), "language and society are born together. . . . To misuse words is a derogation of society and indeed of humanity as taken up in it" (pp. 83, 85). In his book *The Discourse of Modernism*, Reiss demonstrates the central role of language in the divine feudal order of the Christian universe:

> Fundamentally there remains the assumption of an overarching totality within which the word and the world (whether social or physical) are situated at the same level. The dominant model is a collective one in which the sign as a "unit" of meaning or the human as an "individual" in society has no significance at all save as it can be referred to the corporate community or social discourse on the one hand and guaranteed by the Divine on the other. (p. 94)

Science replaced the ideas of language and the corporate community with the ideas of mathematics and objective nature. In this conception words lose their necessary, realistic connection with the sacred (feudal) order and mathematics gains a necessary, realistic connection with the natural (individualized) order. Words had achieved that connection by enabling committed interpretation, as the path to moral knowledge, and mathematics achieved its connection by enabling individualized observation, as the path to rational knowledge. So the focus is changed from interpretation to observation, and mathematics becomes a language of explicit, neutral rationality, a language with no hidden meanings and requiring no interpretation, a language that is really not a language. Science makes observation, not language, the basis for knowledge, and so mathematics becomes something that is both more than and less than a language—more than a language as the privileged path to certain, rational knowledge, and less than a language as a nonsocial, noninvolved path, a path requiring no moral and instructive interpretation. As the "language of nature" mathematics becomes the basis of neutral, objective observations, and through this reliance on mathematics the idea of scientific observation is made to appear simple and unproblematic, as having no inherent involvement with language, human beings, or social life. Mathematics rises above the messy, social notion of language while still grounding knowledge in the necessity of language, and it does this by becoming a new observational language, a language of rational, autonomous minds.

This is a Platonic conception of mathematics, where only pure reason, not ordinary experience, could lead to true knowledge. For science ordinary language becomes a deceptive barrier to knowledge, rather than a sacred source of knowledge, because ordinary language is intrinsically involved in social life and objective knowledge is not. Thus the language of knowledge must rise above ordinary language and experience, and so it must become mathematics, as the rational language of objective nature. Objective nature was unavailable to ordinary experience and could be known only through the proper kind of scientific experience, that is, through mathematical observations. This meant that the idea of experience had to be redefined, so that mathematical experience could become more real and more reliable than ordinary human experience. For science only direct, rational experience could lead to certain knowledge, not the scholastic combination of ordinary experience and rational deduction, since this experience was always misleading and these deductions were always based on faith. Scientific experience had to be completely rational, which meant it had to be completely nonhuman, and it was this kind of experience, at least in theory, that mathematics made possible. For the scholastics valid knowledge could be an issue only of ordinary social experience, while for science valid knowledge could be an issue only of rational, nonsocial experience, the kind of experience made possible by mathematics, as a source of *necessary* rationality. And I am arguing that valid knowledge can be an issue only of reflexive, ecological experience, the kind of experience made possible by language, in the sense of rational efforts at social–natural sustainability.

In order to build the scientific conception on the foundation of mathematics, the early scientists had to change the scholastic focus on *experience* to a scientific focus on *experiment*. For the scholastics the kind of experience that was useful for knowledge was normal, everyday experience, the ordinary experiences of social participants in the sacred community. For the scientists, on the other hand, the only kind of experience relevant to knowledge was mathematical experience, the special mathematical observations of a rational, disinterested nature. This shift from ordinary experience to mathematical observations signaled a shift away from a traditional, moral conception of knowledge, since this idea of ordinary experience meant exactly the traditional experience of feudal rights and obligations, of the divine authority of feudal class relations. These relations could be properly observed by everyone, without any need for special observational help, and they could be properly expressed in the words and concepts of ordinary language, the language of sacred signs and revealed truths. The scholastics reasoned about ordinary experience and language, about "words as signs in the knowledge of God" (Gaukroger 1978, 135). In his book *Explanatory Structures*, Stephen Gaukroger compares scholastic explanation with scientific explanation, and stresses this scholastic notion of experience. "At the level of evidence, sense perception and everyday experience . . . determined the criteria by which the truth and falsity of theories [was] established" (p. 147). Indeed, the use of instruments, such as Galileo's telescope, was proscribed not out of dogmatic fear and ignorance, but out of principle: vision, as it was understood, was the receiving of forms, transmitted from the object, through the eye, into the mind. Thus to interrupt the normal transmission of these forms with a mechanical device, such as a telescope, would be to block vision, to fail to see the world accurately. The mind would receive the forms produced by the lens, as an interference, rather than those produced by the object itself (Gaukroger 1978, 179).

In these terms experience could be a help to knowledge, but only reason could achieve certain knowledge, and reason was strictly an issue of deduction from first principles, the first principles of faith. Reason could only assist faith, since God's mysteries were beyond human reason, and experience, as ordinary experience, could only assist reason, since it was strictly an issue of particulars, and knowledge was strictly an issue of universals. For the scholastics, following Aristotle, the world was made up of unique and particular things, things such as rising and falling motion, fire and water, humans and rocks. Each of these particulars was the manifestation of a different essential form, and each had to be known in its own terms, through its own rational principle. These things could be known in their particulars through ordinary traditional experience, and they could be known in their essence through rational deduction from first principles, with assistance from experience. Thus the world was made up of myriad differences of particular things and essential forms, differences that revealed the endless complexity and mystery of God's moral authority. It was a world centered on the familiar and sacred experience of traditional feudal relations, a world to be correctly interpreted through the divine gift of ordinary language, a world of humans, morality, and faith.

The early scientists had to reject this multitude of essences, as well as the qualitative and detailed attention to particulars on which it was based. They had to observe a universe ordered by regularities, a universe in which subjective, experienced particularities dissolved into objective, rational uniformities. Reason and observation, rather than faith and interpretation, had to become the authorizing basis for knowledge, which meant that experience, as observation, had to be able to lead directly to necessary, demonstrative knowledge. So the mind had to have internal and deductive as well as external and inductive access to the universe; there had to be an a priori as well as an observational connection between the mind and nature. This connection had to give us Godlike knowledge, rather than only opinions and appearances, so it had to be fully rational. In particular, nature had to have a structure of uniform, lawlike regularities, not a structure of miracles, mysteries, and moral interventions. Nature had to be experienced as uniform and regular, as a matter of necessity, and this was the only kind of experience that could count for knowledge. The ordinary experience of unique events and particular differences had to be discredited so that the disinterested experience of underlying rational laws could be validated.

Even more than the scholastics, the scientific thinkers needed to base the idea of knowledge on a conception of experience, but they needed a controlled, restricted sense of experience, not the untrained experience of normal human life. Galileo, for example, "constantly insists that what he calls 'raw experience' is absolutely useless. 'Experience' is only usable when it has been ordered *before hand* by a mental calculus" (Reiss 1982, 202). And Francis Bacon (1960) agrees:

> For experience, when it wanders in its own track, is . . . mere groping
> in the dark, and confounds men rather than instructs them. But when it
> shall proceed in accordance with a fixed law, in regular order, and
> without interruption, then may better things be hoped of knowledge.
> (p. 96)

The new scientific idea of experience had to capture the explanatory necessity of the natural regularities (the forms) while at the same time denying any explanatory significance to the countless particularities (the appearances) that are found in nature. For example, falling and rising motion had to become, for purposes of explanation, simply motion, without any explanatory concern for whether something was moving toward heaven or away from heaven. With this idea of experience scientists could assume uniform regularity even though ordinary experience might indicate vast differences. It was in this way that Galileo solved the classic problem of the pendulum's motion, which had always been seen as combining two fundamentally different kinds of motion, each with a fundamentally different explanatory principle. It was also in this way that Newton combined the heavens and the earth into one uniform explanatory system, thus destroying the defining particularity of Christian knowledge and so bringing reason and order to the universe.

This is an important point to understand, as science has tended to dim our appreciation of this explanatory reliance on particulars. As humans we always experience particulars, such as John and Peter, water and ice, peasant and lord, rising and falling motion, the heavens and the earth. Most versions of knowledge have focused on and extended these particulars, while science has denied and dissolved them, focusing instead on the idea of "experiencing" their common, underlying uniformities. Today in the context of science we may have a hard time appreciating the immense explanatory pressure applied by particular things and events, but the idea that peasants and lords were essentially the same, or that the heavens and the earth had the same basic laws, was staggering, in that such ideas contradicted all human experience. Such ideas changed the world, legitimating new social institutions and generating remarkable technology, and we have generally accepted these ideas as correct, which means we have generally discredited the notion of achieving knowledge from attention to particulars, except in the "soft" areas of interpretation, such as art, literature, and therapy. Through science we have changed our sense of experience, allowing the scientific "experience" of uniformities to replace almost completely our confidence in the ordinary "experience" of particulars. Science has indeed been remarkable and insightful, but it has also been ecologically destructive, and it is my argument that we must begin to regain some of our *explanatory* respect for certain particulars — air, water, ozone, threatened species, limited resources — if we are to achieve an ecological, sustainable knowledge, a "wild" knowledge.

Science required a new kind of experience, a kind that would be able to reach behind the appearance of particular differences between objects in order to find the underlying uniform similarities within those objects. These would be the similarities arising from the real, fundamental properties of objects, the properties that "truly" inhered in and characterized those objects. Only this kind of experience could reveal the "true," underlying structure of objects and events, a structure that is hidden from ordinary, misleading experience, and only mathematics could make this kind of experience possible. The essential properties of things and events were defined as exactly those properties that could be described by mathematics, and in this way the hidden and underlying order of the universe, the necessary order, was established as being fully and exclusively mathematical. In this universe only the mathematical properties of objects truly inhered in those objects, properties such as extension, weight, number, and motion. In ordinary experience other properties might *seem* to be a part of certain objects—for instance, color, smell, warmth, and beauty—but these properties could not be described mathematically and thus did not truly inhere in those objects at all. Rather, these were the confusing, misleading properties that distorted ordinary experience, properties that we would mistakenly attribute to the objects themselves but that were in fact only in our minds. Through ordinary experience our minds would *add* the subjective appearance of nonmathematical properties to the objective reality of mathematical properties, making it seem as though all these properties were inherent in the objects themselves. This was the problem with ordinary experience: it would make us see a confusing, particular world, a world that was not really there, and only mathematical experience could enable us to see the true, uniform world, the world of scientific knowledge.

These two kinds of properties came to be known as the primary and the secondary qualities, where the primary qualities were true and mathematical and the secondary qualities were false and mental. Virtually all of the originators and designers of the new scientific perspective relied on some form of this primary/secondary distinction, including Kepler, Galileo, Descartes, Locke, and Newton. It was a distinction that defined nature in terms of the possibility of demonstrative knowledge, since mathematics could be seen as having the kind of rational certainty required by the scholastic analysis of forms, the certainty of a priori truth, a certainty comparable to that of faith. As John Herman Randall (1940) writes, "Modern science was born of a *faith* in the mathematical interpretation of Nature, held long before it had been empirically verified"

(p. 235). E. A. Burtt (1954) discusses the significance of the primary/
secondary distinction in depth, and summarizes it this way:

> Till the time of Galileo it had always been taken for granted that man
> and nature were both integral parts of a larger whole, in which man's
> place was the more fundamental. . . . *Now, in the course of translating this*
> *distinction of primary and secondary into terms suited to the new mathematical*
> *interpretation of nature, we have the first stage in the reading of man quite out*
> *of the real and primary realm.* (p. 89)

Among other things, the primary/secondary distinction implied that
the true and objective world of nature was only mediately, rather than
immediately, knowable. Nature was characterized as well hidden from
normal experience: as a reality it was formal and austere, permitting only
of carefully trained and guided investigation. Scientific observation had
to be done through rigorously prepared spectacles, the spectacles of
mathematical relations. In this way nature was envisioned as directly accessible to mathematical observation, while at the same time, and for the
same reason, it was envisioned as inaccessible to ordinary observation, to
normal and immediate experience. It was an interesting conundrum: in
order for knowledge to be fully a function of human reason and observation, as opposed to faith and authority, reason and observation had to
be shorn of their human qualities. If truth was to become an issue of individual human minds, then those minds had to deny all their human
tendencies and become uniformly detached and mathematical.

Mathematics could be used to resolve this conundrum because in the
scholastic context mathematics could be presented as characterizing the
essential, necessary form of objective nature in the same sense that ordinary language (as sacred signs) had been accepted as characterizing the
necessary form of the divine universe. For this reason mathematics made
possible the quite remarkable claim that *a kind of* direct and necessary observation could be made of a world that, by definition, could not be directly observed, at least not by ordinary observation and experience. The
problem was to establish a method for doing this kind of specialized,
mathematical observation. For this the primary/secondary distinction
was not much direct help, since it was really an effort to discredit ordinary experience, not to define a mathematical method. This distinction
served to define the necessary universe as mathematical, but only in the
sense of how to *interpret* ordinary experience, essentially a scholastic concern. Science needed the universe to be defined in this way, as strictly

mathematical, so that the knowing mind could be directed away from all confusing social concerns and toward the necessary mathematical concerns. But science also needed a practical way to direct the scientific mind properly, a practical way to see mathematical reality, a practical observational method. The primary qualities referred to physical properties that could be abstracted from normal perception and mathematically described, but physics required an idea of physical properties that could *only be perceived* mathematically, and this was achieved through the idea of the experiment, where observation itself became mathematical.

A New Reality

Through the idea of the experiment, pure mathematical observation was able to replace ordinary, everyday observation as the experiential basis for achieving knowledge. If ordinary experience became scientific experiments, then observation would be focused exclusively on the mathematical properties of objects, thus excluding the secondary properties from the very idea of observation. In this way the scientific experiment did not simply redefine "true" reality, as the primary/secondary distinction did, it also redefined observable reality, so that both reality and observations could become truly scientific. The explanatory point of an experiment was to be able to observe something that would not, and perhaps could not (as in Galileo's thought experiments with frictionless planes), normally occur. For experimental physics reality consisted of natural processes that could be observed only through physical experiments, so that only scientific observation could truly and necessarily encounter the natural order. In this way the idea of knowledge was categorically detached from any explanatory involvement with the ordinary experience of human beings living in a human social world. Knowledge became exclusively an issue of mathematical reality, and that reality became exclusively the province of experimental observations. This idea of experimental reality was first developed and articulated by Galileo, and Gaukroger (1978) describes its explanatory effects:

> Something has happened to reality here: or, more strictly speaking,
> something has happened to the criteria by which something is
> established as being real. A situation which does not occur in reality
> is no longer equivalent to a situation of which we have, or could have,
> no direct experience. (p. 220)

The only observations on which knowledge could be properly based

were observations that no one other than scientists could make, by definition, and yet these same observations could be understood, with the
conceptual help of mathematics, as being *direct*, as being the product of
pure and unfiltered perception. This was the explanatory payoff of combining a mathematical definition of objective nature with an experimental definition of proper observation: a hidden and necessary reality could
now be understood as immediately accessible to direct scientific observation. In this way science could make the hidden mathematical order of
nature rationally observable, an explanatory strategy that essentially
identified the idea of observation with the idea of mathematics, insofar as
observation was directed at reality and could lead to knowledge.

> Experimentation is not something which simply accompanies the
> mathematical treatment of physical problems, it is a necessary condition
> of the mathematisation of a physical problem. Because experiment has
> this role, the "reality" which is dealt with in the mathematical treatment
> of a problem is not that of everyday experience: it is the "reality" of
> carefully controlled physical experiments. (Gaukroger 1978, 221)

It is this combination of mathematics and observation that defines and
characterizes physics and, by extension, all of modern science. Physical
concepts—atoms, electrons, force, mass—are formulated exactly according to how well they will work in a theory that is amenable to experimental
testing, not according to how well they describe and explain the world we
experience. Such concepts may refer to a physical impossibility—a frictionless plane, a point-mass—or they may refer to a physical incoherence—
wavicles, quantum jumps—but they still become explanatory of our world
and thus legitimating of our actions. Physics does not explain the world we
live in, the world of physical experience and physical possibility. Rather, it
explains a mathematical world, a world that can be measured precisely but
that cannot exist, a world that separates the idea of knowledge from the experience of human social life. This is the world of experimental science, a
world that Morris Kline (1985), in a discussion of science and mathematics,
also recognizes as essentially fictional:

> Modern science has been praised for eliminating humors, devils, angels,
> demons, mystical forces, and animism by providing rational
> explanations of natural phenomena. We must now add that modern
> science is gradually removing the intuitive and physical content, both of
> which appeal to the senses; it is eliminating matter; it is utilizing purely
> synthetic and ideal concepts such as fields and electrons about which all

we know are mathematical laws. . . . Science is rationalized fiction, rationalized by mathematics. (p. 199)

This fictional, mathematical world, then, was the world that the early scientists believed could be known with deductive certainty, a world in which mathematical observations could form a necessary connection between the rational mind and objective nature. As science has progressed, this world has become more elaborately mathematical and more apparently fictional, but it is still the same scientific world as that proposed by Galileo and completed by Newton, a world where mathematics rather than human life defines the ideas of knowledge, reason, and reality. In this sense science has changed very little over the years, despite the appearance of many theoretical changes. In physics, whether mechanistic, relativistic, or quantum, and in biology, whether molecular or evolutionary, the world is still assumed to be structured by mathematics, just as it was at the beginning. For Galileo (1957),

that great book which ever lies before our eyes—I mean the universe— . . . is written in the mathematical language, without whose help it is impossible to comprehend a single word of it. (pp. 237-38)

And Descartes (1983) agrees:

I do not accept or desire in Physics any other principles than in Geometry or abstract Mathematics; because all the phenomena of nature are explained thereby, and certain demonstrations concerning them can be given. (p. 76)

Today, three hundred years later, the same image—mathematics as the language of nature—underlies scientific knowledge. Albert Einstein (1945), speaking in 1933, stated:

Our experience hitherto justifies us in believing that nature is the realization of the simplest conceivable mathematical ideas. I am convinced that we can discover by means of purely mathematical constructions the concepts and the laws connecting them with each other, which furnish the key to the understanding of natural phenomena. Experience may suggest the appropriate mathematical concepts, but they most certainly cannot be deduced from it. Experience remains, of course, the sole criterion of the physical utility of a mathematical construction. But the creative principle resides in mathematics. In a certain sense, therefore, I hold it true that pure thought can grasp reality, as the ancients dreamed. (p. 274)

And Richard Feynman, writing in 1967, commented:

> To those who do not know mathematics it is difficult to get across a
> real feeling as to the beauty, the deepest beauty, of nature. . . . If you
> want to learn about nature, it is necessary to understand the language
> that she speaks in. She offers her information only in one form. (p. 58)

This view of mathematics originated as Christian necessity, then became scientific necessity, and then became scientific empiricism, meaning
a kind of scientific magic. Mathematics had to be *necessary* in order to dissolve ordinary experience into scientific observation, but this necessity
could only be part of a Christian world and had no place in scientific
knowledge. Thus one of the last achievements of the Christian God, as
the author of a moral, human universe, was to sanctify the reality of an
indifferent, natural universe, a universe where mathematical truths were
available to rational minds. These minds were the conceptual consequence of mathematical necessity, and as these minds began to explain
nature, as rational observers, they also began to legitimate a new social order, as rational, market individuals. In this sense it was the belief in scholastic necessity, not the direct experience of nature, that made scientific
knowledge possible and thus that legitimated scientific social practices.

Mathematics made this scientific combination of necessity and observation possible, and it did this by appearing as the embodiment of neutral, indifferent rationality. Mathematical rationality could explain the universe, as a matter of necessary structure, but presumably this was a form of
rationality that did not depend upon faith and mystery and thus was independent of any supporting social assumptions. More precisely, however, the
mathematical definition of rationality managed to hide its inherent social assumptions behind the conceptual slippage between God and nature, as
changing references for knowledge. And as God (and necessity) has slipped
from credibility, these assumptions have been able to hide more completely
behind the institutionalized legitimacy of objective nature, even though this
has meant that mathematics must increasingly appear as magic. Mathematics has played a quite deceitful role in scientific knowledge, since its *necessity*
defined objective nature, as rational order, and yet that same *necessity* is incompatible with objective nature, as empirical observation. As we will see
in the next chapter, this deceit has led to myriad conceptual mysteries within
science, mysteries that derive from the social and ecological incoherence of
the mathematical idea of rationality.

FIVE

The Knowing Individual

For the early scientists the rational necessity of mathematics could connect the rational mind to objective nature with certainty, but this connection depended on the authority of God, and science began to undermine that authority. As science moved out of the necessary domain of faith and into its own more empirical domain, its certainty as knowledge began to be questioned. With Berkeley and Hume this questioning began with a focus on the assumption of privileged observations, but soon the privileged rationality of mathematics was also challenged, since observation was defined in terms of mathematics. Generally these two epistemological issues have been discussed separately, with observation carrying most of the *scientific* weight, but fundamentally they are the same issue, as Morris Kline (1980) has shown in his book *Mathematics and the Loss of Certainty*. Is mathematics really the revealed logic of the eternal order, or was it simply an artificial creation of human reasoning, or perhaps simply a formal way of expressing abstractions from experience, maybe even a formalization of human, and perhaps incorrect, intuitions? If mathematical explanations were to become genuinely scientific, rather than scholastic, then the mathematical order had to be seen as an empirical *characteristic* of nature rather than as an a priori *form* of nature. Mathematics had to become an empirical aspect of nature, which meant that it could no longer serve as science's epistemological equivalent of God. Rather, the epistemological weight had to come down on the presumed perceptual purity of scientific observations, and the two epistemological failures were inevitably linked.

Even with the loss of mathematical certainty, however, the physicists have resolutely continued their absolute reliance on mathematics as providing the underlying structure, the basic *form*, of empirical reality—objective nature. Only now, as we have seen, they are more or less amazed at its structural presence in nature, at its magical explanatory ability. Werner Heisenberg (1958), for example, discusses the problems of using familiar physical concepts, such as orbits or density: "When this vague and unsystematic use of the language leads into difficulties, the physicist has to withdraw into the mathematical scheme and its unambiguous correlation with the experimental facts" (p. 179). He does not, however, question the remarkable "correlation" between "the mathematical scheme" and the "experimental facts." And biologist Jacques Monod tries to solve the problem of mathematics scientifically. For Monod (1971), evolution has selectively imprinted the experience of all of our ancestors over the eons into our human brains, giving our brains the ability "to simulate experience subjectively so as to anticipate its results and prepare for action" (p. 154). This is the "simulator," the basis for language and reason, and its evolutionary language, as opposed to individual, cultural language, is mathematics, the language of true experience.

> Great thinkers, Einstein among them, have often and justly wondered at the fact that the mathematical entities created by man can so faithfully represent nature even though they owe nothing to experience. Nothing, it is true, to individual and concrete experience; but everything to the virtues of the simulator forged by the vast and bitter experience of our humble ancestors. In systematically setting logic face to face with experience, according to the scientific method, what we are in fact doing is confronting all the experience of our ancestors with that actually facing us. (Monod 1971, 158)

Thus Monod finds that evolution, rather than God, can now "guarantee" a necessary correspondence between the rational mind and objective nature.

Where Monod finds evolution, others find relativism or technology or simply belief. Mathematics still guarantees scientific knowledge because mathematics defines scientific observation, and even though the necessity of mathematics is gone, the belief in mathematics remains. Science has now legitimated its own institutional practices, and these practices require that nature be defined as mathematical, because the legitimating notions of knowledge, reason, and reality depend upon this definition. The idea of God-ordained necessity helped to legitimate science as it arose amid feudal turmoil, turmoil that included Protestantism, new trade routes, more centralized power, and plundered wealth from over-seas. But as science began to create its own social imagery—around rea-son, the individual, and the market—this legitimating idea of necessity no longer made sense, and scientific knowledge began to be both insti-tutionally embedded and epistemologically mysterious.

The mysteries are all quite familiar—the mysteries of mind and body, of free will and determinism, of realism and idealism, and so on. These are the mysteries of scientific knowledge, mysteries that seem capable of generating endless esoteric discussions, much like the Christian mysteries of the Trinity. In one sense—the sense of a coherent, ecological knowledge—these are the mysteries of language, or rather of the absence of a reference to language in scientific knowledge. Science denies any concep-tual involvement with the idea of language, relying instead on the idea of pure, objective observation, which means tacitly relying on the idea of the pure, neutral rationality of mathematics. For science, then, the knowing mind must be directly juxtaposed with mathematical nature, so that objec-tive knowledge is understood as strictly an issue of the mind observing na-ture, and not as an issue of language somehow mediating between the mind and nature. If knowledge is an issue of language, then both the idea of the knowing mind and the idea of natural reality become aspects of language, and both ideas have to be understood reciprocally in terms of their mutual involvement in the organizing structure of language. That is, the idea of the mind and the idea of nature have to be understood first of all as *ideas*, in the sense that ideas are interconnected by the structure of language, not as inde-pendently existing realities that must be somehow (magically) connected by mathematics if knowledge is to be possible. If the idea of the mind is lin-guistically connected with the idea of nature, then knowledge becomes a hu-man issue of sustaining the possibility of social-natural interactions, through the organizing use of language. But if the mind is somehow directly con-nected with scientific nature, then the mind must be part of the mathemat-ical reality of an objective universe, and this makes the ideas both of mind and of knowledge very mysterious, even incoherent.

I will return to this issue of language later, but first we must see how the mysteries of science arise from its explanatory attention to mathemat-ics, so that they can then be analyzed through an explanatory attention to language. In a more "scientific" sense, then, the mysteries of science re-sult from the mysterious role of the knowing, rational mind, the mind that can somehow directly observe natural reality without really being a part of that reality. If knowledge is not an issue of language, then it must be strictly an issue of detached, isolated minds, minds that are irrelevant to but somehow objectively connected with an indifferent, lawlike universe. Mathematics has made this conception acceptable, by providing the explanatory basis for such a connection, but it has not made this conception coherent, not in a world without God-ordained necessity. Rather, the incoherence of this idea of the mind has been hidden behind a belief in the rationality of mathematics, a belief that makes mathematics appear as magical, as not really a part of language and yet as like a language. Mathematics is the "language of nature," "the language of evolution," "the language of experimental facts," and yet it is not a language, not in any social sense, so that scientific knowledge does not have to depend on an analysis of language, as an enabling conceptual resource. All that science requires is an analysis of nature, a belief in mathematics, and a method of experimental observation, together with embedded institutional legitimacy. The idea of observation may be a problem, since it implies the idea of the observing mind, but the epistemologists can discuss observation without considering language, mathematics, or social theory, and so the mind can retain its mysterious place within the scientific conception.

In scientific knowledge refining the method of mathematical observation (experiment) becomes the focus of genuine explanation, while in scientific epistemology certifying the reliability of neutral observations becomes the focus of philosophical discussion. In all of this the idea of the mind, as the locus of observation, continues lurking just out of sight, appearing explicitly only in the more strictly philosophical/moral discussions: free will, mental acts, intentionality, the idea of the person, and so on. But in all these discussions, and in the scientific discourse generally, the mind must appear as isolated and detached, because it is defined in terms of its ability to know reality directly, as an individual mind, without involvement with other minds, language, or social life. The mind must appear individualized and detached because otherwise the idea of the mind would be defined in terms of its relationship to other minds, its *social* relationship, and a reference to social life would come flooding back into scientific knowledge. But scientific knowledge has excluded the idea of social life from the idea of valid knowledge by definition, as its characterizing achievement. Social life cannot be a necessary aspect of natural reality, since nature would work the same mathematical way without it, so objective scientific knowledge cannot depend on an inherent reference to social life, even in terms of a social mind. There must be an observing mind in the scientific conception, but this mind can only be detached and autonomous, a passive, uninvolved receptacle of objective observations.

Of course, there should not need to be a reference to the mind at all, since mathematical nature should also continue to work the same way without human observers, even as detached minds. (This is why quantum mechanics seems to cause great conceptual problems for scientific knowledge, since quantum mechanics suggests, contrary to scientific definition, that the mathematical laws of nature are not independent of human observation.) But the idea of knowledge always entails the idea of a knower, and so the mind must always be included somewhere in the scientific conception of knowledge, the mind as the necessary locus of knowledge. Thus the mind must be conceptualized as inherent in the idea of knowledge but also as independent of the idea of nature. As a result, science has conceptually neutralized the mind as much as possible, making it completely neutral, passive, and detached, while also endowing it with exactly the receptive qualities for objective observation and knowledge, the qualities of mathematical rationality. This is why the reference to the mind must be hidden behind the idea of mathematics in physics and behind the idea of observation in epistemology, and this is also why the scientific idea of mind is incoherent, and why it generates so many of the famous, intractable mysteries of scientific knowledge. The idea of knowledge implies the idea of the mind, and the idea of the mind implies the idea of human beings, including the ideas of social life, language, institutions, legitimacy, production, environmental dependence, and the like. But science denies these latter implications as inherent aspects of knowledge and tries to hide its own necessary reference to the mind in order to do so, and it is for this reason that science becomes conceptually incoherent and ecologically indifferent.

The Scientific Image of the Individual

It is the scientific idea of the detached, individualized mind that generates the social and legitimating idea of the rational, autonomous individual, the individual of market society. This is the "natural" individual of the state of nature and the social contract, an individual who has "natural," a priori characteristics, an individual who is logically prior to any social order, in the sense of individuals generating society, rather than society generating individuals. This individual is inherently a rational, detached observer of nature, and so all resulting social involvements must follow from that basic assumption. Mathematical knowledge, not social involvement, defines this individual, so that all social involvement must be a secondary artifact of scientific knowledge. This is how physics incorporated the implicit social commitments of market society, and this is why "the most immediate effect of Newton's ideas was in the economic and political field," as Bernal (1971, 489) has commented. In this conception the individual stood directly between nature and society, with mathematical nature being exactly the defining characteristic of the rational individual, and with individualistic society being exactly the necessary consequence of the rational individual. The reference to nature established the basic idea of the individual, and the reference to the individual established the basic idea of society. This had revolutionary consequences, of course, as the legitimating reference for political authority became the rational individual, not the sacred tradition. Through the idea of nature the individual, not the tradition, came to define the idea of reason, so that individuals could begin to criticize traditional authority legitimately, in the name of reason.

In the Christian conception it was language that stood between nature and society, with God being the sacred (traditional) reference that held it all together. The sacred, revealed truths of ordinary language connected the mystery of God's universe with certain, demonstrative knowledge, knowledge that included the proper social morality, and these linguistic truths could be understood only through faith in God, meaning faith in traditional authority. Thus it was the individual's ability to be properly moral (traditional) that was problematic, not the society's ability to be properly rational (natural). Indeed, there was no comparable notion of the scientific individual, not in the sense of autonomous individual reason and interests. This point is made by Timothy Reiss (1982) as he compares the medieval and the modern notions of "will":

> In medieval theory . . . *will* could only be associated with the
> "passions" and opposed to a rational understanding tending toward
> knowledge of God: untrammeled human "will," assuming it thinkable,
> could only lead to error and falsehood. (p. 58)

In this conception human reason was by definition the denial of individual achievement. Reason was an issue of ordinary language (traditional order) and it manifested God's presence, not individual presence. Individuals were fully *inside* God's social-natural order, and this was an order they could interpret, accept, or defy from within, as involved participants, but not an order they could criticize, control, or explain from without, as neutral observers.

Science creates the idea of the self-contained, self-defining individual, the individual who is logically prior to the social order. From now on the social order must be shaped to accommodate the "natural" characteristics of the individual, rather than the individual shaped to accommodate to the sacred social order. This individual is rational, in the sense that reason is now strictly a function of the individual's direct (mathematical) relationship with nature. The scientific (market) individual is created by the mathematical idea of reason.

> This notion of *self*—"individualistic," "psychological," "possessive," and the willful image of God in man—did not exist before. It has now been born. *Self* and *reason* go together. They are given to us as the *origin* of all right discourse. (Reiss 1982, 326-27)

The scientific mind is essentially outside and independent of the world it observes; it "possesses" knowledge of that world from an external and privileged position, a position of detached, Godlike observation, with the implication of Godlike authority and control. Thus the scientific individual is "naturally" oriented toward observation, domination, and control, rather than being morally oriented toward interpretation, involvement, and participation.

> The new scientist *imposes* the discursive *I* upon the world outside him. He is a conqueror enforcing his will, a man ravishing a woman. . . . Descartes will hypostatize that *I* of discourse into the psychological self of possessive individualism, as Hobbes will into the political self. (p. 189)

In this conception the individual becomes the independent locus of and authority for knowledge, but only as a hypostatized rational mind, not as a real, historical individual, not as an involved social participant. The scientific authority of men like Galileo and Newton did not come from their unique individual abilities to see the truth, for this would have made their authority sacred and irrefutable. Rather, their authority came from their formal ability to observe objective nature, and this ability was available to all individuals through the scientific method. Scientific knowledge was an abstract issue of rational minds and objective nature, not of particular, chosen "disciples" or "prophets," and this meant that scientific authorities such as Galileo or Newton could also be criticized in the name of reason and nature. The abstracted individual, as rational mind, became the authority for knowledge, not the particular, historical individual, and this kind of rationality was available equally to everyone, as a function of external, uniform nature. In this sense the rational individuals of scientific knowledge are also equal individuals, equal before nature and thus equal with respect to the legitimating notions of knowledge and reason. The scientific method implies the associated idea of rational equality, since all individuals must be seen as equally capable of achieving rational, mathematical knowledge, strictly as an issue of "natural" individual capacities. So the scientific idea of objective nature implies an incipient political commitment to individual equality, where individuals are "naturally" equal in more fundamental ways (rationality) than they are socially unequal. As Thomas Hobbes (1958) put it in 1651:

> Nature hath made men so equal, in the faculties of the body, and mind;
> as that though there be found one man sometimes manifestly stronger in
> body, or of quicker mind than another; yet when all is reckoned
> together, the difference between man, and man, is not so considerable,
> as that one man can claim to himself any benefit, to which another may
> not pretend, as well as he. (pp. 104-5)

The political consequences of this idea of equality are immense, and they derive from the scientific idea of a rational mind observing mathematical nature. In one sense this political implication of scientific knowledge is well known, since liberal politics and market economics were derived directly from the scientific conception of reason and nature. Indeed, the English political theorists and utilitarians, the Scottish moralists, and the French philosophes were all involved in efforts to extract legitimating implications for individual behavior and social organization from the new physics. But in another sense this political implication is not well known, since scientific knowledge has remained essentially immune from political or social analysis despite its recognized political involvement. Through its image of the rational mind, physics legitimated a new and revolutionary idea of politics and social order, but physics has not been analyzed as a social theory, neither by the anthropologists, the social theorists, nor the philosophers. This social dimension of scientific knowledge has essentially been relegated to intellectual history, where it can be both recognized and ignored. In this way physics can remain immune from social analysis, scientific institutions can remain legitimate, and social theory can continue to privilege the scientific notions of nature, reason, and the individual. Without an analysis of physics, social theory is left with only a *scientific* conception of social life, where social life can be understood only in terms of the "natural" characteristics of the a priori individual. In particular, social theory is left with no central explanatory focus on the idea of language. Language becomes simply another particular aspect of social life, with its own specialized discipline, and linguistics joins psychology, economics, politics, and so on as a distinct and restricted analytic domain. From this scientific perspective all aspects of social life, including language, politics, and technology, must be understood in terms of the fundamental reference to objective nature, which means in terms of the a priori, logically prior mind, as that mind characterizes the "natural" individual of scientific knowledge.

In the context of science both social theory and history hold themselves in homage to the scientific conception of nature, and this conception of nature makes itself immune, as physics, from any coherent social or historical criticism, since scientific nature is socially indifferent. In this conceptual context the political contributions of physics can be analyzed only as intellectual history, since these contributions can have no conceptual relevance to the validity of physics itself, as the knowledge of nature. This is the scientific perspective on itself, and from this perspective the history of science is typically told retrospectively, as though science has had its own independent conceptual continuity, from the early ancient scientists to the present. In this way many medieval and Greek theorists can be interpreted as having been true precursors of science, despite their explanatory commitment to nonscientific conceptions of nature and explanation. It is in opposition to this kind of history that Reiss offers his analysis, showing that such a historical story can be told only through selective hindsight, that is, through the use of modern criteria to isolate, retrospectively, certain aspects of works that were originally part of a very different discourse. The modern, scientific discourse involves a fundamental explanatory change from the medieval, traditional discourse, a change that radiates through such diverse conceptual domains as natural science, economic theory, and religious belief:

> The result of this change is called "puritanism" in one type of discourse, "capitalism" in another, in another "positivistic science," in yet another "neoclassical literature," elsewhere "modern" philosophy, and so on and

so forth: all these are parallel types of a single class of discourse. (Reiss 1982, 304)

From this perspective scientific knowledge is part of a new and quite pervasive explanatory discourse, a discourse that establishes the conceptual and legitimating bases of modern society. And such an analysis supports the idea that physics is as much about social life as it is about natural processes. However, the social analysts of modernity, including Reiss, are primarily concerned with illustrating the literary and historical dimensions of the scientific discourse, not with criticizing physics for its legitimating deception and its ecological incoherence. In general the analytic immunity of physics remains intact, even though the inherent social commitments of the scientific conception are apparent. Reiss argues that we have accepted an explanatory commitment to the willful individual as part of our social acceptance of the scientific discourse, and he concludes that this discourse involves confused and deceptive notions of both nature and the individual. He does not, however, move this analysis into a critique of physics, but rather leaves it as a literary, discursive analysis of intellectual history. This is not a criticism of Reiss, because such a critique is not his project. Rather, it is a comment on the continued analytic privilege of physics and the general absence of any such critical project. Scientific knowledge can be fully analyzed and criticized from a social perspective only to the degree it is approached anthropologically, which means it must lose its self-defined explanatory privilege. Physics must be recognized as primarily a legitimating social theory, and thus as fundamentally mistaken about nature, mistaken because it fails to understand that both nature and physics are conceptually intertwined with the possibility of social life. Physics must be analyzed as mistaken about itself, just as religion has been analyzed as mistaken about itself, since this is the basic implication of demonstrating the inherent political and institutional involvement of scientific knowledge. This critical move is not made, however, not by historians such as Reiss, Burtt, and Jacob, who reveal the social definition of objective nature; not by philosophers such as Rorty, Putnam, and Hacking, who demonstrate the conceptual incoherence of scientific epistemology; and not by social theorists such as Weber, Habermas, and Foucault, who point out the institutional contradictions of scientific rationality. As a theory of nature scientific knowledge remains unassailable, and so it continues to define our legitimating notions of knowledge and reason.

Quantum Physics and the Mind

Meanwhile, our supportive environment continues to deteriorate under the institutional impact of this deceptive and incoherent version of knowledge. Moreover, our scientific idea of nature also begins to deteriorate, even in its own explanatory terms. More exactly, the scientific idea of nature begins to reveal its own conceptual incoherence, not simply as the epistemology of neutral observations but as the physics of detached observations, the physics of observing fundamental particles. This is the incoherence of quantum mechanics, where the notion of an external and detached mind becomes the notion of an internal and involved mind, as a reference to human consciousness enters into the physical description of natural laws. In quantum physics the basic assumption of classical physics has been conceptually challenged, the idea that objective nature operates in accordance with mathematical laws that are independent of human observation and involvement. The epistemological conundrums of observation have now become the experimental conundrums of observation, as physics has been forced to incorporate the idea of the observing mind into the idea of objective nature. But physics has *defined* objective nature as categorically independent of mind, so that physics begins to dissolve its own conceptual basis, and the incoherence of objective nature becomes evident. For Werner Heisenberg (1958), "modern physics has perhaps opened the door to a wider outlook on the relation between the human mind and reality" (p. 202); for Sir James Jeans (1930),

> the universe begins to look more like a great thought than like a great machine. Mind no longer appears as an accidental intruder into the realm of matter; we are beginning to suspect that we ought rather to hail it as the creator and governor of the realm of matter. (p. 158)

As we have seen, a reference to the observing mind has always been an integral part of the scientific conception. Knowledge requires a knower, and the idea of objective nature has always been conceptually connected with the idea of a knowing mind. But objective nature has always worked independently of the mind, so that the necessary reference to the mind could effectively be ignored with respect to the knowledge of nature. For science the mind has always been a logical but not a physical part of objective nature and, accordingly, the mind has had only a tacit, disconnected role in the explanation of natural processes, a role as a passive receptacle for neutral observations. As the defining characteristic of the rational individual, this mind has had decisive political and economic importance, but this social role has been derived from the *scientific* image of rational, neutral detachment from mathematical nature, and now that scientific image must be recognized as fundamentally incoherent, even within physics itself. I have argued that this legitimating image of the rational mind has always been incoherent in social and ecological terms, but quantum physics tells us it is also incoherent in its own terms, the terms of scientific nature. The scientific mind cannot make sense even of nature, much less of knowledge, reason, and social life.

According to quantum physics, the mind that used to be passively disconnected from mathematical nature is now actively involved in mathematical nature. And this is not a bizarre and esoteric branch of physics, but is in fact the central core of physics, the physics of lasers and silicon chips, the physics of compact discs and home computers. Nature is still fully mathematical (not social-natural, not ecological, not reflexive), but now the mind is a causal, substantive determinant of physical events, rather than only a tacit, formal reference for neutral observation. Both matter and events are seen as being physically controlled by the conscious act of observation, so that human consciousness is now understood as an active participant in the mathematical laws of nature. For P. W. Bridgeman (1964), this means that physical explanations can no longer discount the observing mind:

> Wave mechanics marks a great advance over former theories in its recognition that the act of observation is an essential feature in any physical situation. In the background of this recognition there appears to be a curious and perhaps unavoidable combination of physics and philosophy. The recognition that knowledge of a system, without which no theory is possible, is meaningless unless there is an observer, is philosophical in spirit. This philosophical recognition formerly appeared to be without physical pertinence and could be merely disregarded, but the new physical point of view of wave mechanics means that it can no longer be ignored. (p. 121)

For Eugene Wigner (1967), consciousness became the central explanatory term in physics:

> When the province of physical theory was extended to encompass microscopic phenomena, through the creation of quantum mechanics, the concept of consciousness came to the fore again: it was not possible to formulate the laws of quantum mechanics in a fully consistent way without reference to the consciousness. . . . The very study of the

external world led to the conclusion that the content of consciousness is an ultimate reality. . . . The principal argument is that thought processes and consciousness are the primary concepts, that our knowledge of the external world is the content of our consciousness and that the consciousness, therefore, cannot be denied. On the contrary, logically, the external world could be denied—though it is not very practical to do so. (pp. 172, 176–77)

Mathematical nature was defined as absolutely external to the mind, since the central explanatory point of mathematical nature was to divorce the ideas of truth and reality from any reference to human influences and human choices. Nature was defined as working independent of human involvement, so that the universe could be seen as a rational machine rather than a moral test. But now human choices and influences have entered mathematical nature as part of physical causality, and yet the explanatory idea of mathematical nature remains essentially the same, as the mind is somehow added to the mathematical equations. So now mathematical nature must be understood as being exactly what it was defined as not being, something that is determined and shaped by human consciousness and commitments. As one might expect, this situation has led to considerable explanatory confusion and conceptual incoherence, as scientists and philosophers have tried to understand the implications of quantum physics for the idea of knowledge. According to C. F. von Weizsäcker (1973), physics should focus more on the idea of knowledge than on the idea of nature:

> Knowledge exists as well as matter exists, and knowledge is perhaps even more important because we know about matter in the form of knowledge, but we do not know about knowledge in the form of matter. It is not symmetrical. Knowledge is really the more basic concept. (p. 744)

Similarly, philosopher Roger Trigg (1980) comments on the explanatory dilemmas raised by physicist John Wheeler, and suggests that knowledge may be an issue more of understanding people than of understanding nature, providing knowledge is still possible:

> Continued references to the importance of consciousness have another important result. It looks as if sciences about men must underlie any understanding of "the world", if the scope of science is made explicitly dependent on man's capabilities. Yet even these sciences will presumedly depend on man's consciousness. As Wheeler himself remarks— "consciousness can analyze the world around, but when will

consciousness understand consciousness?" We seem to be involved in the most disheartening of vicious circles. (p. 159)

Trigg's book is titled *Reality at Risk*, and he concludes that some approximation of the classical idea of natural, external reality can still be saved through careful conceptual attention. Others, such as Wheeler, Wigner, and Heisenberg, disagree, suggesting rather that the idea of nature must be reformulated, with the mind as an active physical participant. In any case, physics has created a profound conceptual muddle, and it has done so by following out the experimental logic of its own conceptual assumptions, the assumptions of a passive, detached mind observing an independent, mathematical nature. Virtually without exception the efforts to resolve this muddle have focused on how the basic idea of mathematical nature can be adjusted to incorporate the conscious mind. This is what the physicists try to do, by building the consciousness function into the mathematical laws, and this is what the philosophers try to do, by showing that a certain degree of explanatory idealism can be made compatible with scientific realism. The idea of objective nature has always required an implicit, epistemological reference to the observing mind, and now it requires an explicit, physical reference to the observing mind. Such a reference may have made the notion of natural reality incoherent, but it has not had much *practical* effect on the explanatory assumptions and procedures of physics. In essence, physics has simply added the causal mind to objective nature and gone on about its business. Now, however, this business can no longer aspire to rational credibility or conceptual coherence; it can aspire only to institutional legitimacy and technical proficiency. On its own terms physics has become a form of explanatory magic, a magic that supports the individualized, technical institutions of science rather than the traditional, moral institutions of religion.

The discussion of quantum explanations still takes place within the conceptual framework of "the mind observing nature," and this is a *scientific* framework, the framework that defines objective nature as a function of the detached, rational mind. It is this standard, individualized mind that physics has tried to integrate into natural causality, the only mind (the only image of a knower) that is compatible with scientific knowledge. First this mind was necessary to *define* objective nature, as independent of consciousness, and then it became a physical determinant, as consciousness, in the same objective nature. This made the scientific idea of nature blatantly incoherent, but the alternative was to decide that the entire scientific conception was incoherent, and the credibility of this conception is a matter of institutional commitments, not of explanatory coherence. So physics generally muddles on, continuing to accept the idea of mathematical nature even in the context of explanatory magic. The quantum discussion, in both physics and philosophy, has focused entirely on trying to maintain, at least for practical purposes, the idea of objective nature, and this idea requires the complementary idea of the rational, individualized mind, so this mind has been brought into physics without much critical notice. The idea of nature has been the analytic focus, not the idea of the mind, because it is only in terms of this individualized mind that scientific knowledge is possible, and it is only in terms of this mind that the institutions of scientific knowledge can be legitimated.

But this idea of the mind has always been incoherent, as has the associated idea of objective nature, and now this incoherence has simply become more apparent, even at the level of physics itself. Our modern industrial institutions are clearly committed to physics, despite its conceptual problems, but these same institutions are also generating social and ecological incoherence, and so the need for a *social* critique of physics is also becoming more apparent. Such a critique involves analyzing the idea of the mind from a social, ecological perspective, rather than trying to maintain the idea of objective nature, from an individualized, scientific perspective. From an ecological perspective the source of quantum incoherence, and of scientific incoherence generally, becomes fairly obvious, since the idea of the mind is clearly a *social* notion, and it brings all sorts of social involvements and commitments into the idea of objective nature. Physics cannot admit these social involvements and commitments, however, and remain physics. So, as the mind becomes more integrated into physics, physics must become more incoherent. Physics can recognize the mind only to the degree it is pure rational consciousness, with no inherent relationships with other minds and thus no associated commitments of morals, values, sex, legitimation, organization, ecology, and so on. Only such a mind can objectively observe mathematical nature, and yet no such mind is conceptually coherent, so the idea of mathematical nature cannot be conceptually coherent. The idea of consciousness entails the idea of social life, which means that quantum physics has brought a reference to social life directly into the physical conception of nature, to the degree that consciousness is now a factor in physical explanations, a factor in the mathematical equations.

The Reference to Language

Minds refer to human beings, and human beings refer to social life — to language, knowledge, organization, authority, sexual difference, social-natural interactions, and so forth. In effect, physics has brought all of social life into the idea of objective nature and not noticed, and this makes physics incoherent, not to mention mistaken about nature. If the mind determines natural events, then social life determines natural events, and the possibility of social life, not simply the possibility of detached consciousness, must become a reference for the knowledge of nature. If minds are integral to natural processes, then social life is integral to natural processes, and nature must be understood ecologically, as an issue of sustaining the possibility of social-natural interactions. According to quantum mechanics, consciousness is a necessary aspect of the natural universe, and this means that human social life is a necessary aspect of the natural universe, so that natural processes must be understood in terms of their relations to social actions, including legitimated institutions, sexual practices, authorized knowledge, productive technology, and so on.

In a sense, this should have been obvious all along, because the knowledge of nature is always an issue of *knowledge*, and knowledge is necessarily an issue of social life. Physics tried to define knowledge as independent of social life and social actions, in order to escape from the sacred traditional commitments of religion. But it went too far, as it tried to make knowledge independent of social life in the abstract, rather than simply independent of particular sacred traditions. This was an explanatory mistake, and this mistake began to be revealed first in the incoherence of epistemology and then in the incoherence of physics, as the social notion of knowledge began to intrude into the objective notion of nature. In response the scientists and philosophers turned increasingly to explanatory sleight of hand and conceptual magic, in order to protect the legitimating success of science from its apparent incoherence. Then this explanatory mistake began to be revealed in the ecological incoherence of scientific institutions, and even the legitimating success became less convincing. If knowledge is first of all about knowledge, as von Weizsäcker suggests, then it is first of all about the possibility of knowledge, which means it is first of all about sustaining the possibility of social-natural interactions. According to quantum mechanics, then, knowledge must be ecological and reflexive if it is to be coherent, if it is to make rational sense of a universe that includes knowledge. Thus knowledge must be social-natural, and it must legitimate ecological practices at the same time and with the same rational validity that it explains natural processes. The only idea of knowledge that can be made coherent is ecological knowledge, and even the conundrums of quantum physics, if they are taken seriously, point to the same conclusion. Physics was right to reject the rigidity of sacred social-natural interactions, but it was wrong to reject the necessity of a formal social-natural conception of knowledge, and it is toward such a conception that even physics is beginning to turn, despite its own fundamental commitment to objective nature.

Physics still resists this reflexive turn, despite the conscious mind now participating in physical nature, because it is definitively nonsocial, and thus it cannot recognize that the idea of one mind entails the idea of other minds, and that the idea of many minds entails the idea of social life. Knowledge is an issue of language, and so language makes minds possible, as knowing, conscious observers and actors. But *language* is a thoroughly *social* term, in the sense that language use is available only to social participants. The idea of language entails the idea of organized social life, and so conscious, language-using minds (individuals) are necessarily social; the idea of one mind logically entails the idea of other, socially organized, minds. As real, particular individuals, these minds are always socially connected through traditions, institutions, values, history, and the like, but they are also always formally and abstractly connected through the idea of language, since it is their shared use of language, as a formal structure, that makes them minds. And this is where physics, and all of scientific knowledge, makes its fundamental mistake. The idea of the mind is necessary to science, but it can be only an independent, self-referring mind, a mind whose rationality is completely without social reference or involvement. And yet the possibility of one mind entails the necessity of other, socially organized minds, through the enabling reference to language. Physics needs to conceptualize the mind as independent of language and social life, and this is what has made it incoherent.

This is why physics must depend on a magical reference to mathematics, where mathematics can be both a language and not a language, the "language of nature" but not a language of social life. Language makes knowledge possible, so scientific knowledge, like any version of knowledge, must necessarily incorporate a formal reference to language, as the enabling ground of knowledge. The idea of language, however, implies social relations and involvement, and scientific knowledge must exclude any reference to social relations and involvement, so science must incorporate a magical idea of language, where knowledge can be both linguistic and nonsocial. Mathematics makes this possible, or at least the Platonic-scholastic-scientific idea of mathematical necessity makes this possible. If mathematics is identified as detached, nonsocial rationality, then it can have the rational properties of a language without the social properties of a language, so it can be the "language of nature" and provide the basis for objective scientific knowledge. But it cannot really be seen as a language, even as pure rationality, because any such reference to language tends to make the idea of knowledge appear as social and active rather than as individual and passive, as an issue more of linguistic necessity than of detached empiricism. So the image of mathematics as the "language of nature" becomes more a romantic metaphor than an analytic reference to language. In particular, scientific knowledge hides the formal and social idea that mathematics is a language behind the empirical and individualized idea of mathematical observation, so that the individualized idea of observation, rather than the formal idea of language, becomes the establishing reference for scientific knowledge. This is a magical notion of observation, however, because it requires a detached, nonsocial mind, a mind that can reason as a self-contained individual, with no necessary involvement in any linguistic community. And this idea of observation depends on a magical idea of mathematics, where mathematics can enable knowledge outside of any social context, where mathematics can be a rational language without being a social language, and indeed without being a language at all.

As we all know, this conception of knowledge was quite successful at legitimating social institutions, the institutions of the rational individual and market society. It never made any logical sense, however, except as part of a historical effort to discredit and replace the political authority and class relations of the feudal social order. The mathematical magic underlying this conception could remain conceptually hidden (the epistemology of observations) or at least pragmatically ignored (the physics of consciousness) until that conception began to undermine its own social legitimacy, through ecological indifference. But it was always magic, since the reference to mathematics was always a reference to the formal structure of language, and this reference could never be scientifically recognized.

Both religion and science have incorporated a fundamental reference to language into their respective ideas of knowledge, implicitly recognizing that knowledge is inherently an issue of the formal structure of language. But both have distorted that formal reference, interpreting it instead as a substantive appeal to a *particular form* of language, and so referring the idea of knowledge to a sacred, magical form of language rather than to the formal structure of language. For religion this magical language has always been the ordinary, traditional language of daily life, where knowledge of the magical words gives knowledge of the sacred social–natural order, with its necessary moral commitments to traditional acceptance and ritual. And for science this magical language is mathematics, where the magic of perfect observation gives knowledge of the external natural order, with its necessary technical commitments to individualized criticism and efficiency.

If knowledge is to be made coherent, however, it must begin to articulate its inherent reference to language as a formal structure, rather than to some particular form of language as magical access. As a formal structure, language must be recognized as generating the possibility of knowledge, in the sense that knowledge mediates between the possibility of human action and the experience of natural processes. In this sense language would be seen as the necessary ground for knowledge, a ground that is logically prior to either the ritualized language of religion or the mathematical language of science. As the reference for knowledge language must be understood as a formal *enabling* structure, a structure that constitutes the possibility of individuals and social life, in the sense of enabling the possibility of knowing, acting beings. In this sense individuals cannot be understood as the fundamental "atoms" of social life, and thus as having inherent "natural" characteristics. Rather than the idea of the individual being referred to nature, the idea of the individual must be referred to language, where individuals are understood as constituting and referring to one another, just as words are understood as constituting and referring to one another. This is the real implication of quantum mechanics, the idea that physics must be understood as an issue of the constituting structure of language, not as an issue of individual, autonomous minds. As physicist Bruce Gregory (1990) comments in his book *Inventing Reality: Physics as Language:*

> Physics shows us that while the world shapes us, the language that we use shapes the world. We might even say the language we *are* shapes the world, for language undoubtly defines us more profoundly than we can begin to imagine. (p. 200)

Language constitutes the possibility of social actions, and thus it constitutes the possibility of successfully organizing human actions with respect to the world of natural processes, a world that is *experienced* as independent of human actions. It is in this sense that language mediates between actions and the world: it provides the possibility of *knowing* the natural world, the world with which language users must successfully interact. Language always constitutes our world, the world we know, the world we live in—not in the sense that the world is language, or that language controls the world, but in the sense that the structure of language must be an inherent part of any world we can know. If knowledge is to be possible, the structure of language must be compatible with the structure of the world, and in this sense the world must be linguistic. Knowledge must be an issue of language before it is an issue of external nature, and the *idea* of nature must be understood as first of all an aspect of language, so that the *idea* of nature is understood as a necessary aspect of the way in which language successfully mediates between actions and the world. It is in this sense that both social theory and natural theory must be explicitly referred to the formal structure of language, as constituting the possibility of both. And it is in this sense that the idea of knowledge can generate a social-natural theory, where the validity of knowledge must involve a formal judgment of successful social-natural mediation, successful in the sense of sustaining the possibility of language, the possibility of social life.

In the final two chapters I will return to this idea of language as a formal mediating structure, a structure that can generate a reflexive and ecological conception of knowledge. The structure of language must become an explicit, formal reference for knowledge, rather than an implicit, magical reference for knowledge. When it does, knowledge will become abstractly social-natural, rather than traditionally social-natural or abstractly natural, since language is inherently a social-natural structure, a structure that mediates between the possibility of social actions and their dependence on natural processes. Just exactly how this linguistic structure accomplishes this formal social-natural mediation will be the subject of the last two chapters, but the basic idea of language as an abstract social-natural reference for knowledge can be understood more directly, in terms of the medical reference to health. As the legitimating reference for medical knowledge, the idea of health involves the necessity of sustaining the formal possibility of individual health, the formal possibility of individual-natural interactions. And this is what a reference to language must do, on a broader conceptual scale: establish an idea of knowledge committed to sustaining the formal possibility of language, and thus committed to sustaining the formal possibility of social-natural interactions. The medical analogy illustrates the basic idea of a reflexive reference for knowledge, the idea that assertions of knowledge must always evaluate their own validity in the context of social sustainability, just as medical knowledge must always evaluate its validity in the context of individual health. This means that the idea of knowledge can be made coherent only if it is made abstractly social-natural, so that the criteria for validity become committed to the achievement of technical proficiency *in the context of legitimating sustainable practices*, just as we now hope is the case with medical knowledge.

All this suggests that social theory must become as central to the idea of knowledge as natural theory, and indeed it suggests that social theory must become more fundamental than natural theory, as Roger Trigg has pointed out might be the case. Knowledge must be more about social legitimation than natural explanation because it is only through appropriate social legitimation that the possibility of knowledge can be sustained, that language can sustain its own possibility. In the context of science we have generally taken social theory to be sort of the bastard son of knowledge, the black sheep of science, since *real* science is done with mathematics and is focused on passively observing the regular, uniform order of nature. But if knowledge is to become coherent, social theory must begin to take a different role, and in particular it must stop defining itself as a struggling branch of science, a definition that continues to privilege scientific nature and to denigrate social theory. Social theory must begin to question its own conceptual, scientific assumptions, the assumptions that derive the idea of social life from the idea of the individual and that derive the idea of the individual from the idea of nature. Social theory, including political and economic theory, has generally been committed to this basic scientific conception, and this conception can be challenged only by challenging the defining notion of objective, mathematical nature. This is the notion that entails the image of the rational, autonomous mind, the mind of the logically prior individual, and so this is the notion that establishes scientific social theory, as well as the notion that legitimates scientific social institutions. It is here, with a critique of objective nature, that social theory must begin to make the idea of knowledge more coherent and consequently to make social legitimation more ecological. And social theory must begin to do this by investigating more ecologically (less scientifically) the formal structure of language, as the enabling basis for the possibility of knowledge, and thus as the enabling basis for our ideas of nature and social life and rational social-natural interactions.

The explanatory tension between a scientific and an ecological conception of knowledge is the tension between a reference to an autonomous, rational mind and a reference to the formal structure of language. Similarly, the explanatory tension between the scholastic and the scientific conception of knowledge was the tension between the reference to a sacred, traditional language and the reference to an autonomous, rational mind. In the scholastic-scientific case the conceptual transition was generated by a social and political crisis in the feudal order, and it was resolved by a new social-natural vision, where traditional certainty became critical individualism. I am suggesting that another historical crisis is emerging today, a technological and ecological crisis, and that another such conceptual transition is required, another social-natural vision. This must be a reflexive vision, a vision of ecological sustainability, a vision in which both the traditional-natural commitments of religion and the technical-natural commitments of science can be combined and transcended. The conceptual change from a religious world to a scientific world was profound, and a similar profound change to an ecological world is now required. In his discussion of the emergence of science, E. A. Burtt (1954) has managed to capture some of the sense of the earlier transition as a religious world became a scientific world:

> Note . . . the tremendous contrast between [the scientific] view of man and his place in the universe, and that of the medieval tradition. The scholastic scientist looked out upon the world of nature and it appeared to him a quite sociable and human world. It was finite in extent. It was made to serve his needs. It was clearly and fully intelligible, being immediately present to the rational powers of his mind; it was composed fundamentally of, and was intelligible through, those qualities which were most vivid and intense in his own immediate experience—colour, sound, beauty, joy, heat, cold, fragrance, and its plasticity to purpose and ideal. Now the world is an infinite and monotonous mathematical machine. Not only is his high place in a cosmic teleology lost, but all these things which were the very substance of the physical world to the scholastic—the things that made it alive and lovely and spiritual—are lumped together and crowded into the small fluctuating and temporary positions of extension which we call the human nervous and circulatory systems. . . . It was simply an incalculable change in the viewpoint of the world held by intelligent opinion in Europe. (pp. 123-24)

The transition to science involved an incalculable conceptual change from the image of a committed traditional participant to the image of a critical natural observer. We must now begin another such incalculable change, a change from the image of a critical natural observer to the image of a critical social-natural participant, a participant in a world of language, nature, and social life.

SIX

Scientific Social Theory

The new rational mind of scientific knowledge had its most direct effect on the legitimation of new social institutions, not on the understanding or the technology of natural processes. This legitimating effect was expressed in the development of social theory, first as political and economic theory and later as a broader discipline focusing on the general structure of social life. As nature became mathematical, social life became problematic, because it needed to be understood rationally, not traditionally, and yet it seemed to be infused with morality, and morality was contrary to rationality. Natural laws did not have to be legitimated, but social laws did, and thus moral recommendations were required. But where could these recommendations come from, since both tradition and religion were discredited, nature was morally indifferent, and the "natural" individual was autonomous, with no social or moral involvement? Moreover, how could there be scientific (nonmoral) knowledge of social life if social life included an inherent moral dimension? Indeed, how could there be social life at all in a mathematical universe? What made it possible, what held it together, and how should it be arranged, in a world of objective nature and detached observers? In the world of scientific knowledge new kinds of institutions had to be legitimated and new theories of social life had to be developed, institutions and theories that derived their credibility from the rational idea of nature, not from the traditional idea of God.

More exactly, these institutions and theories had to derive their credibility from the foundational scientific idea of the autonomous individual, the individual containing the detached, observing mind. Objective nature made this mind necessary, and in turn this mind, as a human individual, made social life possible. So in a scientific world social life has to be understood and legitimated in terms of this individual. All of scientific social theory (that is, all social theory that accepts the scientific version of nature) depends upon some version of this individual, even the work of theorists who claim to have rejected individualist assumptions, such as Marx and Durkheim. The "natural," a priori individual is the only image of the human being that is compatible with scientific knowledge, and so it is through this notion of the individual that science has legitimated its own social institutions and theories. This is an individual who is logically prior to social life and whose defining characteristics are derived strictly from nature, not from social involvement. In particular this is an individual who is *nonlinguistic*, an individual who can know the universe strictly through observation, and so without the social implications of linguistic involvement. In the conceptual context of this individual, social theory has tended to ignore the issues of language and reflexivity in favor of a focus on objectivity and individual motivations, including individual needs, individual desires, and individual meanings. Also, our scientific institutions have tended to ignore the issues of ecology and sustainability in favor of commitments to technology and control, since these latter commitments are inherent in the "natural" individual.

In this chapter I will look at how this scientific individual enters into our legitimating social conceptions, and I will focus on an analysis of three dominant theoretical concerns: the issue of postulating "natural" individual motivations; the assumption of an inherent tension between the individual and the society; and the question of whether the understanding of social life requires a special kind of rationality, a moral, social rationality as opposed to a mathematical, technical rationality. These three issues have structured the development of scientific social theory, and all of these issues derive from the effort to build a coherent conception of social life on the privileged explanatory assumptions of scientific knowledge, the assumptions requiring an a priori, logically prior scientific individual. For scientific knowledge the individual, as detached, observing mind, must be an explanatory given, and so social life must somehow be "explained" in terms of this "natural" individual, an individual characterized by inherent, "natural" motivations. Also, social life must be somehow external to and constraining on the individual, and it must be understood as having a special relationship to rationality, since scientific rationality is defined as being nonsocial. Each of these issues reflects the explanatory problems of scientific social theory, and I will consider the first two—individual motivations and the individual-social tension—in this chapter and the third—the dilemma of rationality—in the next. The issue of individual motivations is essentially the issue of institutional legitimation, since legitimate institutions must be constructed in accordance with the inherent interests and motivations of "natural" individuals. And so we will look first at how the scientific individual was first "motivated" to legitimate the market and then was later "motivated" to legitimate the rejection of the market, in the name of socialism.

As a legitimating effort, scientific knowledge was first understood as endorsing the institutions and values of the market, and later, in the face of unexpected market brutality, scientific knowledge was reinterpreted, by some, as endorsing the rational criticism of the market, including a commitment to the institutions and values of socialism. In the market argument the scientific individual was found to be "naturally" compatible with individual competition, contractual relations, private property, and wage labor, and in the socialist argument the same scientific individual was found to be "naturally" compatible with communal production, centralized planning, socialized property, and party authority. In both cases the "natural" characteristics of the scientific individual were used to recommend the respective versions of necessary institutions, and in both cases these "natural" characteristics were seen as endorsing the same basic individualized values, the values of freedom, equality, progress, and rationality. These are values that are inherent in the idea of the scientific individual, values that must be used to legitimate any scientific institutions, and they are in clear contrast with such more traditional values as virtue, honor, respect, and stability. Generally, we are familiar with the emergence of these new institutions and values, but we are not as familiar with them as *scientific* institutions and values. Generally, we do not see these social developments as necessarily dependent on physics, as the new science of nature. Our standard histories of political and economic thought tend to trace these new social ideas from Machiavelli through some sequence of Descartes, Hobbes, Locke, Smith, and Bentham, with occasional stops for Leibniz, Ricardo, Voltaire, Condorcet, and other specifically *social* commentators. To the degree that Galileo, Newton, and natural science are mentioned at all, it is generally as defining a separate and authoritative intellectual development, not as involved in the central intellectual ferment underlying the rise of modern social and political institutions.

This kind of intellectual history is a remarkable tribute to the legitimating success of science, since we are now less aware, as social theorists, of the political role of physics than were these early political theorists, the ones who developed our modern social discourse. All of these early theorists discussed the politics of physics more than we do today, an indication of how successful science has been in legitimating its own conceptual privilege. But physics has always been involved in social legitimation and social theory, and this involvement needs to be rediscovered. In this chapter I will discuss this social involvement, and I will argue that a fundamental reference to objective nature, through the autonomous individual, necessarily underlies the development of both scientific social institutions and scientific social theory.

It is easy to see how the image of the scientific individual generates the characteristic scientific values of freedom and equality. The scientific commitment to freedom replaces the feudal (and Greek) commitment to virtue, as the central moral reference for social life. If individuals are fully self-contained, and logically prior to society, then they are "naturally" free and are "naturally" motivated to seek and defend that freedom against all social constraints. On the other hand, if individuals exist only in terms of their authorized place in a sacred traditional order, then they are "morally" motivated to practice virtue, by accepting their place and maintaining the rules of that sacred order. Similarly, the scientific commitment to equality replaces the feudal commitment to class position as the central political reference for social life. If these autonomous individuals are all fully rational, then they are all capable of knowing the truth for themselves, and they are not obliged to accept received authority on faith. In this way all individuals have an equal, "natural" claim on truth and reason, and no "sacred" social inequalities can make any sense. Individuals are more "naturally" equal than they are socially unequal, and the demand for social equality must begin to legitimate political authority. On the other hand, if individuals must accept the sacred class order as a matter of absolute faith and individual salvation, then maintaining class duties and privileges becomes the central legitimating requirement for political authority.

Freedom becomes the central moral appeal of scientific society, and in his classic statement about it, John Stuart Mill (in Mill and Bentham 1961) asserts that liberty

> comprises, first, the inward domain of consciousness; demanding liberty of conscience in the most comprehensive sense; liberty of thought and feeling; absolute freedom of opinion and sentiment on all subjects, practical or speculative, scientific, moral, or theological. (p. 486)

He generalizes this position with the claim that "mankind are greater gainers by suffering each other to live as seems good to themselves, than by compelling each to live as seems good to the rest" (p. 487). Now, while this argument may seem reasonable and appealing on the face of it, it rests on a distinction that is not only historically new but that can become coherent only in the context of scientific nature. Mill is assuming that the specific commitments of each individual consciousness — conscience, thoughts, feelings, opinions, sentiments — all exist and are clearly established independent of any social involvement. In general, he is assuming that each of us, as autonomous individuals, knows what "seems good to us" inherently, and that social participation can only distract us from this, not define it for us. For Mill — and for Hobbes, Locke, and the entire tradition of autonomous rationality — social constraints may be necessary, but they are not constitutive: they are only legitimate as an enabling context for independent individuals, a context that therefore can be justified only in terms of the separate and logically prior consciousness of individuals. Thus Mill's argument about liberty rests upon a grounding conception of the autonomy of individual consciousness, a conception derived from the idea of objective nature.

With respect to equality, Galileo presented the characteristic scientific challenge by claiming that individualized reason and observation gave him better access to truth than millennia of sacred traditional authority. This challenge created the discursive space for individual equality with respect to truth and reason, and this discursive space in turn created a political space for the idea of legitimate individual equality, an equality based on reason and nature. In this way the legitimacy of the social order began to be referred to the "natural" individual, rather than the morality of the individual being referred to the sacred social order. In this new political space, as Hobbes assumed, all individuals could be seen as being formally equal (through rational access to truth) in more important ways than they were substantively unequal (through talent, strength, class position, and so on). Clearly, this scientific notion of rational equality before nature was derived from the Christian notion of moral equality before God. But the Church had made the heavenly commitment compatible with absolute class privilege in mundane, earthly life, whereas the scientific commitment was explicitly mundane and earthly (natural) and thus could not be manipulated to legitimate feudal class structure. It was this necessary commitment to earthly equality contained in the idea of objective nature that political theorists such as Hobbes and Locke asserted as a legitimate, rational challenge to the class order of feudal society.

Both freedom and equality, as social values, were derived from the assumption that individuals are logically prior to and autonomous from social institutions. But this was a formal assumption, concerning the abstract individual, so that the problem arose as to what kinds of specific institutions could possibly be compatible with these "natural" individuals, that is, with their "natural" freedom and equality. No clear solution to this problem was necessarily contained within the foundational image of rational, autonomous individuals observing objective nature, since this foundational image itself was defined as independent of any specific institutional content. This image could be used negatively to criticize the class arrangements of feudalism, in the name of individual equality, but it could not be used positively to authorize a particular institutional alternative, because these "natural" individuals were logically prior to all institutions. As pure scientific minds these individuals were only passive rational observers, and to legitimate a particular institutional arrangement they had to be active rational seekers of something, active individual desirers of gain, pleasure, fulfillment, and so on. The foundational image could serve as a basis for institutional legitimation only to the degree that an additional assumption of "natural" individual motivations could be imposed on that image, and no such specific motivational assumption was necessarily inherent in the scientific image of a passive, rational observer. As a result, the inherent scientific commitments to individual freedom and equality have been abstractly available, in principle, for the legitimation of different, and often incompatible, visions of scientifically necessary institutions, such as those of capitalism and socialism. From one set of motivational assumptions the values of freedom and equality can be seen as legitimating the market, while from another set of such assumptions the same values can be found to legitimate the socialist rejection of the market.

In general there have been two basic kinds of motivational assumptions. In one, individual motivations are seen as having no inherent moral content, so that social life becomes strictly an issue of technical order, not an issue of moral commitments. In the other, individual motivations are seen as having explicit moral content, so that social order becomes an issue of meeting inherent moral commitments. In the first, the "natural" motivations of individuals in society are seen as being directly comparable to the natural motions of matter in nature, so that the proper social order becomes directly comparable to the necessary natural order, as an issue of neutral rationality. In the second, individual motivations are seen as having a special moral dimension that separates social life from natural processes, so that social order becomes an issue of a special moral rationality. The first version includes the legitimation of the market, as rational and nonmoral, and the second version can be understood only in the context of this first, market version of individual motivations.

Legitimating the Market

The problem for the new scientific social thinkers was how to conceptualize the "natural" motivations of autonomous, scientific observers. As scientific minds, these individuals had no social involvement, so social life had to be the result of "natural" individual drives toward social participation. These drives would be inherent characteristics of autonomous individuals, and as such they would determine the only kind of social order that would make rational (scientific) sense, the only social order that would be compatible with "natural" individuals. Thus these postulated motivations would be able to add specific institutional content to the general scientific values of individual freedom and equality. And the most obvious and familiar version of individual motivation was the assumption of rational individual self-interest, the assumption of the market individual. The scientific individual was already a rational, autonomous observer, so all that was necessary was to add the idea of a rational, autonomous desire or interest. This desire would be a "natural" characteristic of individuals, and it would push them to participate in social relations in order to satisfy that desire, as an issue of rational self-interest. The idea of rationality came from mathematical nature and the idea of self-interest, as social motivation, came from the image of a priori, self-contained individuals, individuals who were the only rational authorities over their own inherent desires. But still the idea of rational self-interest had to be given some concrete institutional content, in the sense of what such an individual would really want from social relations. And this content was given by the specific institutional assumption of private property, the idea that "natural" individuals would be rationally motivated to accumulate property, as a matter of inherent self-interest.

It was this new idea of private property that added specific institutional content to the general idea of rational individual self-interest. This was the content of market relations, where individuals would "naturally" seek to maximize their property, through rational, contractual interactions. This idea of private property, as C. B. Macpherson (1973) comments, "is largely an invention of the seventeenth and eighteenth centuries, and is fully appropriate only to an autonomous capitalist market society" (p. 122). Macpherson goes on to dissect this market idea of property into three basic components: first, that a property right is exclusive, alienable, and individually controllable, so that individuals can exclude others as well as buy and sell property; second, that property involves a right to a material thing, rather than a right to revenue; and third, that an individual has property rights with respect to his or her own labor, in the sense that labor, like land and capital, becomes alienable, and thus can be bought and sold.

The first component defines property as strictly an issue of individual interests and choices, rather than as a set of social privileges and commitments. Under feudalism a right to property involved the traditional obligations of class and kinship, and the economic function of land was not separable from its symbolic and ritual function in the divine social-natural order. In the scientific world, however, property rights had to be stripped of their traditional class commitments, so that these rights could be understood as referring only to individual self-interest and as involving only "natural," material things, things with no moral dimensions. Thus for Hobbes (1958) there is a "natural right of every man to everything" (p. 110), an idea that completely undermines the feudal order and that was derived directly, via Galileo, from the scientific image of rational, autonomous individuals. Since this idea of property is a "right of nature," the entire market conception of government, contracts, competition, and individual accumulation follows from it, as the only institutional arrangement that is compatible with the "natural" individual.

The second component—that property involves a right to a material thing, rather than a right to revenue—reinforces the first, making property an issue of individual control rather than social obligations. But it also expresses another fundamental institutional commitment of the scientific conception, a commitment derived from the idea of external, detached nature. If nature is objective, then the rational mind becomes a detached, uninvolved knower of nature, a knower of strictly material things and events. This means that the scientific individual becomes an external *possessor* of objective knowledge. Scientific knowledge can be utilized with moral impunity, since there can be no reflexive effects upon nature itself. The scientific individual possesses a knowledge of nature that is independent of moral or social dimensions, and therefore the material things of nature can be possessed in the same way. The idea of knowledge becomes the idea of rational ownership, since knowledge is strictly an issue of autonomous individuals and nature is strictly an issue of neutral material things. Thus the basic assumptions of scientific knowledge imply the legitimacy of private property, a legitimacy that, among other things, tends to make scientific institutions ecologically indifferent. Science changed a universe of moral commitments into a universe of mathematical events, and in this universe the only rational human attitude is one of possessive domination and technical manipulation.

This image of detached possession and control also provided conceptual support for the third component of private property, the idea that individuals have property rights to their own labor, that human labor enters into the market as an alienable commodity. The foundational image implied the famous conceptual separation of the mind from the body: the rational mind observing the objective material world, of which the body, but not the mind, was a part. It was easy to turn this epistemological mind-body dualism into the institutional idea that the rational mind had proprietary rights and control over its own physical labor. As Marx understood, this idea was instrumental in freeing productive activity from the feudal complex of traditional rights and obligations. In the context of science and capital, individuals no longer produced goods from within a network of social commitments, they sold their labor in an individualized market. Moreover, if everyone "naturally" had property (labor) to sell, then the requirement for formal equality before the market was met, despite the obvious and oppressive inequalities of property. If labor is property, then everyone is born with equal access to the market, as a formal, "natural" characteristic of individuals. Thus the idea of private property could not only reveal the "natural" legitimacy of market institutions, it could also indicate how those institutions would satisfy the formal scientific commitment to individual equality.

> The concept of property as nothing but an exclusive, alienable,
> individual right not only in material things but even in one's own
> productive capacities was thus a creation of capitalist society: it was only
> needed, and only brought forth, when the formal equality of the market
> superseded the formal inequality of pre-capitalist society. (Macpherson
> 1973, 130)

The idea of private property added the institutional content of the market to the scientific image of the rational, autonomous individual. As property maximizers, individuals would be motivated to compete with one another through rational contracts, to form a government to enforce those contracts and protect property, and to be fully rational with respect to the productive use of property. Individuals were "naturally" free but they were also "naturally" insecure, since each was exposed to theft, betrayal, and attack from the others. Thus they could become rationally free, secure, and prosperous only by accepting the institutions of the market, the only institutions that were compatible with the "natural" individual. In their "natural" condition, as perfectly free and inherently rational, these individuals would inevitably create disorder and instability, the "war of all against all." But their inherent rationality would make them realize that surrendering some of their "natural" freedoms to the right kind of government would create a condition of rational freedom, a condition of stability, prosperity, and maximum individual rationality. If individual motivations were left unconstrained, there would be chaos; if they were overconstrained, through religion, tradition, class privilege, and so on, there would be stagnation and decay. But these "natural" motivations could be rationally ordered through the appropriate market institutions, and the result would be a rational, individualistic, and nonmoralistic social order, where pure individual self-interest would lead to stability, prosperity, and progress.

This was the remarkable, even miraculous, thing about the market: it could create a rational social order out of "natural" autonomy, distrust, and disorder. This was Adam Smith's (1909) idea of the "invisible hand," the idea that in the context of the market

> it is his own advantage, indeed, and not that of the society, which [the
> individual] has in view. But the study of his own advantage naturally, or
> rather necessarily leads him to prefer that employment which is most
> advantageous to the society. (p. 349)

This meant that the "natural" desires of autonomous individuals could be rationally ordered in the same sense that the natural motions of uniform matter were rationally ordered. With the appropriate institutions, social life could be as rational as nature. In this way mathematical nature could legitimate market rationality; the rational laws of the market could have the same force and necessity as the rational laws of nature. Moreover, this market order was not an issue of moral commitments, any more than the natural order was an issue of moral commitments. The market had the same neutral, mechanistic rationality as nature. The rational social order was a good thing, but only in the sense that the rational natural order was a good thing, the sense of the value of order over disorder. This was the indifferent morality of order as such, the morality of mathematical necessity, not the morality of sacred (traditional) purposes, goals, or privileges. Just like the natural order, the market order required no moral commitments, it required only neutral, rational constraints on the "natural" motivations of autonomous individuals. And this meant that the social morality of market relations could be identified with the mathematical rationality of objective nature. The market was definitively rational, in the neutral sense of natural order, and thus it was necessarily the only acceptable, appropriate institutional order for "natural" individuals.

In the context of scientific legitimation this idea of a neutral, "natural" morality becomes quite important. It means that a morality of market relations can be derived from the neutral, nonmoral rationality of nature. But this is simply a morality of order itself, as a fragile, necessary thing, not a morality of fulfillment or completion or salvation. In the scientific-market context, order as such, as a technical goal, becomes the inherent moral reference, and this is a morality that is not a morality, a morality of technical stability as opposed to a morality of meaningful commitments. This morality can recommend market institutions, but only in the sense that anything else would be disorder, not in the sense of a moral commitment to purpose or fulfillment. In its effort to be strictly scientific, the argument for the market tries to hide a moral commitment behind the idea of natural necessity, and it does this by making moral assumptions about individual motivations—property, self-interest, and so on—and then presenting them as "natural" motivations, motivations that partake of the neutral rationality of nature. These are the motivations of the market, and they are added to the foundational scientific individual as "natural" characteristics. As we will see, Marx adds a different set of "natural" characteristics to that individual and finds in that individual the "natural" motivations to socialism.

The market is probably the most logical and certainly the most dominant strategy for social legitimation to come out of scientific knowledge. The scientific individual is rational and autonomous and the market individual is rational and autonomous. Also, science makes the knowledge of nature appear as individual property and the market makes material nature appear as individual property. So when market theory adds the assumption that individuals are "naturally" motivated by a limitless desire for property, then market institutions seem to arise naturally out of the scientific conception of truth and reality. But this is not the only version of social legitimation that is compatible with scientific knowledge, and indeed other versions soon arise, more or less against the market, since the market never seems to work quite as rationally and miraculously as envisioned. As market institutions begin to take hold, many analysts find them to be oriented more toward selfish disorder than toward rational order, and the basic assumptions of the market begin to be challenged. But these market assumptions are always challenged from within the defining scientific conception of knowledge and nature, which means that the only assumptions that can be challenged are those concerning the "natural" motivations of autonomous individuals. The assumptions of mathematical nature, of the detached mind, and of nonlinguistic knowledge are never challenged, so that all efforts at scientific social legitimation are conceptually committed to the foundational scientific image of detached, logically prior minds, the image of the a priori individual.

The legitimating support for the market is derived from the assumption that individual motivations are rational and nonmoral. But it is also possible to assume that the "natural" motivations of autonomous individuals are both nonmoral and nonrational, and from this assumption there is an even greater commitment to the "natural" necessity of social order as such. In this case the individuals are still seen as motivated by limitless desire, but now this desire is irrational and sensual rather than rational and acquisitive. Individuals are "naturally" out of control, rather than "naturally" rational. Accordingly, social order becomes absolutely necessary, rather than only maximally rational, because now individuals are motivated by inherently destructive tendencies rather than by "natural" rationality. This is the perspective of theorists such as Durkheim, Freud, and the functionalists, and a legitimating version of this theoretical perspective has been used by both conservatives and fascists in market society. Durkheim (1951), for example, finds that human nature is substantially the same among all men, in its essential qualities. It is not human nature which can assign the variable limits necessary to our needs. They are thus unlimited so far as they depend on the individual alone. Irrespective of any external regulatory force, our capacity for feeling is in itself an insatiable and bottomless abyss. (p. 274)

And for Freud (1961),

instinctual passions are stronger than reasonable interests. Civilization has to use its utmost efforts in order to set limits to man's aggressive instincts and to hold the manifestations of them in check. (p. 59)

These are theorists who tend to find an absolute need for social order, as such, rather than a need to criticize and disrupt one set of institutions in order to create better, more moral institutions. The general need for order, as such, becomes more important than the particular experience of inequality and injustice, and so once again a morality of order is established in the face of "natural" tendencies toward chaos and disorder.

In this case, however, the need for social order is not something that individuals will necessarily see for themselves, since they are driven by irrational desire, not by rational self-interest. Thus this version of individual motivations legitimates far more centralized control in the name of order for its own sake, and this legitimation of control begins to make more sense, particularly to those with political power. Soon market relations begin to appear less as spontaneous, miraculous order and more as requiring centralized control in order to maintain the appropriate structures of power and privilege. This irrational version of individual desires allows centralized control over individuals for their own sakes, whereas the rational version of the individual allows only the centralized control that individuals have rationally accepted as in their own self-interest. As social analysts begin to realize that social life is far more complicated than simply contractual relations between rational individuals, this assumption of irrational desire starts to permeate social theory, since it makes the controlling social institutions far more important. This irrational version of the individual is compatible with the market (limitless desire), but it legitimates even greater institutional authority, in the name of order. In both versions of the individual, however, there is a morality of order as such, as the need for social order becomes a "natural," rational demand. And this is the neutral rationality of mathematics, the indifferent ratio-

nality of nature, not the moral rationality of the good life, the good society, or individual fulfillment.

Legitimating a Moral Order

Some theorists, however, argue that social order must involve a special,
moral rationality, a rationality of goals and fulfillment, rather than of
mathematical laws. This would be a rationality of human beings, not a
rationality of nature, and it would impose a moral imperative on social
organization, rather than simply announcing the morality of order as
such. From this perspective individual motivations contain an inherent
moral dimension, the dimension of a "natural" human meaning, or essence. Individuals are "naturally" motivated to fulfill this essence, and
thus social life must be directed toward and organized around this "natural" motivation. From this perspective social order is justified only insofar as it can satisfy and fulfill this "natural" human essence, and this is
not an essence of limitless desire, whether rational or irrational. Rather, it
is an essence of human completion, human development, human social
participation, an essence that can provide a truly moral basis for criticizing social institutions in the name of the individual. As Macpherson
(1973) puts it:

> A concept of man as essentially an exerter and enjoyer of his own
> powers had to be asserted. Life was to be lived, not to be devoted to
> acquiring utilities. The end or purpose of man was to use and develop
> his uniquely human attributes. A life so directed might be thought of
> as a life of reason or a life of sensibilities, but it was not a life of
> acquisition. (p. 32)

This idea of the individual reinserted a notion of purpose into the understanding of scientific social life: society had the purpose of fulfilling
the human essence, and it had to be morally directed toward that goal.
This essence was "natural," and thus it could be known rationally, scientifically, and while objective nature was still absolutely nonmoral, social life could now be seen as having an inherent moral dimension, the
dimension of individual fulfillment. Clearly, this idea is related to the
Christian idea of individual salvation and it works as an effort to bring a
more human, moral reference into the austere rationality of the market.
But it also works to present a social solution to the classic scientific
dilemma of the mind and the body, since now social life can enter a different explanatory domain from natural processes, a domain where a ref-

erence to morality can make sense. With this assumption social theory is categorically separated from natural science, and social life is no longer subject to the same kind of neutral, scientific analysis as nature, where rationality is mathematical and indifferent rather than moralistic and purposeful. This analytic strategy develops with Hegel, who begins to explain social life in terms of purpose, through the specifically social notions of history and culture (spirit). And after Hegel scientific social theory begins to diverge around this strategy, around whether social life can best be explained in terms of a mathematical, scientific notion of rationality or a specifically social, moral notion of rationality.

Among other things, this is a divergence over the legitimation of social institutions. Like the idea of individual motivations generally, the idea of a motivating human essence needed filling in with specific motivational commitments, so that specific social institutions and actions could be legitimated in the name of individuals seeking to fulfill this fundamental human essence. In Germany, Marx followed Hegel with a radical critique of the market, and in England John Stuart Mill and others developed a liberal critique of the market, a critique directed toward humanizing the market.

> The quality of life in the market society was seen by moralists as different as Mill and Marx, Carlyle and Saint-Simon, Ruskin and Green, the German moralists and the English Christian Socialists, to be little short of an insult to humanity. Those of the critics of market morality who still hoped to retain some of the values of liberal individualism thus thought it . . . morally right to assert a higher set of values than those of the market.
> This meant asserting an equal right of every individual to make the most of himself. (Macpherson 1973, 34)

In the liberal critique of the market, individuals are not motivated by a limitless desire for property, but rather by a desire for human fulfillment, and that fulfillment can be best achieved through the structure of private property and the market. However, if the market is left to its own rational (mathematical) mechanisms, it will provide only greed and oppression, not human fulfillment. Accordingly, the market must be rationally controlled and directed, in a more moral and social sense of rational. Individual access to private property is an important aspect of human fulfillment, but the market tends to concentrate on access to property and to disdain individual human needs, so that government must systematically intervene in the market in the name of the individual, by providing welfare protection, unemployment insurance, and health care; by preventing discrimination and enabling competition; and so on. The liberal tries to make the rationality of the market compatible with a moral human essence, but this is a difficult if not impossible task, since market rationality, like natural rationality, is defined as nonmoral, and since the market will always concentrate power and property, through its rational, indifferent mechanisms.

This is the issue around which much of modern American politics revolves, as the conservatives tend to think the market should order itself and the liberals tend to think the government should endeavor to control and humanize the market. In effect, the theoretical tension between a scientific or a moralistic rationality for social life becomes the central political tension of the market, as the debate focuses on what individuals are really like, what is best for them, when are they most free and equal, and what is the appropriate role of the government. In this debate the market is always the fundamental reference for an acceptable social order, and this means that the fundamental reference for rationality is always scientific, mathematical rationality, the neutral, mechanistic rationality of the market. This is why Marx had to reject the market in order to complete the legitimating image of a moralistic human essence, and this is also why Max Weber is such a pessimistic liberal theorist. For Weber the market defines the idea of rationality, and this rationality will inevitably dehumanize social relations in the name of efficiency and technical control. Bureaucratic indifference organizes the market "without regard for persons" (Weber 1958, 215), and so the liberal tragedy results, the tragedy of rationality versus human values. As Weber establishes it, the analysis of bureaucracy suggests that the market can be organized and controlled only in the direction of greater efficiency and less humanity.

Karl Marx, on the other hand, argues that the inhumanity of the market is an offense against rationality (albeit historically necessary) and that the market must be rejected and replaced in the name of a social, human rationality. For him the market is not compatible with the "natural" human essence, and in particular that essence is not compatible with the idea of private property. Individuals are "naturally" producers, not accumulators, and so they are fundamentally characterized by their need to control the products of their labor. It is an offense against their "natural" essence to let others control those products, and thus individuals cannot rationally or morally sell their labor as property. Marx used this idea of the human essence to legitimate a fundamental critique of the market and to recommend the institutions of socialism, where everyone would work for everyone's profit and all individuals would, at least in principle, control the products of their own labor. Marx used a social, moralistic rationality to criticize the "natural," scientific rationality of the market, but he also claimed a scientific basis for his moralistic rationality. This enabled his followers to legitimate a scientific bureaucracy and technology as the basis for a centralized moral authority, rather than as a response to an emergent market rationality. Marx questioned the rationality of the market but not the rationality of science, and this made it possible for him to authorize a specific set of rational institutions in the name of the "natural" individual. Marx realized that scientific rationality was not fully compatible with human social life, but he appealed to science to defend a moral rationality, and thus he gave scientific legitimacy to a moralistic vision.

Where the market developed excessive centralized power in the name of controlling "natural" individual desires, socialism developed excessive centralized power in the name of enabling the "natural" human essence. Both became committed to their respective versions of the "natural," rational order, the only order that could be derived from the inherent characteristics and motivations of "natural" individuals. In the name of science and the "natural" individual, both Marx and the market theorists legitimated a particular set of social institutions as absolutely rational, in the same sense that science and nature are rational. More precisely, they both utilized an implicit reference to the mathematical rationality of nature to decide that social order has the same necessity as natural order, and thus to deny the need for a reflexive, ecological reference for knowledge and social legitimation. The necessary structure of "natural" social institutions can be derived from the objective knowledge of "natural" individual motivations, and so social practices do not need to be legitimated in terms of reflexive evaluation and criticism and in accordance with the ecological criteria of sustainability.

The Individual-Social Tension

Through these different versions of individual motivations, social theory created different strategies for social legitimation and social explanation. In all of these versions social theory has accepted the scientific version of objective nature, as the valid basis for reason and knowledge, and thus social theory has revolved around the idea of the autonomous scientific individual. Because this individual is logically asocial but empirically social, social theory has generally focused on the relationship between the individual and the society, with the individual being in various stages of tension and conflict with society. This tension is inevitable, and it makes social order somewhat problematic, at least theoretically. This is the famous problem of social order: individuals are "naturally" free and society imposes external constraints on them, constraints that both inhibit freedom and enable individual rationality, fulfillment, and so on.

This vision of an individual-social tension permeates scientific social theory, with social analysis always directed toward what kind of institutions will best resolve this tension, through organized efforts to meet the "natural" individual needs that generate it. Different theorists locate this tension along different social dimensions, but they all incorporate it in some analytic form and it always implies that social practices must be arranged in accordance with the inherent desires or essence of the "natural" individual. In effect, the individual becomes comparable to the corpuscles (atoms, particles) of nature, and society becomes the external, constraining structure (laws) that creates order. And this is exactly the image that Hobbes used, explicitly following Galileo, to first state this individual-social tension and the problem of social order. Hobbes assumed that individuals were naturally in motion (limitless desire), just like Galileo's corpuscles, and that society constrained and ordered those motions, just like the laws of nature. Since then there has been a scientific problem of social order, where "natural" individuals are generally understood as inherently restricted by external social constraints, rather than linguistic individuals being understood as inherently social-natural. Science and nature are definitively nonsocial, so that if individuals are conceptualized as "natural," then social life must become an explanatory puzzle, since it is composed of individuals and yet is categorically detached from nature. Society must be understood in terms of individuals, and yet it must also be understood as external to individuals, and this generates the individual-social tension, while also making the idea of social life ambiguous and confusing, from a scientific perspective. In essence, the individual-social tension makes the idea of society problematic in order to avoid making scientific knowledge problematic, since conceptualizing individuals as truly social would contradict the idea of an objective, mathematical nature. And this vision of scientific nature is protected by requiring social life to be conceptualized as an artifact of logically prior, "natural" individuals, regardless of the confusion this imposes on the conception of social life.

In the case of Hobbes, Locke, and the market tradition, the individual-social tension is obvious: rational, self-interested individuals are constrained by social laws and contracts. But the theoretical reaction against the market involved an effort to see the individual as less self-interested and more inherently social, so that social life could be understood as more than only rational agreements among selfish, calculating people. Social theory became an effort to understand the richness and complexity of social life in an explanatory context that defined the basic ideas of reason and knowledge in terms of mathematical nature. This meant that social life had to be seen as a more necessary part of the scientific individual, more necessary than the idea of the rationally organized market. The complexity of social life had to be somehow inherent in the "natural" individual, and so the individual had to be somehow enabled or completed by social constraints, not simply made more secure by them. In effect, the individual had to be seen as a locus of conflict between inherent "natural" desires and necessary social tendencies, with the social tendencies enabling full humanity but always being fragile and problematic and always being felt as external constraints. Thus, for Durkheim (1951), "inextinguishable thirst is constantly renewed torture," and "since the individual has no way of limiting [the passions], this must be done by some force exterior to him" (pp. 247-48). Society is this force, and while society enables full humanity it can do so only "by the power of external coercion" over the "unlimited desires" of individuals. Thus for Durkheim any social order is better than no social order because the morality of social order as such is necessary to control the insatiable demands of "natural" individuals.

Max Weber is more pessimistic, finding that the enabling social constraints of religion are being overrun by market rationality, as it encourages "natural" individual self-interest. He finds the same kind of individual-social tension, only now the tension is between "societal action" and "communal action," or between class interests and status honor. Societal action "is oriented to a rationally motivated adjustment of interest" and communal action "is oriented to the feeling of the actors that they belong together" (Weber 1958, 183), so that the tension is between individual interests and social values. Like the market theorists, Weber finds individuals to be motivated by rational self-interest, but unlike them he finds the pursuit of rational interests to be in conflict with the possibility of human commitments and communal identity. So once again individual desires are in conflict with social life, only this time the individual desires are winning and social life is becoming less social and more technical. From this perspective Weber can suggest that the rational institutions of the market, such as bureaucracy, are necessary in terms of the "natural" individual, but that they are also debilitating, in terms of a human, communal quality for social life.

Both Durkheim and Weber find the individual-social tension to be necessary and irresolvable, as do the market theorists, but Marx finds it to be contingent and resolvable, at least in principle. For him this tension is historical, rather than inherent, and it will disappear after capitalism has made its productive-technological contribution and been overthrown. Before socialism, however, this tension is pervasive, since individuals can never fulfill their "natural" human essence when the productive institutions are oppressive and exploitative, and only these kinds of institutions are possible in the context of scarcity. Individuals are producers by "nature," but production will always be an issue of class exploitation, and thus "natural" individuals will always be in conflict with their constraining institutions, until history comes to an end. Marx analyzed capitalism in terms of an individual-social tension, and he thought that socialism would resolve that tension, but in fact he provided theoretical support for the party's effort to establish an absolute moral order, and to coerce individuals to accept that order, since if no individual-social tension was possible then there could be only recalcitrant and misguided individuals. For Marx the individual-social tension under capitalism provided the basis for a legitimate criticism of capitalism, but since there could be no such tension under socialism then no such legitimate criticism was possible, and the party could claim absolute control, in the name of history.

Each of these theorists legitimates a slightly different kind of social practice, but all of them accept the ideas of scientific knowledge, scientific nature, and scientific technology. Thus they all build their productive bases on the same technology and their legitimating bases on the same idea of knowledge. In particular, they all try to analyze and explain social life by assuming a fundamental tension between the individual and the society, a tension that is conceptually required by the autonomous individual of scientific knowledge. Science requires an explanatory commitment to individualism, in the sense of a "natural," a priori individual, an individual who is logically prior and essentially external to any social order. For Freud this individualism takes the form of the desiring "id" conflicting with the constraining "superego," and for George Herbert

Mead it takes the form of the spontaneous and unique "I" struggling against the obedient and collectivist "me." The list of social theorists employing this explanatory individualism could go on, as John W. Meyer (1986) remarks:

> All modern systems are rooted in individualism; its form merely varies. Even the socialist world resolutely and overtly roots its theory of value and its political doctrine in individual action, in the benefits that the individuals in its present or future population will attain. The mediation itself, of course, takes place through some communal vision—a party here, a picture of the future community there—nevertheless the difference between this and the liberal European or American forms of individualism should be seen as one of degree rather than of kind. (p. 212)

In scientific social theory, social knowledge is referred back to natural knowledge, and natural knowledge assumes a world that is made up of fundamental particles of matter (atoms, corpuscles) in constant motion, with that motion being constrained and ordered by the laws and forces of nature. In this model individuals become the fundamental particles of social life, and the laws and institutions of society become the constraining forces that impose order on those individuals. Hobbes used this scientific model explicitly, and succeeding social theorists have used it more implicitly, through an explanatory reliance on an individual-social tension. In this model there are basically two aspects of the individual that become crucial for social theory. First, all individuals, as fundamental particles, are assumed to be uniform, which means they are all assumed to be equal. The "natural" equality of individuals becomes a central reference for scientific social theory. Second, all individuals, as fundamental particles in motion, are assumed to require constraint and control by external social forces. So the necessity of order also becomes a central reference for scientific social theory. It is possible, then, to categorize social theories according to their conceptual focus on one of these two references. If they focus on the idea of equality, with Marx and the liberal theorists, then they tend to think that social order should be criticized and improved in the name of equality. If they focus on the idea of order, with Durkheim, Freud, and the market theorists, then they tend to think that the established institutions should be protected against disruption and change in the name of order. Thus the scientific model sets up the order-conflict debate in social theory, just as it also sets up the agency-structure debate.

What is not set up by the scientific model is a focus on the idea of sustainability, through a reference to an ecological version of reason and knowledge. Because of its homage to objective nature, social theory cannot make knowledge an issue of social analysis, and so it is left with the social residues of scientific knowledge — the "natural" individual and the external necessity of social order. In particular, social theory can conceptualize the individual only in terms of "natural," inherent motivations, not in terms of the enabling structure of language, and thus social theory cannot incorporate a reflexive reference to social-natural interactions. As language users, human beings are always adjusting their actions and ideas (institutions and knowledge) according to the effects of those actions and ideas, but as "natural" individuals they are simply trying to achieve the "proper" social order, an order that can be known with scientific certainty in terms of their "natural" characteristics. Moreover, these "natural" characteristics can legitimate an enormous amount of social control. They can be known scientifically, and thus they can be used in the name of reason and truth to force individuals to act in their own "real" interests, that is, to be more "naturally" equal, to accept the "proper" institutions, and so on. A reference to language, however, as opposed to nature, can only legitimate sustainability, which means that no one can ever "know" the truth with certainty. They can know only the reflexive consequences of efforts at institutional sustainability, and so they can argue only for an ecological rationality that is context dependent, they cannot argue for an objective rationality that is context free. Through a reference to language not only can the individual be seen as inherently social but social life can be seen as inherently an issue of natural processes, of the natural environment, and as inherently open to criticism, as we will see. Social theory has legitimated objective and technological institutions in the name of the "natural" individual, and now it must begin to legitimate reflexive and ecological institutions in the name of a linguistic individual.

The reliance on the "natural" individual raises another and even more fundamental problem for social theory, the problem of rationality. If nature is objective and the individual is "natural," and social order must be understood in these terms, then what kind of rationality is available to understand and explain social life? The universe is rational in the mathematical, nonmoral sense and social life is part of the universe, so therefore a strictly scientific rationality must be appropriate. But we can do something about social life in a way that we cannot do something about natural processes, and so a more moral, instructive rationality must be appropriate. This is the dilemma of rationality: Does the analysis of social life require a different kind of rationality from the analysis of nature, and if so what kind of rationality and where does it come from? As long as social theory accepts physics, it must also accept a fundamental reference to mathematical rationality as the ordering principle of the universe and as the basic structure of valid knowledge. But social theory seems to be a different explanatory domain from physics, and social life seems to require a different explanatory strategy, a more involved, less detached, strategy.

In particular, social life seems to require a more critical strategy. In social life the idea of rationality is not only descriptive, it is also legitimating, so that institutions that simply claim to be rational for the sake of legitimation may need to be criticized in the name of a true, or authentic, rationality. But a social rationality can be critical in this sense only if it is based on an image of what social life ought to be if it is to be truly rational. So a critical rationality must be a moral rationality, but it must also be a scientific rationality, since its institutional recommendations must have the moral weight of "natural" necessity. But a scientific rationality cannot be a moral rationality, by definition. Thus there are the horns of an explanatory dilemma: either science is not rational or the legitimating, moral rationality of social life must somehow refer back to the mathematical, nonmoral rationality of nature. In this book I am arguing for the first horn: science is not rational because it is not ecological, and scientific rationality is not coherent because only a reflexive reference to sustainability can make the idea of rationality coherent. But scientific social theory has generally accepted the second horn, with all its conceptual incoherence, because nature has been given over to physics, with the result that all knowledge, including social theory, must be referred to the mathematical rationality of nature. This means that a moral rationality must be made scientific, and this is possible only if institutional recommendations can be derived from the scientific study of social life. Thus we are back at the "natural" characteristics of a priori individuals as the only basis for deriving a critical rationality for social life. And this is generally what social theory has attempted, with either continued order or more equality being recommended for "natural" individuals.

In social theory the need for a critical rationality has revolved around the need to criticize, in the name of reason, the social implications of scientific knowledge, including the market, individualism, bureaucratic indifference, technological control, and loss of cultural identity. But how can you criticize the social implications of rationality in the name of rationality unless you redefine the idea of rationality? This has been the dilemma of social theory, a dilemma I will explore in the next chapter. The ability to have a critical, nontraditional attitude toward social life is one of the social implications of scientific knowledge, but scientific knowledge also makes it virtually impossible to criticize the legitimating notion of scientific rationality, and this is the problem. In social life the idea of a social rationality must be used against the idea of a natural rationality, and yet no notion of social rationality can make sense in the context of science. Much of critical social theory has been focused on trying to develop such a social, moral rationality, but always in the conceptual context of physics, always by giving away nature to mathematics. In the following chapter I will discuss this critical effort, and I will argue that a critical rationality must reject scientific rationality as incoherent. A critical rationality must be ecological, and so it must be referred to the idea of language, rather than to the idea of nature.

SEVEN

The Dilemma of Rationality

One of the central differences between scientific knowledge and religious knowledge is that science can legitimate the possibility of internal criticism against its own theories, whereas religion cannot. Science does this by assuming that reality is abstract rather than specific and therefore that the knowledge of reality is the knowledge of an abstract, formal order rather than the knowledge of a specific, substantive order. The formal order, of course, is mathematics—mathematical nature, mathematical rationality—as opposed to the substantive order of religious knowledge—traditional practices, ordinary language. By identifying reality with a formal order, science can use one mathematical theory to criticize another mathematical theory, just as relativity is a criticism of Newtonian mechanism, or quantum mechanics is a criticism of relativity, and so forth. This criticism and replacement of specific theories is possible within science because the formal (mathematical) reference for valid knowledge is always maintained, whereas it is not possible within religion because there is only a specific (traditional) reference for valid knowledge, and it can be maintained only absolutely, ritually. Science enables the internal criticism of particular mathematical theories, but it does not enable the criticism of a mathematical idea of knowledge, any more than religion enables the criticism of a traditional idea of knowledge. Scientific knowledge refers to a true reality that is as final and absolute as the true reality of religious knowledge, but scientific reality is compatible with the possibility of internal criticism because it is abstract and formal, whereas religious reality is not.

In particular, scientific reality is nonsocial, and criticism is always a social issue. Criticizing theories always involves criticizing people, and when one theory of reality supports one particular social group, criticizing that theory also involves social criticism and social legitimation. Religious reality always includes specific social practices, and so any criticism of a religious theory necessarily involves a criticism of social authority, institutional order, and so on. But scientific reality is defined as nonsocial, so that internal scientific criticism involves no issues of social authority and legitimation, by definition. Scientific knowledge is based on a reference (mathematics) that is clearly *formal* and that is asserted (and accepted) as being *nonsocial*, and this means that internal criticism is made possible as a strictly nonsocial, nonpolitical concern. In this way science distinguishes itself from religion and introduces the possibility of legitimate criticism into the idea of knowledge, and it can do this only because it asserts such an austere, nonsocial, nonlegitimating idea of criticism. In scientific terms this is only a formal and detached commitment to criticism, not a social and legitimating commitment, but the idea of legitimate criticism quickly escapes this scientific formality and enters into the political practice of scientific social life.

Despite its professed social indifference, science manages to legitimate the external possibility of social criticism in the same way it legitimates the internal possibility of theoretical criticism, by establishing a formal reference for reason, a reference that cannot be identified with and "tamed" by any particular social practices. In its original religious context, however, science could assert such a formal reference only by defining it as categorically nonsocial, and thus as not a threat to the religious version of social rationality, the sacred rationality of the established tradition. Of course, this scientific idea of reason immediately became available for social criticism, particularly the criticism of the established tradition, but this could only be social criticism in the name of a nonsocial rationality, which means in the name of a nonsocial and essentially technical idea of individuals and nature. In effect, science replaced a substantive sacred reality (the traditional order) with a formal sacred reality (mathematical nature), and this new reality brought with it its own legitimating commitments to the "proper" social institutions, the institutions of the "natural" individual. Both versions of reality involved specific, but quite different, images of legitimate social practices, but the scientific version of reality was defined formally, rather than ritually, and so it could establish only a formal framework of legitimation rather than the specific details of legitimation. This was the formal legitimating framework of technical proficiency and "natural" individuals, a framework derived from the formal rationality of mathematical nature, and it could legitimate only a certain general set of technically rational institutions. But the critical issue, in terms of the possibility of criticism, is the idea of a general, formal set of institutional possibilities, as opposed to a specific, ritualized tradition.

Through a formal reference for reason, science legitimates the possibility of rational criticism, even in terms of a limited critical domain, and yet this possibility of criticism is not dependent upon the scientific idea of reason, with its commitment to mathematical nature and "natural" individuals. Rather, the legitimacy of criticism is dependent only upon the idea of a formal reference for reason, and it is this aspect of science, rather than its image of nature, that must be incorporated into a coherent and ecological idea of knowledge. Mathematical nature is a formal but not a coherent reference, because it mistakes a form of language for "true" reality, and so a reference must be found that is both formal and coherent, and that reference must be the structure of language. In these last three chapters I will argue that if the idea of knowledge is to be coherent it must be referred to the formal structure of language, and that such a reference will establish a *critical* and *ecological* idea of reason, an idea that is coherent, unlike the scientific idea, because it is reflexive. And this means that the scientific ability to legitimate a critical idea of reason must be analytically distinguished from the scientific idea of mathematical reason. In science the idea of mathematical reason makes criticism possible, but it is not the only way to make criticism possible, and the formal structure of language will legitimate an even greater, "wilder" commitment to criticism.

I will argue, then, that we should abandon the image of a mathematical universe as incoherent, but that we should keep the idea of a formal reference for knowledge as the basis for a critical idea of reason, and that this formal reference should be the structure of language. It is in this sense that the commitment to a critical idea of reason is the most profound social implication of scientific knowledge. This is the commitment that transformed the formal possibilities of social life, while the idea of mathematical nature simply legitimated one substantive version of institutional content in the name of one particular version of reason. But there are other, more coherent, versions of reason, and there are other, more ecological, versions of institutional content, and to find them we must detach the idea of reason from the idea of nature, which means from the idea of mathematics. Science identified these ideas, but they are conceptually independent, and if this independence is recognized then a coherent idea of reason can be used to criticize the scientific idea of reason and a coherent idea of knowledge can be used to legitimate coherent and ecological institutions.

Through the formality of mathematics, science legitimated the internal criticism of its theories in the name of reason, but what about criticizing social actions and values in the name of reason? Scientific knowledge undermined the sacred tradition and introduced a legitimating reference to rationality, but this was the nonsocial rationality of objective nature, and so it was not an appropriate basis for social criticism, by definition. In effect, science introduced the legitimacy of criticism into social life, through the idea of reason, but provided no coherent reference for social criticism. Science can legitimate internal criticism as long as all scientists accept and operate within the same formal conception of reality, the idea of mathematical nature. From within this conception scientists can criticize and replace each other's theories as long as they all use the same criteria of mathematical observation, mathematical experiment, and mathematical order. In theory, however, scientific rationality is strictly about nature and has no application to social life, and this makes the scientific idea of social criticism quite ambiguous. So as the scientific ideas of reason and criticism made their obvious and necessary move into the legitimation of social actions, the question arose as to what kind of rationality could provide a coherent reference for social criticism.

In the Christian context the strict scientific idea of rationality was sufficient, because it could finesse the sacred authority of tradition. Against the moral, traditional rationality of the Church the new nonmoral, mathematical rationality could be quite effective, since it could disrupt social authority while claiming to glorify God. So the first legitimating uses of scientific reason and criticism came in the name of the perfect scientific individual—the rational, autonomous individual, the individual with "natural" motivations toward rational self-interest, the individual "naturally" seeking to maximize private property, the market individual. The market was legitimated against feudal tradition in the name of strict scientific (mathematical) rationality, and this is why the early theorists of the market were so insistent, and so impressed, that a rational social order could be established independent of moral strictures. The market did not need morality, it simply needed to provide a rational order to the "natural" motions of "natural" individuals and a free and equal, prosperous and progressive social order would result. Thus in the context of a society legitimated by tradition and faith, the new scientific rationality could provide a basis for moral and institutional criticism without appearing to be a moral, social rationality. Reason was replacing tradition, and so the only criticism necessary was the criticism of superstition in the name of reason. Pure, neutral rationality dictated the necessity of the market, and once it got started social life would have the same rationality as nature, and there would be no requirement for a specifically *social* rationality.

But how could there be a rational criticism of the market if the market was already rational? This was the problem that confronted the critics of the market, as the market order began to appear less and less rational, in the sense of less morally legitimate. Science had legitimated the possibility of rational criticism, and the market order, with its increasing exploitation and dislocations, required criticism. But the market was supposedly a consequence of rationality, not of tradition, and so how could rational criticism be turned against a rational order? In the context of scientific rationality (mathematical nature) there was only one possibility: the "natural" individual had to be different from what the market theorists had presumed, and then the market would be based on a scientific mistake. In this case the market would not be rational, since it would not be compatible with the "natural" individual, and it would be subject to rational criticism. And so social theory began to postulate a different individual, such as an individual who was "naturally" motivated by irrational desire rather than by rational self-interest. This was the strategy of Durkheim and Freud, and it legitimated greater social concern and control in the name of reason, as the indifferent individualism of the market became increasingly oppressive. As Durkheim understood, this strategy stressed the importance of moral commitments, since only such commitments could constrain the brutal self-interest of the market. But for Durkheim and Freud morality became simply a technical requirement for social order, as a way of controlling the "naturally" irrational individual, and so for them scientific rationality remained the objective, nonsocial reference for social criticism. In effect, the individual had changed but the logic had not. Now scientific rationality endorsed order as such, as a technical achievement, rather than only the market order, as a rational achievement, and once again science could be seen as making legitimating recommendations in the name of neutral nature.

Both the rational and the irrational individual were efforts to make scientific reason applicable to social life, and both legitimated a necessary image of rational social order in the name of thoroughly nonsocial individuals. But some theorists began to suspect that individuals were more inherently social than this, and that the nonsocial rationality of science was not really appropriate for social life, either as the rationality of the market or as the rationality of necessary moral constraints. Scientific rationality was defined as indifferent to human life, and some theorists, such as Weber, began to think that its institutional recommendations would also be indifferent to human life. For Weber nature and mathematics still defined rationality, but this rationality would inevitably undermine the human quality of social life, so that social life could become more rational only by becoming more inhuman. The human, communal quality of social life depends on commitments to moral values, and rationality will disrupt any such commitments, since it is strictly an issue of "natural" individual interests, market interests. Like Durkheim and the market theorists, Weber managed to apply the scientific idea of rationality to social life, but he accepted its nonsocial, nonhuman implications, and thus he saw rationality as making social life more efficient but less enjoyable. You could not criticize rational (market) society in the name of rationality, but you could criticize it in the name of human beings.

Because he understood scientific rationality, Weber had to give up on the idea of a good society that was also rational, but other theorists wanted to legitimate a good, moral society in the name of rationality. These theorists wanted to use the critical idea of rationality as a basis for institutional legitimation, in the sense that the appeal to rationality involved a definite moral commitment. They also saw humans as requiring a moral order, but this would be a specific and necessary moral order, a moral order of human fulfillment, not the morality of order as such. This would mean that the appeal to rationality would legitimate a specifically moral set of institutions, institutions that would fulfill the "natural" moral essence human beings. This is the position of Marx, where an image of a social and productive human essence is asserted against the market image of strict individual self-interest and accumulation. Marx tries to define a (true) social rationality as a basis for criticizing the (mistaken) individualist rationality of the market, but he tries to do this in the name of science, so that he must assert a thoroughly social, moral rationality in the name of a thoroughly nonsocial, indifferent rationality. He wants to criticize the indifferent, oppressive institutions of the market in the name of a committed, human rationality, but the idea of rationality, as a critical reference, has been defined by science, and it is an indifferent, nonhuman rationality. Marx must either abandon the rationality of science or appeal to it, and he cannot abandon it because he seeks the authority of science for his social analysis. So he locates his social rationality within natural rationality, where the laws of history are like the laws of nature and individuals need certain institutional arrangements, for their "natural" fulfillment, whether they know it or want it or not.

Rationality and the Critical Theorists

Marx presents the idea of a critical, social rationality, but he ties it to an image of the "natural" individual, an individual who is more social than self-interested but is still defined by "natural" motivations. This is the productive individual, the individual who makes the idea of private property irrational and immoral. For Marx, scientific rationality can understand this individual, create a specifically social, moral rationality, and legitimate the socialist rejection of private property. The only problem is that socialism must then be legitimated by scientific rationality, and scientific rationality is by definition nonsocial and nonhuman. This is the problem that confronted the critical theorists of the Frankfurt school, theorists who were sympathetic to Marx's call for a critical rationality but who were unable to accept his scientific version of it. For Marx, scientific rationality could create the good society simply by disallowing private property, and the critical theorists thought it was more complicated than this. Marx envisioned scientific socialism, and while the critical theorists agreed that private property was an important obstacle to the good society, they did not think it was the only obstacle. They thought the main obstacle was scientific rationality itself, a rationality that was indifferent and nonhuman. They agreed with Weber that scientific rationality was not particularly good for people, but they disagreed with his claim that scientific rationality was the only kind available and therefore that only a dehumanizing society could be legitimated in the name of reason. They thought, rather, that a good, human society could be legitimated in the name of reason, but that this had to be a moral rationality and that such a rationality could provide the basis for the critical rejection of scientific rationality.

Thus the critical theorists, including prominently Adorno, Horkheimer, and Marcuse, had the task of developing and articulating this critical, moral idea of reason. But they did not want to attack physics, as the rationality of objective nature. Rather, they wanted to attack only the social ramifications of this scientific rationality, and so they tried to develop a social rationality that was superior to scientific rationality with respect to social life, not with respect to nature. As a result they could mount only a *social* critique of science, not a *social-natural* critique. They had to focus on the social, not the ecological, consequences of science, and they had to do this from within the scientific conception of knowledge, since they had accepted the scientific version of nature. Thus like most other social theorists they analyzed social life from the perspective of the a priori individual. For them this individual was characterized by "consciousness," and this was a social consciousness, in the sense that individuals "naturally" sought meaningful social relations, not the relations of alienation and domination fostered by scientific rationality. For the critical theorists individuals needed something like the social commitments of traditional, religious societies only without the inequality, so they projected a society that would maintain the scientific commitment to equality but without the scientific individualism and exploitation. This critique, however, became more of a moralistic rejection of scientific society than a positive institutional recommendation, since they basically wanted the social benefits of science—technology, equality, rationality—without its social indifference, and they could find no way to distinguish one from the other. They began with scientific assumptions—objective nature, the a priori individual—and then tried to base a social, critical rationality on these assumptions, and they were left in a romantic, analytic muddle. They continued to define both rationality and social life in scientific terms and then demanded a more humane version of them, but all they could finally do was express disapproval of some scientific consequences in the name of other scientific consequences.

The critical theorists sought an objective reference for a social rationality, but they continued to accept the scientific reference to objective nature, and so the only *social* reference they could find involved the a priori individual. In their case this was individual consciousness, and it was a version of the inherent scientific commitment to "natural" individual equality. Thus they focused on a "critique of domination" (meaning inequality), but their own arguments made their criticism seem futile, since they could not clearly distinguish the rationality they opposed (the rationality of domination) from the rationality they endorsed (the rationality of equality). As Jürgen Habermas (1984) puts it, Horkheimer and Adorno "believe that even the critique of instrumental reason remains tied to the model that instrumental reason itself follows" (p. 389). These theorists were trying to criticize the social effects of science from within a scientific conception, so they could only mount an impassioned rejection of science in the name of the fulfilled individual. In particular, they could not criticize scientific rationality from the perspective of an ecological rationality, and so they could not replace the scientific conception of a "natural" individual with a reflexive conception of a linguistic individual.

Following in this critical tradition, Habermas has argued that a critical rationality must be referred to the idea of language, not to a notion of individual "consciousness." In his terms, we must

> give up the paradigm of the philosophy of consciousness—namely, a subject that represents objects and toils with them—in favor of the paradigm of linguistic philosophy—namely, that of intersubjective understanding or communication—and put the cognitive-instrumental aspect of reason in its proper place as part of a more encompassing *communicative rationality*. (p. 390)

This communicative rationality is grounded in the formal structure of linguistic communication, a structure that always presumes, in principle, an equal, nondominating relationship between speakers. Thus the reference to language can establish a critical, normative rationality, since "the utopian perspective of reconciliation and freedom is ingrained in the conditions for the communicative sociation of individuals" (p. 398). This means that the institutions and practices of domination can always be objectively criticized in the name of communicative rationality, since any institutional distortion of formal linguistic equality is contradictory to that necessary social rationality. In this way Habermas feels he can reject the "reification of consciousness" and ground a critical rationality in an objective and truly *social* reference to language.

Since I am arguing something quite similar, it might seem that Habermas has already done my work, and indeed I believe he has begun to push social theory in the (linguistic) direction it must go. Finally, however, he fails to recognize the truly constitutive role of language, and so remains firmly within the framework of scientific social theory. In particular, he continues to privilege the scientific notion of objective nature, arguing, as in the quote above, that communicative rationality must somehow accept and incorporate the instrumental rationality of science. In fact, he retreats from the position of Horkheimer and Adorno, arguing that they find too much social fault with science and that science is really only the technical control of nature. "But the conceptual apparatus of instrumental reason is set up to make it possible for subjects to exercise control of nature and *not* to tell an objectivated nature what is to be done with it" (p. 389). This means, in effect, that the idea of objective nature is basically neutral and does not carry with it specific social recommendations. And in an earlier work, he states that the function of science is technical control and that "for this function, as for scientific-technical progress in general, there is no more 'humane' substitute" (Habermas 1970, 88). So Habermas tries to have it both ways, a linguistic rationality and a scientific rationality; this means that he misunderstands the significance of language and that he remains conceptually committed to some version of the a priori individual, the individual of scientific knowledge. Like other critical theorists, Habermas worries about structures of domination rather than structures of sustainability, and so like them he must finally assert more of a moralizing criticism of industrial practice than a coherent conception of a social and critical rationality.

In contrast, I am arguing that the scientific ideas of knowledge and nature are incoherent, and that rationality must be understood as fully an issue of language, not as an issue of language with respect to social life and as an issue of mathematics with respect to nature. From my perspective, nature must be understood reflexively, through a reference to language, not objectively, through a reference to mathematics, and this means that scientific rationality must be criticized in the name of reflexive nature, not accepted in the name of objective nature. Habermas continues to give away nature to physics, and so he can criticize the institutions of science only from within the social assumptions of science, that is, from within the assumptions of "natural" individual characteristics and "natural" individual equality. All scientific social theorists presume some "objective" formal basis for "natural" individual equality — rational self-interests, irrational desires, productive needs, self-consciousness, and so on — and then they project a legitimating (and critical) image of the "necessary" institutions for these "natural" characteristics. For Habermas, individuals are formally equal before language, as an inherent, "natural" characteristic, and this formal equality becomes the basis of a linguistic critique of unequal and distorted communication.

All this can mean, however, is that scientific institutions should be criticized in the name of the "natural" individual, because this reference to language can refer only to these formally equal, a priori individuals. These are the individuals who use language to communicate, and it is finally on these individuals, not on a conception of social life, that Habermas rests his critical rationality. Communication becomes strictly an issue of the formal necessity (but institutional distortion) of linguistic presumptions about individuals (honesty, sincerity, and the like), and so even the idea of communication refers back to the "natural" (linguistic) characteristics of individuals. Habermas thinks that he has provided a truly social reference for rationality through the idea of language, but this reference can be truly social only to the degree it reflects the enabling conditions for social life (and thus for language), not the enabling conditions for formal individual equality. Language is about sustaining its own social-natural possibility, not about equal individual access to communication, and so a linguistic rationality must be a reflexive, sustainable rationality, a rationality based on an ecological, not an objective, conception of nature.

All of these theorists, including Marx, try to ground a critical, social rationality on some version of an "objective" reference to individual characteristics, characteristics that are variously defined in terms of production, consciousness, or communication. This critical reference is supposed to be "objective" in the same sense that the scientific reference to nature is objective, and so the underlying conceptual support for this social rationality is always the scientific idea of mathematical nature. In general, social theory has allowed science to define the basic legitimating idea of rationality, and the most obvious way to see this is to notice that none of these theorists has felt obligated to complete the argument about social rationality with a fundamental critique of physics. Physics has always defined the technical, nonsocial rationality of science, and so it would seem that any social critique of this rationality would have to focus on physics. Otherwise it is possible only to assert two separate, contradictory kinds of knowledge, with the scientific knowledge of natural reality being the most fundamental. And this is all that these critical theorists can assert, since they are unwilling to challenge the objective, technical rationality of mathematical nature. Despite the demand for a critical rationality, mathematics always remains mysteriously explanatory and physics always remains neutrally valid. So they are left in the position of defining the good society in terms of the social commitments of science (the objective, "natural" individual) and then criticizing the social commitments of science in the name of this good society.

From this perspective, then, scientific rationality can be blamed for the loss of community, the evisceration of meaning, the triumph of technique, the disenchantment of the world, the ideology of domination, the sterility of bureaucracy, the destruction of the environment, the perfection of control, the end of evolution, the threat of annihilation, and so forth. Generally these analyses are forceful and convincing, yet they never seem to lead to a social analysis of physics. But the idea of a social rationality can only be an oxymoron as long as physics remains privileged, and physics will remain privileged as long as its legitimating mathematical magic remains hidden. This is the legitimating magic of experimental observation, the magic that defines objective nature and the individual mind as complementary necessities, the magic of the "natural" individual. This mathematical magic is hidden behind the foundational idea of observation, and while this idea has now been recognized as incoherent, it continues to support the explanatory validity of scientific knowledge. So it is here that scientific rationality needs to be challenged, not at the conceptual level of alienation and domination but at the conceptual level of observation and mathematics, the level of physics. And this can be done only in terms of a social-natural rationality, a rationality based on ecological coherence rather than objective nature, a rationality that replaces the reference to observation with a reference to language.

A Critical and Ecological Rationality

The theoretical criticism of scientific rationality — whether of the market, bureaucracy, technology, or whatever — has primarily focused on its political uses, not its conceptual assumptions, because scientific rationality has essentially defined the legitimating, critical idea of rationality. At its origins scientific rationality was successfully critical of traditional authority, but now we need another kind of rationality to be successfully critical of science, and yet science is still accepted as defining the idea of rationality. So we need an idea of rationality that can be critical of scientific rationality, according to formal and necessary criteria, criteria that incorporate the social and legitimating dimensions of the idea of rationality. These would be the "objective" criteria the critical theorists sought, and such criteria can be found only if the idea of rationality is decisively detached from science, which the critical theorists failed to do. Scientific rationality contains no such necessary social criteria, since scientific rationality requires detached individuals and therefore is compatible with various (individualistic) social directions according to their various presumptions about individual motivations. But when the idea of rationality is detached from science, its inherent social criteria can be recognized, because the idea of rationality is clearly about *legitimating sustainable social actions*, in the same sense that medical rationality is about sustaining social actions. The idea of rationality is about sustainability in the same way that medical rationality is about health, and so its inherent social criteria are the criteria of ecological coherence and reflexive evaluation, the criteria of legitimating sustainable institutions. And these are the criteria that cannot be recognized from within scientific rationality, because this rationality can legitimate only technical manipulation, not sustainability.

The critical theorists wanted to develop a critical rationality for social life while still respecting the natural rationality of science. In contrast, I have suggested that we separate the rational legitimation of criticism from the scientific conception of nature, and that we base the idea of rationality on the former while rejecting the latter. This would identify the idea of rationality with the (social) possibility of criticism, not with the postulated image of an objective (natural) reality, as science has done. Science legitimates internal criticism by postulating a *formal* and *nonsocial* image of objective reality (mathematical nature), and in this way rational criticism can appear as having no involvement with the normative issues of social legitimation. But criticism is always an issue of social legitimation, and so scientific knowledge inevitably creates the dilemma of rationality, the dilemma of justifying a critical, social rationality in terms of an indifferent, natural rationality. This dilemma cannot be resolved from within the scientific conception, so that science both legitimates criticism and makes it incoherent, in the sense that critical disputes about legitimation can find no common rational grounds for discussion. In a world explained by science there can be no objective social criteria for criticism, only competing, legitimating assumptions about the "natural" individual, so that critical debates about "the good society" can only become absolute assertions of various "objective" moralities. Science makes the idea of criticism incoherent because its image of nature is incoherent, but this image also makes the idea of criticism legitimate, and it is this aspect of science that should be retained, not its particular definition of nature.

The idea of criticism is about both legitimation *and* reflexivity, whereas the idea of an objective reality, as a critical reference, is only about legitimation, and this is why we must pay more attention to the scientific endorsement of criticism and less to the scientific idea of nature. The image of an objective reality, whether the gods or nature, can legitimate social actions, but not the criticism and discrediting of that reality as a result of those social actions. Such a reality is not recognized as a legitimating *idea*, which would mean that it could be evaluated and changed in the context of the social actions it generates and endorses. Rather, it is recognized as an absolute truth, known with incorrigible certainty, so that social actions can only try to conform with its necessary structure. But the idea of criticism is always about legitimating social actions *reflexively*, in the sense that it must always continue to be *possible*, even when it has been successful at discrediting certain social actions and legitimating new ones. This is why science creates the paradox of rationality, because it both legitimates criticism and denies its social relevance, through the idea of a formal and nonsocial reality. And this is why religion must deny the possibility of criticism, because religious reality is inherently social and so any legitimation of criticism would involve social criticism.

In this sense science legitimates criticism but denies reflexivity, and thus it denies the possibility of a reference to sustainability, an ecological reference. Religion, on the other hand, tries to legitimate sustainability by denying criticism, on the tacit assumption that the tradition is sustainable and ecological, since it has worked so far. In the scientific context this can make religion look remarkably respectful of nature and ecology, as various romantic interpreters of tribal "sensitivities to nature" have suggested. But in fact this is only traditional devotion, not ecological attention, which is why traditional societies have often internally disrupted their own ecological base and also why they are so completely vulnerable to external disruption from scientific societies. Religion tries to incorporate an ecological reference that is absolute and noncritical, and this makes religious societies unable to adjust easily to rapid and disruptive change, from internal or external causes. On the other hand, science tries to incorporate a critical reference that is absolute and nonecological, and this makes scientific societies unable to adjust easily to their own commitment to systematic ecological disruption. With its technical, nonecological reference, scientific knowledge can do more absolute damage more quickly, but with its sacred, noncritical reference, religion is more absolutely vulnerable and exposed, and in any case a noncritical knowledge is not viable in the context of a critical knowledge. Religious societies can only collapse in the face of the social failure of their legitimating realities, but scientific society has the possibility of rethinking its legitimating reality, because it is committed to the idea of criticism.

Religion cannot be ecological because it cannot be critical and science cannot be ecological because it also cannot be truly critical, which is also why it is inevitably confused about rationality and social life. Religion relies on a substantive reference for knowledge—traditional practices, ordinary language—and in this conceptual context no rational criticism is possible, only rational support. Thus religious knowledge is absolutely "tamed" by its substantive conception of reality, in the sense that the legitimating idea of knowledge has been completely captured by a particular set of traditional practices, so that only these practices can be legitimated in the name of reason. But science relies on a formal reference for knowledge—mathematics, objective nature—and in this conceptual context the idea of knowledge becomes less "tame" and more critically available. In this scientific context certain different, and even incompatible, forms of social practices—such as socialism and capitalism—can be legitimated in the name of truth and reason, since now objective reality is formally detached from any specific institutional arrangements. It is still an objective reality, however, and this means it is compatible only with certain formal kinds of institutional arrangements, the arrangements entailed by mathematical nature, the arrangements of "naturally" motivated individuals and of maximum technical proficiency. Scientific knowledge is not substantively "tamed" by a traditional reality, but it is still formally "tamed" by a mathematical reality, and thus it can legitimate only technical, non-ecological, and nonreflexive institutions.

The idea of knowledge is primarily about legitimating organized social actions, so that social life can be productive and reproductive and sustainable. In this sense the idea of knowledge is primarily an issue of social legitimation and only secondarily an issue of defining an image of reality on which to base social legitimation. But any "tamed" version of knowledge, whether science or religion, will always derive social legitimation from an absolute image of a "true" reality, and this will make it unable to legitimate social institutions reflexively, that is, as a continuing critical issue of their own ecological effects. Such an absolute image of reality will always contain inherent institutional commitments—traditional order, "natural" individuals, technical indifference—but it will also make these commitments inaccessible to criticism, since they will not be seen as institutional recommendations but rather as objective necessities. It is in this way that the idea of knowledge becomes unable to criticize itself, despite its apparent social effects, and it is in this sense that such versions of knowledge must be understood as institutionally "tamed."

The alternative, of course, is for knowledge to become "wild," in the sense of truly critical and reflexive. Knowledge would become "wild" when it is no longer referred to some absolute, unassailable reality but to its own continued possibility, as a reflexive issue of legitimating sustainable social practices. Thus a "wild" knowledge would legitimate criticism absolutely, as the only way to prevent itself from being institutionally "tamed" by a particular version of "true" reality. More exactly, a "wild" knowledge would legitimate equal critical access for all individuals, regardless of their location within a legitimated social order. But this would not be the anarchy of critical access for its own sake, according to whatever particular references these critics might claim as important—freedom, stability, profit, control, technology, and so on. Rather, it would be an ecological critical access, meaning a critical access that is primarily committed to maintaining the reflexive possibility of critical access. A "wild" knowledge would legitimate reflexive criticism as its primary commitment, and it could do this only through a formal reference to sustainability, which means through a reference to sustaining the formal possibility of social-natural interactions. The critical reference would be to a formal ecological rationality, since only through such an ecological reference could the formal possibility of social life, and critical access, be sustained.

This would mean that any particular set of social institutions, together with their particular versions of knowledge and truth, could always be legitimately criticized in the name of the necessary, formal conditions for ecological knowledge and ecological sustainability. Of course, this would require that such formal conditions could be coherently articulated and specified, at least to the degree that debates and disagreements over the legitimacy of social actions could be rationally resolved, according to these formal and shared ecological criteria. If this could be done, then it would provide a *necessary* reference for a normative, legitimating rationality, a reference that could both legitimate criticism absolutely and establish a common rational ground for the evaluation and resolution of criticism. Such a reference would be *necessary* in the sense that it would be inherent in the ideas of knowledge and reason, to the degree that those ideas are made coherent through a reflexive reference to their own continued possibility. So a "wild" knowledge would establish a necessary, legitimating rationality, a rationality that would derive an absolute social commitment to criticism from a formal social-natural commitment to sustainability.

All this would depend upon the possibility of articulating the formal structural conditions for conceptualizing and organizing sustainable social practices, the conditions grounding the critical, ecological reference for knowledge. These conditions would be formal and structural in the sense that mathematics is formal and rational, the sense of a *structural form* that defines both the conditions for legitimacy and the conditions for legitimate criticism. In this case, however, the structural form would define the conditions for reflexive knowledge and sustainable institutions, rather than the conditions for objective knowledge and individualized observation. The structure of mathematics provides a formal but ostensibly nonsocial reference for scientific knowledge, and this reference legitimates a limited and incoherent commitment to criticism, as well as a technical and incoherent idea of social life. A critical, ecological knowledge, then, must depend on a reference that is both *formal* and *social-natural*, and this reference, I am arguing, can only be the formal structure of language, where language is understood as enabling the possibility of social life and thus the possibility of social-natural interactions.

In this sense language has a formal structure, just as mathematics has a formal structure, only it is the formal structure of human actions, social life, and reflexive explanation, rather than the formal structure of logical indifference, technical relations, and objective explanation. We are not used to thinking of language in this enabling, social-natural sense, because we are used to thinking of it scientifically, where it is generally seen as simply another tool or resource or characteristic of the "natural" individual. Generally, we see language as something that individuals use or communicate with or represent the world through, and so we see it, objectively, as something that is logically subsequent to the a priori individual. Generally, we do not see language, reflexively, as something that is logically prior to the social individual, in the sense that language, as a formal structure, enables the possibility of social life and thus of acting, knowing individuals. It is in this *social* sense, however, that we must begin to analyze the formal structure of language, and not strictly in the technical (individualized) sense of syntax, semantics, phonetics, and speech acts.

In this social sense, then, language is the structure that enables knowledge and reason, and so the idea of knowledge must be understood in terms of the structure of language, rather than the structure of language being understood in terms of a scientific notion of objective, natural knowledge. If knowledge refers primarily to language, rather than nature, then knowledge is primarily about understanding its own formal possibility, and knowledge becomes reflexive. If knowledge refers to objective nature, as science would have it, then the idea of knowledge becomes incoherent, because objective nature does not contain the possibility of knowledge (social life, reason, language, and so on), by definition. Scientific knowledge requires a detached, nonsocial knower, which is why it generates a plethora of conceptual mysteries. Physics cannot explain itself, which means, in effect, that we can understand our universe (scientifically) only to the degree we are not in it, to the degree we cannot understand ourselves. But if knowledge is recognized as an issue of language, it is recognized as reflexively referring to its own possibility, and in this way knowledge becomes an issue both of successfully explaining natural processes *and* of successfully legitimating social actions, and of doing both at the same time, reciprocally. For scientific knowledge, objective explanatory "success" means achieving local technical proficiency, means–ends "success," with no *social* reflexivity. But for ecological knowledge, reflexive explanatory "success" means explanations that can sustain their own possibility, through the generation of ecological technology and critical, sustainable institutions. The reference to language makes knowledge a reflexive issue of social–natural interactions, rather than an objective issue of natural observations, and in this way knowledge can become both critical and ecological, as well as coherent. That is, through a reference to language, knowledge can become "wild."

In the following chapters I will explore this reference to language in more detail, and I will show how the formal, enabling structure of language contains a set of formal, structural requirements for sustainable institutions and technology. In particular, I will show how these structural requirements include such institutional commitments as equal critical access, organized diversity, and secure social spaces for all individuals. This discussion will require a somewhat eclectic view of language, as language is analyzed in terms of its inherent ecological strategy rather than in terms of its biological organization in the brain or its specific cultural manifestations or its objective universal structure. Also this ecological analysis of language will generate a somewhat unusual analysis of social life, as individuals and institutions are conceptualized in terms of the inherent ecological goals of linguistic structure, rather than in terms of the inherent objective motivations of "natural" individuals. This may seem to be a strange way to think about individuals and institutions, as well as about reason, knowledge, and nature, and indeed it will be strange, and complicated and abstract, from the perspective of scientific social theory and scientific knowledge. But in fact it is a quite familiar, as well as necessary, way to think about these matters, at least in one explanatory domain, and that domain, of course, involves the issue of health, with its associated notions of medical knowledge and rationality.

The Formal Conditions for Sustainability

Health is an issue of sustaining, at the individual level, the formal possibility of social-natural interactions, not of technical proficiency, and thus we are used to thinking about health reflexively. The idea of health legitimates medical practice, and yet medicine cannot categorically define health, not in the same way that science has categorically defined nature. Health is as much an issue of social participation as of physical functions, and this means that social participants always have some legitimate authority over decisions about their own health. As a result, medicine cannot define and manipulate health technically, not in the same sense that science can define and manipulate nature technically. Health is a reflexive judgment about social actions, not an objective judgment about physical procedures, and so individuals always have, in principle, a legitimate authority for criticizing medical knowledge, despite the fact that medical knowledge will generally be accepted and respected. Medicine certainly has substantial cultural authority, but individuals still have legitimate critical access against it, in the name of health, and this is what makes medical knowledge reflexive. Medical knowledge can legitimate certain physical technologies in the name of health—penicillin, Valium, estrogen, the IUD, the swine flu vaccine, mastectomies—but individuals can also discredit some of these technologies against medical knowledge, also in the name of health. Thus we are used to thinking of knowledge reflexively, just as we are used to legitimating institutions, technology, and equal critical access reflexively, all in the name of health.

And health is a formal structural reference, exactly the kind of reference that can legitimate both specific institutional practices *and* continued critical access against those practices. Medicine—and therapy, nutrition, and the like—can only try to maintain the formal structural conditions for health—physiological functioning, language, rationality, and so on—while only individuals can complete the substantive achievement of their own health through social involvement. Medicine is not about achieving a particular cultural version of individual-natural interactions, but about achieving the formal structural conditions for sustaining individual-natural interactions, and this is why medicine presents such a good model for a reflexive, critical idea of knowledge.

This does not mean, of course, that medicine is always open to legitimate individual criticism in the name of health, or even that medicine is always primarily concerned with health. Like all social institutions, medical institutions will be primarily concerned with maintaining their own social position and authority, and this concern can often take precedence over a concern for maximizing health. Two points need to be made about this inherent institutional logic, however. First, medicine tends to be more responsive to external criticism than most other institutions—government, corporations, education, and so on—because of the reference to health. The reference to health makes medical practice accountable on grounds that are immediately and legitimately available to everyone, and this enables the possibility of effective criticism against entrenched institutional authority, as we have seen in such cases as acupuncture, holistic medicine, nutrition, and women's health issues.

Second, in scientific medicine the reflexive reference to health must be combined with the objective reference to nature, since the explanatory framework is thoroughly scientific. This means that medicine is also pushed toward objective, physical definitions of health and toward technical proficiency for its own sake. It is as scientists, not as health-givers, that doctors become technical manipulators and unassailable authorities, and it is exactly against this scientific detachment that patient outrage and criticism are directed, in the name of health. Science and health fit uneasily together, and we have tended to think of health, not objective nature, as the anomalous reference. I am suggesting the reverse, that the reference to health is more fundamental and that a reference to *sustainability*, as the social generalization of health, should be recognized as the only coherent reference for knowledge. In this way all knowledge, including medical knowledge, can be made thoroughly reflexive and critical, and science will no longer be able to legitimate detached technical authority.

Science has certainly become the dominant authority in medical knowledge, and it is an authority that radiates from all the institutions of modern society—productive, political, economic, and educational. Science defines our legitimating idea of knowledge, and so it is not surprising that the institutions of scientific medicine can often override the critical notion of health. What is more surprising is that the idea of health can still generate effective critical leverage against scientific medicine even in the midst of thoroughly scientific institutions and values. This can happen because the reference to health is more fundamental than the reference to objective nature, and indeed all the institutions and ideas legitimated by objective nature are really about the possibility of achieving health, not the possibility of achieving neutral knowledge. Social explanations and social actions have always been about maximizing health, in the sense of stability, order, prosperity, control, and so on, and different cultural versions of knowledge have always been more or less successfully directed toward this goal. Whatever the cultural setting, the criteria for valid knowledge have always included some version of sustaining individual health, since knowledge is always about reflexively sustaining its own possibility, through individuals, and individual health has always been experienced as fragile and problematic. As human beings we have always known that health is important and uncertain, and so we have included it in our conceptual efforts at social legitimation, making sure that our institutions generally respect, protect, encourage, and treat it. This is why the idea of health can still be effective against scientific medicine, because maximizing health is fundamentally what science is all about, even though science cannot admit it.

We have not, however, generally thought of sustainability as fragile and problematic, not as a formal possibility. As individuals, we have routinely known about the formal conditions for health and illness—nourishment, rest, language, participation, danger—and we have routinely incorporated a reference to these conditions into our idea of valid knowledge, through the idea of health. But as societies we have not routinely known about the formal conditions for sustainability, the conditions of available resources, environmental compatibility, carrying capacity, ecological values, reflexive institutions, and so on. Religious societies have generally been concerned with their own sustainability, but only as a ritual issue of the sacred tradition, not as a critical issue of formal social-natural possibilities. Religious societies have identified sustainability with their particular tradition, not with formal social-natural conditions, and while this has limited their absolute ecological impact it has also undermined their sustainability, by limiting their ability to change. Scientific society, on the other hand, has simply ignored the issue of sustainability, relying instead on its remarkable abilities to change and to produce. These abilities are derived from the formal idea of mathematical nature, and this idea denies any social reference, so that no issue of social-natural sustainability can be made relevant to the legitimating idea of knowledge. For science nature is impervious to human actions, so that no reflexive concern for sustainability can be made coherent. But this has not been considered an explanatory problem because scientific society has been so productive and flexible that sustainability, unlike health, could simply be taken for granted, as a contingent but expected benefit of objective, indifferent knowledge. In effect, science projected a nature that was not only indifferent but infinite, so that the obvious and formal dependence of human life on natural processes could not become a reflexive, social reference within the idea of valid knowledge.

As we all know, this scientific strategy has been quite successful, both technically and politically, and it has indeed seemed that the formal issues of sustainability could be ignored. Religious societies worried about sustainability in terms of sacred rituals, but scientific society can be cavalier about tradition and change and still retain its social coherence. For scientific society, then, sustainability becomes only a formal issue of resources and environment, and in an infinite and impervious universe this is not an issue at all. Now, however, we are beginning to recognize that our universe—the universe we live in, the universe of our supportive natural environment—is not infinite and impervious, but rather limited and somewhat fragile. Science has been mistaken about this universe, but the problem is that science can neither admit nor rectify that mistake. Indeed, science cannot even talk about the universe we live in, because science has defined the universe as something we are not in. So we must begin to talk about the universe in a different way, in the way that we have routinely and necessarily talked about health. Unlike the issue of health, the issue of sustainability has not been a constant aspect of our ordinary experience, but it is the same kind of issue and has the same necessary relationship to knowledge. Until now the planet has been too big and our actions too small for us to experience, or even consider, the fragility of our ecological relations, as the *formal* social-natural conditions for sustainability. But science has made our actions bigger and the planet smaller, and now we must begin to think consciously in terms of sustainability, just as we have always thought instinctively in terms of health. Now we can destroy our supportive environment, and with it the possibility of knowledge, and so we must begin to incorporate the fragility of nature into our idea of knowledge, into a reflexive idea of knowledge. We must begin to think of social-natural interactions in terms of sustaining our social "body," just as we have always thought of individual-natural interactions in terms of sustaining our individual bodies, and if we do then all knowledge will become an issue of sustainability, just as medical knowledge is an issue of health. If we think of nature as our social "body," then we can refer the idea of knowledge to the formal conditions for sustaining that "body," and in this way we can develop a critical and ecological knowledge, a "wild" knowledge.

Such a reflexive idea of knowledge would provide a critical reference against the conceptual and ecological incoherence of scientific knowledge. But this would require a truly critical idea of reason, and in particular the idea of reason would have to be detached from scientific nature and given a *formal social-natural* reference. This can be done only if we recognize that the scientific idea of reason has always had two distinct, and conceptually independent, components—a formal reference for reason and the particular content for that reference, the idea of mathematical nature. It is the formal component, as I have argued, that legitimates the possibility of criticism, because its formality means that the idea of reason cannot be identified with any particular, substantive set of rituals and practices; it cannot be institutionally "tamed." Mathematics is certainly formal in this sense, and it gives scientific knowledge a degree of critical "wildness." Thus science has legitimated internal criticism by giving the formal component of the idea of reason the particular content of mathematics. Mathematics allows scientific knowledge to be critical of itself and still remain scientific, but it also makes the idea of social criticism incoherent, since criticism is inherently social but mathematics is postulated as being socially neutral. This is the incoherence of mathematical magic, the incoherence of knowledge that cannot know about knowledge, and it permeates the scientific conception, resulting in the legitimation of ecological indifference in the name of the "natural" individual.

In our scientific enthusiasm we have generally accepted this incoherence, with all its conceptual mysteries, as inherent in the idea of reason, and this means we have accepted the scientific identification of mathematical nature with the critical idea of reason. But mathematics is not the only possible formal reference for knowledge, and indeed it is not the "wildest," not the most critical. Language is also such a formal reference, language as a formal structure, language as the enabling structure of social-natural interactions. The structure of language is formal in the same sense that mathematics is formal: it provides a reference for knowledge that cannot be identified with any particular social practices, that cannot be institutionally "tamed." But language provides a much "wilder" reference than mathematics because it is social-natural, and thus it can legitimate and make sense out of social criticism, something mathematics cannot do. Mathematics gives science a degree of critical "wildness" by postulating a formal reality that is ostensibly external to social life, but science is still somewhat institutionally "tamed" by the tacit social commitments inherent in this objective reality—the "natural" individual, constraining society, indifferent technology, and so on. The structure of language, on the other hand, would enable knowledge to become completely "wild," because it would not postulate a true, objective reality at all. Rather, it would postulate a reflexive reference to sustainability, a reference that would legitimate critical access absolutely, in the name of sustaining the possibility of critical access.

In effect, the reference to language would do what the reference to mathematics tries to do but cannot, because the reference to mathematics is based on a conceptual mistake. In the scientific conception mathematics cannot legitimate a coherent idea of criticism because mathematics must be seen as independent of language, in any social sense. Mathematics must be seen as a language that is not a language, and therefore as legitimating magic. This mistake makes science completely confused about reason, criticism, and language, and it is a mistake that the reference to language can correct. Mathematics is an aspect of language, a logical, technical resource of language, and it can support a very effective form of technical, logical knowledge. But mathematics is still a *part* of language, and so the technical rationality of mathematics must be understood in terms of the reflexive rationality of language, rather than being hypostatized as the structure of a "true" (and tacitly magical) reality. Mathematics must be conceptually located within the structure of language, and then technical knowledge can be conceptually located within the structure of an ecological and critical knowledge. In this way technical proficiency can proceed within the context of sustainable institutions, just as medical technology has proceeded within the context of health.

Changing our ideas of mathematics and reason will change our ideas of social life and individuals. We have seen how the scientific conception contains an image of "naturally" equal, autonomous individuals, but if the scientific conception involves two distinct components—the formal and the mathematical—then where is this image of the scientific individual? Each of these components imposes its own distinct image of the knowing individual, and scientific knowledge has combined these two images into one explanatory individual—the foundational individual of objective knowledge, the "natural" individual of social theory. But these two images can be analytically separated, since they are based on analytically separate components, and when they are we get a different picture of knowledge and social life. The first component is the idea of a formal reference for knowledge, the idea that legitimates rational criticism, and this idea implies an image of individuals who are all equal with respect to critical access. If truth is a formal structure, rather than a traditional order, then that truth is always available, in principle, as a reference for legitimate criticism against any of its particular social manifestations. This is what it means for knowledge to be "wild," that no particular set of institutions can *embody* the truth, they can only *argue* for its support, according to the formal, "wild" criteria for rationality. And all individuals can equally argue for its support, in principle, since it is a formal matter of reason, not a ritual matter of revelation. Thus the idea of formal reference for knowledge legitimates the idea of equal critical access for all individuals, and more generally the idea of a formal equality among individuals, because the reference for reason and truth has been detached from received authority and made available to everyone, in principle. This was Galileo's achievement, when he claimed a Godlike knowledge against tradition and the Church, because he claimed it in terms of a formal reference, not in terms of his own unique and privileged contact with divinity. And it was a political achievement because it asserted, in principle, the claim that all individuals can have legitimate critical access against any established beliefs or practices, in the name of reason.

Galileo, of course, appealed to mathematical nature to assert his claim to equal rationality, but such a claim does not depend upon this particular idea of nature, only upon an appeal to a formal, "wild" reference for knowledge. The idea of mathematical nature works as a formal reference, but it also imposes additional social commitments on the image to the individual, and in particular it imposes the idea of the detached, autonomous observer, the idea of the a priori scientific individual. This is the image that science specifically requires, the a priori, "natural" individual, the individual who is external to social life. Scientific knowledge contains an image of individuals who are formally equal and socially autonomous, but while the image of autonomy is derived directly from mathematical nature, the image of formal equality is derived from the formal reference, and that reference could be language as well as mathematics. In other words, the social commitment to formal individual equality is an issue of critical reason, not simply of scientific reason, and so Galileo's reference to objective nature can be replaced with linguistic structure without losing his political claim of equal critical access. However, the autonomous, logically prior individual is a specifically scientific image, and it would be discarded in an ecological, linguistic conception of knowledge.

In effect, scientific knowledge has created two distinct images of the knowing individual, and then compacted them together into one scientific individual. This is the individual who has directed and shaped scientific social theory, an individual who can legitimate a social commitment to equality but only in terms of some particular, postulated set of "natural" motivations and "objective" institutions. But if these two distinct images are conceptually separated, the one that remains coherent — the image of equal critical access — can begin to generate a new approach to social theory, a reflexive, ecological approach. Such an approach would enable social theory to be derived from a reference to the structure of language, as the basis for social-natural interactions, rather than from a reference to the structure of mathematics, as the basis for individual observations of nature. This would mean that social life could be seen as inherently organized, in accordance with the formal structure of language, as opposed to individually motivated, in accordance with independently moving particles, and it would mean that social practices could be legitimated ecologically, rather than technically. Finally, it would mean that the idea of knowledge would no longer contain a dilemma of rationality. Rather, rationality would be understood as a critical issue of sustainability, and social practices would be legitimated by the requirement of equal critical access in the name of reason, a requirement necessitated by a coherent idea of knowledge, a "wild" knowledge.

EIGHT

The Reference to Language

From a religious perspective, knowledge is an issue of ordinary language, as magical signs, and is about maintaining the sacred tradition. From a scientific perspective, knowledge is an issue of mathematics, as absolute rationality, and is about describing objective nature. And from an ecological perspective, knowledge is an issue of the formal structure of language, as reflexive rationality, and is about sustaining its own formal (social-natural) possibility. In this last case the idea of knowledge is no longer referred to some postulated "true" reality, whether of gods or of nature, but rather is referred to the formal enabling conditions that make knowledge possible, the formal conditions that enable social-natural interactions based on knowledge. These formal conditions are based in language, in the sense that language grounds the possibility of knowledge, and thus of social-natural interactions. As we have seen, both the religious and the scientific versions of knowledge incorporate a necessary reference to language, but both also interpret this reference in terms of a particular, privileged language—the language of "true" reality—and so both fail to conceptualize knowledge as a formal issue of language. Both of these failures are instructive, however, since each fails as part of the formal effort of knowledge to sustain its own possibility. Religion focuses on a quotidian, ritualized idea of language in order to stress an ecological concern, but such a noncritical reference can achieve only a devout adherence to sacred tradition. And science focuses on a detached, indifferent idea of language in order to stress a critical concern, but such a nonecological reference can achieve only a cynical adherence to technical proficiency. Knowledge can sustain its own possibility only through a simultaneous commitment to both ecology and criticism, and such a commitment can be made only if knowledge is referred directly to language, as a formal structure, rather than to some disguised version of language masquerading as "true" reality.

The idea of a "true," external reality is derived from the idea of a world that is external to human beings, a world that is independent of human actions. Certainly we experience a world that is independent of human actions, in the sense that the physical world transcends any individual actions. The world of physical events is not determined or shaped by any particular individual actions, and so there seems to be a contingent, problematic relationship between actions and the world. It is this contingent relationship that makes knowledge necessary, since knowledge is exactly the effort to *understand* how an independent world seems to work, rather than an effort to *pronounce* how a dependent world must work. Still, it is never quite clear, for either religion or science, that the world is completely independent of human actions. In a religious conception the "true," independent reality—the gods—can always be addressed and influenced through ritual appeal, which means that reality is reliably responsive to human actions. This means that for religious knowledge, reality is independent of us in the same sense that other people are independent of us: our actions can influence, if not determine, their actions and their actions cannot be explained independent of our actions. Religion sees humans as interacting with their world, rather than simply acting on it, so that the world is seen as both independent and responsive, but only as responsive to ritualized, traditional actions, actions that have a special, magical place within "true" reality.

In the name of reason science dismisses this idea of ritualized influence as magic, postulating instead a reality that is completely impervious to human influence. But then the logic of science, as quantum physics, entails the idea of the observer creating physical reality by collapsing the wave function, and so even physics cannot resist the idea that the world is somehow dependent on and influenced by human actions. This means that science must rely on its own version of magic to explain how it is possible for humans to know a completely independent world with legitimating certainty, and in science, unlike religion, this reliance on magic can only be incoherent. This is the conceptual dilemma of an independent but knowable reality: If we can know it, can it be truly independent? If we can know a truly independent reality with certainty, then our knowing minds must have some inherent correspondence with that reality, and if magic (faith, revelation, and the like) cannot be used to explain that correspondence, then how can it be explained? Scientific thought originally relied on such a magical connection—the scholastic necessity of mathematics—but this magic had to be denied and hidden, and so it became the quantum mysteries of physics and the epistemological mysteries of philosophy. In philosophy and social theory these have been the mysteries of rationalism versus empiricism, realism versus idealism, agency versus structure, free will versus determinism, and so on, mysteries revolving around whether the world is dependent on or independent of the mind. And in physics the magic of observational detachment becomes the magic of observational determinism, as the assumption of a completely independent reality inevitably folds back on itself as conceptual, and then as ecological, incoherence.

If the world can be known, then it cannot be completely independent of knowledge, unless magic is involved. Either knowledge has been magically attached to an independent world or there must be some logical, rational connection between knowledge and the world. In the latter case the possibility of knowledge must somehow be inherent in the world, so that knowledge is *necessary* to the world and knowing about the world is also knowing about the possibility of knowledge. In order to deny any magical (traditional) connection between knowledge and the world, science denied any possibility of such a necessary connection, and this denial resulted in the mysteries and conundrums of rationalism, idealism, quantum mechanics, and so forth. If knowledge is possible, then the world must be somehow necessarily compatible with and amenable to knowledge, but how can this necessary relationship be understood if the world is also experienced as independent of knowledge and human actions? The very idea of knowledge demands that the world be seen as independent of knowledge, since otherwise we would not try to learn about the world, contingently; we would simply tell it what to do, necessarily. As human beings we experience a contingent relationship with the world, but it is contingent only in the sense that knowledge is possible but problematic, not in the sense that knowledge is impossible and useless. Thus we are caught between the contingent experience of a completely independent, unintelligible world and the necessary experience of a responsive, logically connected world. We know that knowledge is substantively problematic but we also know that it is formally possible, and it is only in terms of *both* of these dimensions that the idea of knowledge can escape from a dependence on magic and be made coherent.

The issue, then, is: How are we to think about the idea of knowledge? If we begin with a postulated, independent reality, then we must ask how knowledge of that reality is possible, and so we must also postulate some kind of a priori (magical) connection. This is what both science and religion have done, presuming that a special, magical language has a privileged connection with an otherwise independent and detached reality. From this perspective we must analyze what people, social life, and rationality must be like in the context of this particular, postulated reality, and all of this analysis must be based on a magical idea of knowledge. But if we begin with the possibility of knowledge, rather than with a particular image of reality, then we must ask what the world must be like in order for knowledge to be possible. In this case we must analyze the idea of reality in terms of the more fundamental idea of knowledge, whereas in the former case (science and religion) we must try to analyze the idea of knowledge in terms of the more fundamental idea of reality, a reality we can somehow (magically) "know" as a basis for acquiring knowledge. If we analyze the idea of knowledge *from the perspective of knowledge*, then we will focus on the formal, enabling conditions that make knowledge possible, the conditions that enable knowledge to mediate effectively between human actions and an independent world. But if we try to analyze the idea of knowledge from the perspective of a given "true" reality, then we must always have a magical idea of knowledge, since we must always somehow "know" reality prior to acquiring any valid knowledge.

From the perspective of knowledge, then, we must consider how knowledge is possible, which means we must consider what the world must be like and what human actions must be like in order for knowledge to be possible. In essence, we must first think of "the world" and "human beings" as formal concepts that must be analyzed, rather than as real, given things that are somehow "known" directly. Both the *idea* of "the world" ("reality," "nature," "the universe") and the *idea* of "human beings" ("persons," "actors," "knowers") are first of all *ideas*, and this means that they must be analyzed as conceptual efforts at knowledge, and thus as subject to all the formal conceptual constraints imposed by the enabling conditions for the possibility of knowledge. From the perspective of knowledge the world must be *a certain kind of thing* in order for knowledge to be possible, and this means that the *idea* of "the world" must be conceptually constrained in certain formal ways in order for knowledge to be possible. In order for knowledge of the world to be possible the world must be conceptualized in accordance with certain formal conceptual assumptions, and we can understand these formal and necessary assumptions only by analyzing the formal, enabling conditions for knowledge, not by directly observing the world. If knowledge is possible then the world must be amenable to knowledge, and this means that the idea of "the world" must be conceptualized in a way that is compatible with the possibility of knowledge. In this sense the possibility of knowledge must impose formal conceptual constraints on the idea of "reality," constraints that then enable "reality" to be experienced as both knowable and independent.

Similarly, human beings must be *a certain kind of thing* if knowledge is to be possible, and so the idea of "human beings," of "human actors," must be conceptually constrained by the possibility of knowledge. From the perspective of knowledge, knowledge mediates between actions and the world, and so both "actions" and "the world" must be conceptualized in certain formal, constrained ways, as a condition of knowledge. "Actions" must be understood as capable of being effective on the world, and "the world" must be understood as regularly responsive to knowledgeable actions, and so both of these concepts must be formally constrained so as to support this explanatory reciprocity. The idea of "human actions" must imply the idea of an amenable, responsive world, and the idea of "reality" must imply the idea of effective, knowledgeable actions, and this conceptual, explanatory reciprocity is a formal necessity for knowledge. But this is only a *formal* requirement for knowledge, which means that many different *substantive* explanatory versions of "the world" and "actions" are possible within these formal conceptual constraints, versions such as those of religion and science. Both religion and science conceptualize "actions" that are effective and "a world" that is responsive, and thus both meet these formal, necessary conditions for knowledge. But neither can recognize these formal conditions as a necessary aspect of knowledge, and so both must resort to some magical form of a privileged language to explain how actions connect with the world. From the perspective of a "true" reality the idea of a responsive world can only be magical, since human actions can have no inherent, necessary connection with the independent reality they are directed toward. But from the perspective of knowledge the idea of a responsive world is a conceptual necessity, and so human actions must be recognized as formally inherent in any substantive conception of an independent but knowable reality.

In order for knowledge to be possible, the world and human beings must be certain kinds of things, which means that the world and human beings must be *conceptualized* as certain kinds of things. In particular, the world must be conceptualized as both independent of direct human control and reliably responsive to knowledge-based human actions. Similarly, human beings must be conceptualized as having a *formally necessary* but *substantively contingent* relationship with their world, a relationship through which knowledge is always formally possible but also always possibly mistaken. Such a conception of humans would mean that they can always *affect* their world through knowledge, since the world is formally responsive to knowledge, but that they cannot always *control* their world through knowledge, since the world is substantively independent of all particular versions of knowledge. And this is exactly what the idea of knowledge must mean, as the effort to organize and direct problematic human actions toward the world in such a way as to sustain the possibility of human actions, and thus the possibility of knowledge. If knowledge is possible, then human beings must be the kinds of things that can affect their world formally but cannot control it substantively. In other words, human beings must constantly try to improve their knowledge, and thus their control, of a world that constantly responds to, and thus constantly escapes and redirects, all their particular efforts at knowledge. For human beings knowledge is always possible and necessary, and yet it is also always problematic and contingent, and this means that human beings must be understood in terms of both their necessary (formal) and their contingent (substantive) relationships with their world.

It is this idea of a formal relationship between humans and the world that has been neglected and denied, as both science and religion have postulated only a substantive, independent world, and thus have hidden the formal issues of knowledge behind an image of magical privilege. But if knowledge is to be possible, then there must be a formal and necessary relationship, as well as a substantive and contingent relationship, between human actors and their world. Religion explicitly ties humans to their world, but only substantively, not formally, only in terms of a particular sacred tradition, where only certain magical appeals can elicit responses from the gods. And science explicitly detaches humans from their world, so that nothing about human actions, either in the particular or in the abstract, can possibly be relevant to an understanding of the world. In both cases the possibility of a formal, logical connection between knowers and their world is denied, and then in both cases some kind of magical, necessary connection is reestablished, blatantly in the case of attentive gods and surreptitiously in the case of mathematical nature. And in both cases this magical incoherence in the idea of knowledge imposes a social incoherence in the legitimated institutions, the religious incoherence of a sacred tradition (denial of criticism) and the scientific incoherence of sacred technique (ecological indifference).

Knowledge is possible only if an independent world reliably responds to knowledgeable actions, and somehow this combination of independence and responsiveness has to be recognized and explained within the legitimating conception of knowledge. In both science and religion the independence of the world is taken as a conceptual given, and the responsiveness of this independent world must be explained, through either the attentive gods or mathematical nature. These are not coherent explanations, however, and so they can explain the effectiveness of knowledge only in terms of magic, that is, in terms of a privileged, magical language that can connect humans with a fully independent world. Science and religion both focus the idea of knowledge on the necessity of independence, and so both can have only a magical account of responsiveness. But if we can focus the idea of knowledge on the necessity of both independence and responsiveness, then we can begin to achieve a coherent and nonmagical account of knowledge, an account that makes knowledge an issue of its own possibility, rather than an issue of "true" reality. This would be an account of knowledge from the perspective of knowledge, rather than from the perspective of some postulated reality, an account that focuses on the possibility of mediating effectively between actions and the world, in the sense of sustaining the possibility of knowledge.

From this perspective, then, knowledge is formally about itself, its own possibility, and it is in terms of this formal commitment that any particular version of knowledge will create an image of reality. In this sense the idea of reality must be understood as an issue of knowledge, not the other way around, and any particular image of reality must describe an independent world that will also reliably respond to knowledgeable human actions. From the perspective of knowledge the world is both independent and responsive by definition, not by magic, because both "human beings" and "reality" can be conceptualized only in such a way that knowledge can effectively mediate between them. Thus from the perspective of knowledge there must be a formal, conceptual relationship between humans and their world, a relationship that must formally organize and structure all of the particular, substantive efforts of humans to understand that world. Knowledge is possible only if the world is *necessarily* responsive to human actions, and it is the conceptual structure of this formal necessity that a coherent and nonmagical analysis of knowledge must reveal. This is the conceptual structure that formally and necessarily connects human actions with the world, and it is a structure that is imposed by the abstract possibility of knowledge, a possibility grounded in the human use of language.

Rethinking Language

Knowledge is the socially organized use of language, language directed toward generating effective actions on the world. Language makes *human* actions possible, and so it is the structure of language that underlies the possibility of knowledge. Language is exactly the effort to conceptualize the world in order to act on it, and so it is the abstract structure of language that makes knowledge possible, and thus that imposes the *formal* conceptual constraints on the fundamental ideas of "human beings" and "the world." In this sense it is the abstract structure of language that creates the formal possibility of conceptually mediating between actions and the world, through knowledge, and so it is only through an analysis of language that we can begin to understand the conceptual structure of this formal possibility. The use of language is definitive of what it means to be human, and being human means being able to act on the world effectively. Thus it is only through an analysis of language that we can begin to understand, formally and necessarily, what it means to be human. But what it means to be human is not independent of what the world must be like, in formal, conceptual terms, and so it is also through an analysis of language that we must begin our formal exploration of what the world must be like — that is, of how the world must be formally understood if knowledge is to be possible. It is only through language that "humans" and "the world" become possible, in the sense of concepts, knowledge, and actions, and so if the idea of knowledge is to be made coherent it must first be analyzed in terms of the formal structure of language, the structure that connects humans with their world.

This is a somewhat different conception of language than we are used to, a conception in which language is seen as always actively addressing the world, in a constant, formal effort to sustain the necessary conditions for its own possibility, the conditions of coherent knowledge, effective actions, and social life. More typically we see language as a formal structure (syntax, phonetics, and so on) that is passively available, in particular forms (English, French, and so on) to humans for their use, in such activities as communication, reference, and speech acts. And clearly this is our most obvious and immediate experience of language, as something that can be used more or less well by individuals to communicate, plan, learn, give orders, and the like. Also, science has tended to reinforce this passive view of language, since explanatory attention has been focused on the a priori individual, so that language becomes simply another, secondary attribute of "natural," logically prior individuals. But this is an incoherent idea of individuals and of language, and in order to make the idea of language coherent we must begin to see it as having an *active* formal structure, a structure with the inherent formal goal of sustaining its own social-natural possibility. In this sense language would be seen as imposing formal, enabling constraints on the conceptual possibilities for knowledge, so that all substantive efforts at knowledge would necessarily take the abstract *form* of enabling and legitimating effective human actions. In particular, the structure of language would impose formal conceptual conditions on the basic ideas of "human beings" ("persons," "actors") and "reality" ("the world," "the universe"), so that all efforts at knowledge would necessarily include the presumption that human actions could be effective on an independent but responsive world.

Recently, this idea of analyzing language as active, rather than passive, has been gaining some momentum. As we have already seen, physicist Bruce Gregory (1990) suggests that "the language we *are* shapes the world" (p. 200). Similarly, linguist Derek Bickerton (1990) argues that language is far more than it appears: "Seeming to us no more than the glass through which we see our world, language is in fact the subtle, many-layered lens that created that world—the lens without which all that we know would dissolve into chaos" (p. 257). In his book *Language and Species*, Bickerton explores the origins and role of language, suggesting, as I have, that "language mediates between the world and our species" (p. 226) and that, while the use of language entails the idea of knowledge, it can only be

> "our" knowledge, the knowledge of a particular species at a particular
> stage of its existence, rather than some transcendental revelation of a

deeper reality. . . . What has been called "search for knowledge" might be better and more modestly regarded as a dialogue—among ourselves, and between ourselves and nature—from which we learn whatever aspects of nature and ourselves we may need to know in order to go on surviving and seeking—that being the mode of existence that language imposes on us. (p. 231)

This is an activist, goal-oriented idea of language, and it is shared by philosopher Bruce Wavell (1986), who argues that reason is fundamentally an issue of language, and that linguistic reason is pragmatic and active, a commonsense reason that underlies all other forms of reason, such as science and mathematics:

Common-sense reason is thus the basis for all reason. It is the non-technical, non-specialized form of reason that is employed in everyday life for both theoretical and practical purposes and is implicit in the structure and uses of ordinary language. (p. xxi)

In his book *Language and Reason*, Wavell analyzes the structure of language from this activist, human perspective, as a structure that mediates between "persons" and "reality," rather than as a structure that represents "true" reality. In this analysis, then, he focuses on the necessary conceptual constraints that language imposes on its inherent, bracketing ideas, the ideas of "persons" and "reality" ("humans" and "the world"), and I will utilize his analysis below, in an effort to articulate the necessary conceptual conditions for language to sustain itself. From this activist perspective, Wavell, Bickerton, and Gregory have defined reason, knowledge, and physics in terms of language, as well as consciousness, reality, and human beings, and in much of this they have been joined by supporters of the connectionist movement, the neural network approach to artificial intelligence and the workings of the brain. Jeremy Campbell (1989) has reviewed this analytic approach and has summarized its emerging view of the self: "What we take to be the self is really a network of knowledge, probably the richest there is, that is saturated in language and organized in such a way as to be useful rather than true" (p. 258).

Linguist George Lakoff (1987) also takes an activist view of language, arguing that "there is no unbridgeable gulf between language and thought on the one hand and the world on the other. Language and thought are meaningful because they are motivated by our functioning as part of reality" (p. 292). For Lakoff, scientific objectivism has assumed a detached, God's-eye perspective on reality, and this has led to fundamental mistakes:

> The problem is the external perspective—the God's eye view. We are not outside of reality. We are part of it, *in* it. What is needed is not an externalist perspective, but an internalist perspective. . . . Objectivist philosophy is inconsistent both with the facts of human categorization and with the most basic of requirements for a theory of meaning. . . . The result is a crisis. We need new theories of meaning, truth, reason, knowledge, understanding, objectivity, etc. (pp. 261, 265)

Lakoff believes that biology can save scientific knowledge from the flaws of objectivism, while I would argue that scientific knowledge must be replaced by an ecological knowledge, and that a *social*, rather than a biological, perspective must be incorporated into our idea of knowledge. He agrees, however, that science has always been fundamentally, but tacitly, about language and the mind, and that it has been wrong about them. "The objectivist paradigm is not just about the world. It is very largely about the mind and language . . . [but] *none* of the objectivist doctrines concerning language and the mind can stand up to [empirical] scrutiny" (p. 196). As an alternative, Lakoff offers an "experientialist approach," an

> attempt to characterize meaning in terms of *the nature and experience of the organisms doing the thinking.* . . . Where objectivism defines meaning independently of the nature and experience of thinking beings, experiential realism characterizes meaning in terms of *embodiment*, that is, in terms of our collective biological capacities and our physical and social experiences as beings functioning in our environment. (pp. 266-67)

Thus our linguistic concepts must be seen as both structured and embodied in terms of our specifically human experiences, and it is only through such an analysis that language and meaning can be understood internally, and coherently.

> Our concepts are structured, both internally and relative to one another. That structuring permits us to reason, to comprehend, to acquire knowledge, and to communicate. . . . [And] conceptual structure is meaningful because it is *embodied*, that is, it arises from, and is tied to, our preconceptual bodily experiences. In short, conceptual structure exists and is understood because preconceptual structures exist and are understood. (p. 267)

All of these theorists take an activist approach to language, arguing that language is more about involved mediating and surviving than about detached representing and mirroring. And all of them suggest that language necessarily structures the way we think about ourselves and our world, since language is actively striving to sustain its own possibility, through human knowledge and actions. But none of them moves this analysis of language into an analysis of social life, that is, into an analysis of politics and legitimation, of ecology and technology. None of these theorists seem to realize that language can sustain itself, actively, only through the organizing and legitimation of social institutions, which means through versions of knowledge and reason as *legitimating, organizing* endeavors. If language is analyzed as actively supporting human social life, then it must be seen as the basis for a linguistic, reflexive idea of knowledge, so that knowledge becomes as much an issue of social theory and social legitimation as of natural explanations. This would be a radically different idea of knowledge, knowledge as ecological and social, rather than as scientific and natural, and none of these theorists of language are able to take this radical step. They all manage to resist a move into the messy, value-laden realm of social theory, even though their own analyses of language, as the formal, enabling context of human life, seem to demand such a move.

In essence, all of these theorists tend to retain, implicitly, a scientific, objectivist account of language and knowledge, even as they reject, explicitly, the scientific idea of detached, objective knowledge. Their problem is that they want to be able to discuss language and knowledge intelligibly without also having to discuss politics, values, and legitimation. That is, they want to reject the objectivist account of knowledge on objective grounds, so that they do not have to worry about the legitimating implications of their own account of knowledge. But they can do this only if they can base their analysis of language on objective, neutral grounds, which means on the empirical, observable "facts" of scientific knowledge. Only in terms of such objective, scientific "facts" can they continue to talk about language and knowledge as though they were independent of social theory and institutional legitimation. Thus Bickerton and Wavell base their analyses on an appeal to evolution, suggesting (with Jacques Monod, as we have seen) that evolution has conveniently "arranged" language to mediate effectively between us and our world. This means, in effect, that language becomes an explanatory subset of genetic structure, and that the objective science of evolutionary biology can explain the active structure of language, a structure that then discredits the scientific account of objective knowledge. And Lakoff takes a similar position, appealing generally to scientific biology and in particular to the physiological idea of "preconceptual structures," an idea that is somehow conceptually prior to, and generative of, the possibility of having ideas.

Lakoff is pursuing the general explanatory project of cognitive science, a project he traces from Wittgenstein and Austin to artificial intelligence and the connectionists. As a consequence, his attention is focused on the primary issues of this cognitive project, the issues of meaning and cognition. But these are the issues of a scientific version of linguistic philosophy, and so they tend to refer more to the detached scientific individual than to an active, social-natural conception of language. Meaning and cognition, like consciousness, are issues of individual minds, and they are appropriate to a concern with modeling individual intelligence, whether linguistically, neurologically, or artificially. But they are not the central issues of an activist, internalist account of language, because language is about sustaining its own possibility, through social legitimation. Language organizes social relations in order to mediate effectively between humans and the world, and so any coherent account of language must focus on language as enabling actions and social life, rather than as enabling meaning and cognition. The structure of language generates the structure of social life, not simply the structure of individual consciousness, and so the analysis of language must become the analysis of social-natural interactions, an analysis based on an ecological and critical conception of knowledge.

The Formal Goal of Language

If language is to be analyzed from the inside, it must be analyzed as a reflexive, goal-oriented process, a process with the formal goal of sustaining its own possibility. This means that the social dimensions of language—knowledge, reason, actions, institutions, technology, and so on—must also be analyzed in terms of this formal, reflexive goal of language. The structure of language involves a formal, active logic, and this logic can be used to analyze and evaluate the particular concepts, explanations, and institutions that are generated as part of this linguistic effort to sustain itself. Each of these theorists of language moves toward this kind of internalist analysis, and all of them stop short, from my perspective, of moving far enough, which would mean into a thorough social and ecological analysis of knowledge and legitimation. Nevertheless, they all recognize some fundamental problems with our scientific versions of knowledge, truth, and legitimacy, and they all suggest that it is only through an activist analysis of language that we can begin to correct these problems. Moreover, they all begin to analyze language in this way, as an active, enabling structure that imposes formal conceptual constraints on the explanations and activities of human beings. Thus they are beginning to analyze the legitimating issues of knowledge and reason in terms of language, that is, in terms of what it means for human beings to be able to conceptualize and act on their world. Generally, they stop this analysis short of the move into social theory, through some "scientific" appeal, but this appeal is usually unconvincing, because their own analysis tends to discredit the appeal to science and to imply the need for social and ecological criticism.

So even while they continue to detach linguistic analysis from social criticism, in the name of science, these theorists are developing new and provocative approaches to the study of language, approaches that contain an incipient logic of social and ecological criticism. It is in these kinds of analyses of language that a new and coherent idea of knowledge can be articulated, an ecological, "wild" knowledge. Eventually, analyses such as these will lead to the ideas of knowledge and reason, as well as the ideas of reality, individuals, and legitimacy, being referred to language rather than to nature. And when these ideas are referred to language, our social life will be based on considerations of reflexivity and ecology rather than on considerations of objectivity and technique. These analysts of language, then, have begun the process of developing a new, more coherent conception of knowledge, a conception that must become the basis for a more ecological and sustainable idea of social theory. We have misunderstood language both religiously and scientifically, and now we must begin to understand it ecologically, as Derek Bickerton (1990) comments at the end of his book:

> We can understand neither ourselves nor our world until we have fully understood what language is and what it has done for our species. For although language made our species and made the world we inhabit, the powers it unleashed drove us to understand and control our environment, rather than to explore the mainspring of our own being. We have followed that path of control and domination until even the most daring among us have begun to fear where it may lead. Now the

engine of our quest for power and knowledge should itself become the object that we seek to know. (p. 257)

And knowing about language must involve more than knowing about evolution and the species, and more than knowing about meaning and cognition. It must involve knowing about social life and social legitimation, and in particular it must involve achieving a critical, sustainable conception of social-natural interactions.

I am suggesting, then, that language must be seen as formally seeking to sustain its own possibility, a possibility that requires sustaining the possibility of social life and social-natural interactions. From this perspective language sustains its own possibility through particular assertions of knowledge, where the idea of knowledge always assumes, formally, that knowledgeable actions will be effective on an independent but responsive world. The use of language requires this formal conceptual assumption about humans and the world, which means that there are certain formal constraints imposed on all of our concepts and explanations by the use of language, constraints that make knowledge, action, and social life possible. But the idea of knowledge does not formally require that we explicitly understand these conceptual constraints, within our assertions of knowledge. It requires only that we utilize these constraints, so that we can both incorporate them into our particular idea of knowledge *and* fail to understand them, which means we will think of them as magic. This is what we do with both science and religion. We assume that the world is responsive, since the idea of knowledge requires it, but we can conceptualize a responsive world only in terms of a magical idea of language, because we cannot reconcile the experience of independence with the formal requirements for responsiveness. Thus the formal structure of language pushes us in the necessary direction for effective knowledge, but it does not give us sufficient conceptual conditions for coherent knowledge, for knowledge that is sustainable rather than only effective. In other words, language gives us the *possibility* of knowledge, the *possibility* of acting and thinking; it does not tell us categorically how to act and how to think, for then we would not have knowledge and we would not be human. Language makes us human, in terms of knowledge, actions, and social life, and it does this by providing the formal conditions for knowledge but not the substantive details.

If language makes knowledge possible, then it also makes coherent knowledge possible, knowledge that can sustain its own possibility. This would be a knowledge that is referred to the formal, enabling structure of language, not to a "true" reality that can be known only through a magical language. If knowledge is to be coherent, then it must begin to understand itself as an aspect of language, and this means it must begin to understand the formal conceptual conditions that enable knowledge, the conditions that enable humans to act effectively on their world. This would mean being able to derive both social and natural theory from the formal structure of language, and this is the project I am undertaking here, the effort to understand both social life and nature in terms of language, rather than trying to understand social life and language in terms of nature. This would be an ecological view of nature and society, an ecological knowledge, and it would be ecological because language can sustain itself only through versions of knowledge that legitimate ecological, sustainable actions. Thus if knowledge begins to understand itself in terms of language, then it will begin to understand itself ecologically, and it can do this only by *explicitly* understanding the formal conceptual conditions imposed by language on knowledge, the conditions that make knowledge and social life possible. These are the conditions that enable us to conceptualize the world as both substantively independent and formally responsive, and thus understanding them will enable us to escape from a view of knowledge as magic. And if we begin to understand these formal conditions explicitly, in terms of language, rather than implicitly, in terms of magic, then we will begin to understand ourselves and our world ecologically, because these are the formal conditions for sustainability, the conditions for an ecological, "wild" knowledge.

My remaining theoretical task, then, is to try to explicate these formal conceptual conditions for knowledge, the linguistic conditions that require us to define "ourselves" and our "world" in such a way that effective interactions are possible. The general form of these conceptual conditions has already been suggested, the form imposed by the idea that language is actively about sustaining its own possibility, not passively about mirroring "true" reality or ritually about appeasing the gods. If language is formally about sustaining its own possibility, then it must require the formal conceptual possibility of effective interactions between "humans," as linguistic actors, and "reality," as linguistically acted upon. These must be the fundamental, bracketing ideas, the necessary ideas that establish the possibility of knowledge, and these ideas must be mutually referring, in the sense that each is necessarily defined in terms of the other. "Humans" must be formally defined as able to interact effectively with an independent but responsive "reality," and so what it means to be human must involve an idea of reality, and vice versa. Moreover, these two bracketing ideas must be formally (logically) related in such a way that "humans" can act effectively on "reality," so that the idea of "being human" necessarily involves acting (on the world) and the idea of "reality" necessarily involves independence, responsiveness, and sustainability. My claim, then, is that these are the formal conceptual conditions required by a coherent, and linguistic, idea of knowledge, and that all substantive, cultural efforts at knowledge must assume this formal conceptual framework. Knowledge is possible only if the world is understood as both independent of and responsive to human actions, *and* if human actions are understood as capable of sustaining their own possibility, through knowledge and legitimation.

This is the conceptual framework that knowledge must have, but a closer analysis of language can reveal many more of the formal conceptual conditions that are required by this general framework, conditions such as those governing a linguistic, ecological idea of individuals, social life, and nature. If knowledge is referred to language, then the basic ideas of social and natural theory — such ideas as "individuals," "society," "authority," "technology," and "nature" — will have to be redefined, and when they are they will have an inherent conceptual quality of ecological necessity. When terms such as these are defined religiously they take on an inherent conceptual quality of traditional necessity, and when they are defined scientifically they are given the quality of technical necessity. But when they are referred to language, such terms must reflect the reflexive structure of language, the structure given by the formal, active goal of sustainability. Thus a more detailed analysis of this structure should give us more of the conceptual details concerning the formal conditions that language imposes on these terms. These are the terms through which we explain our social and natural relations, our interactions with one another and with our world, and the analysis of language should give us the formal conceptual constraints that would make these terms both coherent and ecological. This would be the theoretical payoff of a linguistic idea of knowledge — a way of conceptualizing ourselves and our world that is reflexive and ecological, an idea of knowledge that can give normative and critical instructions for organizing sustainable social practices. Language strives to sustain its own possibility, so if we understand our social life linguistically then we must understand it, and legitimate it, in accordance with the formal goal of sustainability. If we analyze language reflexively we should be able to reconceptualize, and legitimate, social institutions and productive technology ecologically.

Such an analysis will require thinking of these basic explanatory terms reflexively, rather than descriptively. We will have to think of these terms — *human beings, individuals, society, organization, nature,* and so on — as having a formal explanatory *goal,* rather than as simply reflecting (mirroring) some preexisting abstract "facts" about reality. The reference to language brings the need for a goal-oriented analysis back into the idea of knowledge, a need that science was specifically designed to purge. But science was designed to purge the idea of particular, substantive goals for nature, of immanent ends and final causes, and a linguistic analysis would require the idea of formal, reflexive goals, the goals of linguistic process, not of particular events or achievements. Broadly, this would be the formal goal of sustainability, and so linguistic theory, analysis, and legitimation would all be subject to evaluation in terms of the formal goal of sustainability, not in terms of the objective "truths" of nature, reality, observation, and so on. And the goal of sustainability would be formal in the sense that it could never be finally embodied by any particular cultural versions of knowledge, technology, institutions, or values. This goal would be reflexive in the sense that the only possible way to achieve it would be the formal legitimation of continued efforts to achieve it, meaning the formal legitimation of criticism above all particular versions of "truth," "reality," and "authority." In terms of sustainability, all particular efforts at knowledge would be seen as inevitably disrupting the particular social-natural context of those efforts, thus requiring that version of knowledge to be constantly reevaluated and criticized in the name of sustainability. The inherent goals of language could be formally achieved only if they could never be substantively achieved, and so they would essentially be the goals of legitimate critical access against all established practices, the goals of "wild" knowledge.

This idea of a formal, reflexive goal would distinguish linguistic knowledge both from religious knowledge, with its absolute commitment to traditional goals, and from scientific knowledge, with its categorical denial of goal-oriented explanations. In particular, it would give linguistic knowledge the human, social dimension that scientific knowledge has always lacked, by definition. Scientific knowledge could replace religious knowledge only by disdaining explanatory goals, and so science has always had difficulty conceptualizing the social world, a world that is intrinsically goal oriented. This difficulty has led to the dilemma of rationality, the dilemma of deriving a critical, social rationality from an indifferent, natural rationality. From the scientific perspective it has been impossible to achieve an "objective" commitment to social legitimation, because nothing about the "objective" world can tell us anything about how to act in social life. Thus we can have only an "objective" commitment to scientific technology, while no "subjective" version of social values can possibly be "objectively" critical of that technology, even in the name of ecological sanity. But if knowledge is understood as *formally* goal oriented, then it can tell humans how to act *formally*, in the sense of legitimating ecological, social–natural criticism against any established version of truth, knowledge, or institutional authority. The idea of a *formal* goal means that linguistic knowledge cannot become religion, but neither can it disdain the issues of social legitimation. A linguistic knowledge must be a *social-natural* knowledge, which means it must recognize the need for *formal* social recommendations as well as for *formal* natural explanations. This is what the idea of a formal goal for knowledge would allow, and it is an idea that has already been accepted with respect to medical knowledge, as the formal goal of health has been used effectively to legitimate medical institutions, technology, and criticism.

Linguistic Motives: Legitimation versus Criticism

Knowledge serves the formal goal of language, the goal of sustaining the social-natural possibility of language through organized, legitimated human actions. From this perspective language must be seen as formally directing human actions, through efforts at knowledge, toward its inherent, formal goal, the goal of sustaining the possibility of such human actions. This seems to be simply another way of saying that humans will characteristically use language to explain their world and survive. But there is a crucial difference between these two perspectives on language, and it is the difference between whether language uses humans or humans use language. Put more precisely, this is the difference between whether we assume the idea of language to be logically prior to the idea of being human or vice versa. In the first case we will try to understand human beings in terms of language, and in the second case we will try to understand language in terms of human beings. In the scientific world we have typically taken the second explanatory strategy, where human beings are taken as a "natural" given and language, knowledge, and social life must all be understood in terms of the a priori characteristics of "natural" individuals. From this perspective humans use language in the same sense that they seek property, act rationally, desire pleasure, and so on; that is, language use can be explained in terms of the inherent, "natural" qualities of individuals. But this means that the idea of being human is logically prior to the idea of language, and this is conceptually incoherent, because the idea of being human depends upon the idea of language. Language constitutes and enables human beings, and so some assumption about language is always involved in any conception of human beings and human action, with the only issue being whether that assumption involves language as magic or language as a formal, reflexive structure.

In the context of science we tend to misunderstand the idea of language, and so we sometimes talk about apes or bees or dolphins as having language. But these animals do not have language, not in the sense that humans do, because if they did they would be able to be integrated into human social life. Having language is not a physical or vocal or symbolic issue, it is an issue of being a part of linguistic social life, and any being who can use language can make a legitimate claim upon human social life. This is what various subgroups have done when they have been socially excluded from acceptance as "fully human" based on racial or sexual or ethnic criteria. There may be a physiological bias against social inclusion, but all beings who use language will tend to become fully included in any human society, since being human is really an issue of social life, and social life is an issue of language. (This is an issue our science fiction writers are constantly raising, in the sense of when androids can be accepted as full and equal social participants.) The same point is made when people who are physiologically human cannot fully participate in human language, because of mental retardation, brain damage, failure to learn a language, or some other reason. This linguistic failure always involves some degree of institutional insulation and protection from full participation in daily social life (for example, driving). It is in this sense that social institutions, including our modern legal idea of human equality, must always accept the priority of linguistic criteria over physiological criteria with respect to the social implementation of ordinary human rights and opportunities. The same is true for children, where linguistic ability and mastery become the crucial criteria for moving from childhood to full social participation. Being human is an issue of participation in human society, and such participation is an issue of language, not of biology. In general, the idea of being human will be extended to all beings who can use language, regardless of physiology, in the sense of full participation in the rights and responsibilities of human society. So if apes and dolphins had a language, then we would not wonder if they had a language. Rather, we would educate them, demonstrate for their rights, reconsider legal protections, and devise marketing strategies.

From this perspective language is not something human beings contingently *have*, so that the idea of being human cannot be logically prior to the idea of language, and animals cannot be both nonhuman and have a language. Rather, language constitutes human beings, so that the idea of language is logically prior to and the idea of being human is dependent upon the idea of language. Human beings—individuals, persons—must be understood in terms of language, and if language is recognized as active and goal oriented, then human beings must be conceptualized as participating in the formal, reflexive goal of language, the goal of sustaining the possibility of social life. This means that humans must be understood as inherently linguistic and interactive, rather than as inherently "natural" and physiological. Humans are constituted by language, not by biology, and so humans must be understood as motivated by language, not by "natural" desires or needs or interests. Humans are inherently active, and so some notion of motivation is necessary, some conception of why individuals act, of what they act toward, of what organizes and directs human actions. In the context of science we have conceptualized motivation as an issue of "natural" individual characteristics, following the foundational idea of the detached, a priori individual. But this is incoherent, because it means that mathematical, indifferent nature must impose inherent goals and motivations on humans, thus making humans a conceptual anomaly within the scientific project. This leads to all the mysteries and conundrums of scientific knowledge, and to the magic required by conceptualizing humans as logically prior to language.

From the perspective of language, however, individuals would be understood as formally motivated by language, where language, unlike scientific nature, is already understood as having an active structure and a formal goal, the goal of sustaining its own possibility. From this perspective individuals would be understood as participating in this formal, goal-oriented structure, and thus they would be understood as motivated by the same formal mechanisms that generate knowledge, social life, and social legitimation. Individuals would be understood as formally motivated to act in such a way as to sustain their own human possibility, the possibility of social life. In effect, humans would be understood as formally compatible with social life, as an issue of language, rather than as formally in conflict with social life, as an issue of "natural," individualized motivations. Individuals would be understood as inherently linguistic and thus as inherently social, in the sense of inherently motivated to sustain the ecological, social-natural possibility of social life. Language would be seen as striving to sustain itself through knowledge, social organization, and social legitimation, as well as through reflexive criticism and delegitimation, and individuals would be understood as striving to know, act, and criticize in order to achieve this formal, structural goal. So individuals would be seen as having linguistic motivations, in the sense of acting in accordance with the formal, structural demands of language, as it imposes its inherent, reflexive goal on people, knowledge, and social life.

From this perspective the theoretical, explanatory tension would not be between the individual and the society, as it has been in scientific social theory, but rather between the linguistic demands for institutional legitimation and the linguistic demand for reflexive criticism. Institutional legitimation is always necessary as the basis for organized social actions, and yet reflexive criticism against those legitimated actions is also always necessary, as an issue of the formal goal of sustainability. Both science and religion have stressed the idea of legitimation over the idea of criticism, and both have failed to understand knowledge as an issue of ecology and reflexivity, focusing instead on knowledge as an issue of absolute reality and truth. And from this perspective individual interests, including individual criticism, will always appear to conflict with the social order, since the social order will always define itself in terms of an ultimate reference to truth and reality. If knowledge is referred to language, however, then legitimation becomes an issue of ecology and sustainability, and thus the reflexive commitment to criticism becomes as central as the organizing commitment to legitimation. These are both central linguistic commitments, and they are clearly in profound theoretical conflict, where legitimated institutions must be able to withstand legitimate criticism and legitimate criticism must be able to undermine legitimated institutions. But this explanatory conflict is enabling and constructive, unlike the explanatory conflict between the individual and society, which reflects no formal goal and can only be a puzzling artifact of indifferent "natural" regularities. The legitimation-criticism conflict is exactly the way that language enables social life, so that this conflict always serves the formal goal of sustainability; that is, it is always available as the basis for constructing and reconstructing sustainable social institutions.

Linguistic social theory, then, would focus on the explanatory conflict between legitimation and criticism, between a legitimating ecological conception of knowledge and the critical ecological evaluation of that knowledge in the context of its institutional, social-natural effects. Social practices would be legitimated in terms of their formal commitment to sustainability, which means in terms of their ability to legitimate reflexive ecological criticism against themselves. Individuals would be understood as the source of this criticism, so that they would be understood as inherently participating in social organizations and as inherently capable of legitimate ecological criticism against those organizations. Individuals would be understood as inherently linguistic, which means they would be understood as inherently motivated by the formal linguistic demands—knowledge, organization, legitimation, criticism—of sustainability. Individuals would be understood as the active, organizing, and critical aspects of language, so that social relationships would be understood in terms of the formal and active dynamics of linguistic structure, rather than in terms of the formal and active dynamics of "natural" characteristics. More precisely, individuals in society would be understood in a way similar to the way words are understood in a language, in the sense that each individual would be understood as logically referring to all other individuals, and no individual could be understood as conceptually detached and self-contained (self-referring), as scientific knowledge would have it. Just as one word can make sense only in the linguistic context of other words, one individual could make sense only in the social context of other individuals, and this social context would be understood as formally constrained and organized by the active structure of language. Individuals would be seen as linguistically motivated, in the sense of formally constrained to act in accordance with this active linguistic structure, and if these motives could be articulated and understood then human beings could achieve a more coherent understanding of themselves and their world. In particular, they could begin to legitimate their institutions on the basis of an ecological and "wild" knowledge, rather than on the basis of a sacred and magical knowledge.

Humans are constitutively linguistic, and they act in accordance with formal linguistic motives, but they do not necessarily understand themselves as linguistic, and as linguistically motivated. Their effort to understand themselves and their world, the effort to achieve knowledge, is inherently linguistic, but a particular (cultural) version of knowledge will not necessarily articulate and recognize its own linguistic basis. Rather, particular versions of knowledge, like science and religion, may find their basis in some sacred version of "true" reality, and thus incorporate an occluded, and therefore magical, idea of language. Such versions of knowledge will always be incoherent, because they will fail to understand themselves. Also, these versions of knowledge will always stress legitimation at the expense of criticism, because they will always understand human motivation, and thus social life, in terms of some absolute, sacred reality, a reality that settles legitimation at the same time that it inhibits criticism. But if knowledge focuses on its basis in language, then it will focus on formal linguistic motives, and it will begin to conceptualize social-natural relations and to legitimate social practices in terms of linguistic motives, rather than sacred, or "natural," motives. In this way knowledge can become coherent, as it begins to achieve a formal understanding of the kinds of actions and organizations that can sustain the possibility of social life, actions and organizations that are as committed to the ecological necessity of disruptive criticism as they are to the social necessity of institutional legitimation. Both social theory and natural theory can become social-natural theory, where particular theoretical efforts are committed to reflexivity and ecology, rather than to objectivity and nature. And in particular, social theory can begin to incorporate a reflexive reference to the natural environment, and natural theory can begin to incorporate a reflexive reference to social sustainability, just as medical theory incorporates a reflexive reference to health.

The final task, then, is to analyze and articulate these formal linguistic motives. If language is committed to sustaining its own possibility, then the formal motives it imposes on human beings—the motives to understand their world and to organize social actions—will be the motives of sustainability. If we can articulate these motives, we will have the basis for an ecological conception of social legitimation and for a "wild," as well as coherent, conception of knowledge. This will be the task of the final chapter, a task involving the idea that language requires us to interact with one another, and to organize social life, in certain formal, structural ways. If we can understand these formal constraints on interaction, we can begin to understand ourselves and our world linguistically, and thus ecologically, and if we cannot, then we must continue to understand ourselves and our world magically, and thus incoherently. The idea of linguistic motives may seem obscure, since we are not used to thinking in these terms, but it is an idea that has already received systematic attention, primarily from philosopher Bruce Wavell and literary critic Kenneth Burke. Both Wavell and Burke recognize language as the basis for all social practice, including the conception of nature, and so I will turn to them for the analytic beginnings of a linguistic social theory. For Wavell, language, not mathematics, is the only coherent reference for reason, and this is a form of reason that involves necessary formal motivations, not simply logical relationships between terms. For Burke, language motivates human actors according to the formal demands of conceptual difference and rhetorical appeal, demands that must be understood as the basis for both social theory and natural explanations. Burke's analysis is literary and eclectic, and as such it is outside of the standard linguistic and philosophic approaches to language, but probably for this reason it is the most social and reflexive analysis of language available, the most consistent analysis of language from the inside, as an issue of enabling social life.

NINE

The Ecology of Language

If knowledge is to be reflexive, it must recognize its own necessary relationship to social action, which means to social legitimation. Knowledge organizes actions on the world, and the only coherent criteria for the validity of knowledge are criteria evaluating the ability of knowledge claims to sustain the possibility of knowledge, through legitimated social actions. This means that if knowledge is to be valid, the world must be conceptualized as a certain kind of thing, as we have seen, and social life must be conceptualized as a certain kind of thing. In particular, social life must be conceptualized as necessarily but only formally related to an independent world, to natural process, and this means that the relationship between social life and the world must be seen as formally necessary but substantively contingent. In these terms social life must be understood as organized around a dual necessity, the formal necessity of sustainability and the substantive necessity of legitimation. Social actions must be legitimated, and they must be legitimated through assertions of valid knowledge, assertions that can generate effective and reliable responses from natural processes. But these specific, legitimated actions must also be formally sustainable, which means that the formal criteria for sustainability must always take precedence over the specific criteria for legitimation. Specific cultural actions must be legitimated in terms of conceptions of "truth" and "reality," but the validity of these conceptions must in turn be evaluated in terms of the formal criteria of sustainability. And according to these formal criteria, actions that are legitimate under certain social-natural conditions may not be legitimate under later, changed social-natural conditions, conditions that result from the effects of those legitimated actions. From a reflexive perspective, the legitimating notions of "truth" and "reality" must be subject to evaluation and criticism in terms of the formal criteria for sustainability.

But these are the notions that legitimate specific institutions, specific cultural practices, so that the legitimacy of established institutions must always be subject to evaluation and criticism in the name of the formal criteria for sustainability. The dual necessity of social life must be understood in terms of an inherent tension, the tension between the substantive legitimation of specific practices and the formal legitimation of sustainable practices. As a cultural issue the notions of "truth" and "reality" will be asserted as absolute, so that specific institutional practices — specific relations of power and privilege — will be accepted as absolute. But as a formal issue these practices cannot be absolute, since they must change the conditions of their own legitimacy. Specific cultural practices will always assert their own legitimacy in terms of a general notion of social benefit, social value — so we get such notions as "We had to destroy the village in order to save it," or "Better dead than red," or "What's good for General Motors is good for the country." And it is through such general assertions of social benefit that the necessity of the formal criteria of sustainability is always recognized, at least implicitly. No established practices can legitimate themselves strictly on the basis of their being established; they must also assert, however cynically, some notion of their general social value, a notion that includes a tacit commitment to the issues of sustainability. But usually this assertion simply hides a commitment to the continued legitimacy of those particular practices, whatever the social cost, where social benefit is defined simply in terms of a specific structure of power and privilege. In particular, there is no way that the legitimacy of the established institutions can be legitimately ("rationally") challenged in the name of a *formal*, "wild" concern with social benefit, or sustainability.

The tension is still there, however, and if the challenge cannot be made legitimately, then it will be made subversively, because social institutions must be organized according to both levels of necessity. They must be able to generate specific organized actions, *and* they must generate these actions in accordance with a formal, general commitment to social sustainability. And there is an inherent tension because legitimate institutions must inevitably disturb the conditions of their own legitimacy, in terms of sustainability. Institutions must either legitimate themselves absolutely, in terms of an absolute, nonreflexive "truth," or they must be able to criticize and reshape themselves, legitimately, in the context of their own social-natural effects, and in accordance with the formal criteria of sustainability. They will inevitably do the former, and simply "believe" that the proper knowledge of absolute "reality" will generate social benefit, unless knowledge is recognized as being reflexive, rather than magical. And if knowledge is recognized as reflexive, then it must be recognized as necessarily legitimating, and thus as necessarily involving an inherent tension between the substantive and the formal requirements for social legitimation. Assertions of knowledge must be able to legitimate social institutions in terms of how actions and the world can be effectively, reliably, and sustainably connected. And they must be able to criticize and delegitimate institutions that have been effective and reliable but have become ecologically irrational, in terms of the formal criteria of sustainability.

Reflexive knowledge must be able to legitimate specific institutions in terms of a conceptual interpretation of reality and nature, and to legitimate the criticism of those same institutions in terms of formal criteria, the criteria that enable the possibility of effective social-natural interactions. We are generally familiar with the requirements for establishing a conceptual interpretation of nature, but we are not generally familiar with the requirements for meeting the formal criteria for sustainability. In particular, we are not familiar with the necessity of continually shaping and evaluating our conceptual interpretations of nature in terms of these formal criteria. In order to do so, we must first articulate these formal criteria, the criteria that require a *formal*, abstract understanding of our world as independent but responsive. These criteria must be formal in the sense that they must remain "wild," they cannot be captured by particular cultural "truths," as either sacred rituals or mathematical techniques. These are the criteria of formal sustainability, the criteria that enable absolute critical access against all established institutions, and so they must remain formal and abstract, not substantive and cultural, not "tamed." These are the criteria of rationality and legitimacy, and so we must be able to find that particular social-natural practices—the hunting of buffalo, the harvesting of forests, the burning of oil—are not absolutely legitimate. Rather, they may be rational (sustainable) under certain historical conditions and not under others, and we can make such judgments only if the criteria for rationality are formal, in the sense of identifying the formal conditions for sustainable social-natural interactions.

These formal conditions are established by language, where our ability to conceptualize the world formally involves us in striving to sustain our own social possibility, as language users. Language requires that language users (humans) interact formally with an independent but responsive world, through knowledge, and so if our idea of knowledge begins to recognize this formal linguistic necessity, then we can begin to make this idea coherent, not magical, because we will make it reflexive rather than "true." In particular, we will recognize that the legitimation of criticism is as central to the idea of knowledge as the legitimation of social organization, and that knowledge must become "wild" if it is to be coherent and ecological. Language can sustain its own possibility only through the legitimation of organized social actions, but particular institutions will always try to capture the legitimating ideas of knowledge and reason, and so the necessity of institutional legitimation must always be held critically accountable to the necessity of formal sustainability. And this can be done only if language is seen as imposing a necessary formal structure upon knowledge and social life, a structure of formal sustainability, not of magical cultural "truths." Assertions of knowledge must be evaluated first in terms of the formal structure of language (sustainability) and then in terms of local technical success (productivity, efficiency, and so on), just as assertions of medical knowledge must be evaluated first in terms of the formal notion of health and then in terms of technical success (keeping the heart working, preventing miscarriages, and so on). And such evaluations must refer to the formal conceptual order that language imposes on the understanding and organizing of social life, and in particular to the formal linguistic motives that language imposes on its users, as the active agents of formal sustainability.

This means that we must achieve a knowledge of language from inside of language, as linguistic beings, as opposed to the scientific notion of a knowledge of nature from outside of nature, as detached individuals. From the inside, language formally organizes our ability to know our world, and this ability depends upon our understanding ourselves as capable of effective, sustainable interactions with our world. Thus from the inside language imposes formal conceptual conditions on our understanding of ourselves and our world, of *persons* and *reality*, and these are the conditions that Bruce Wavell (1986) explores in his book *Language and Reason*. Wavell sees language, not mathematics, as the necessary reference for the idea of reason, so that reason becomes an issue of the necessary conceptual relationship between *persons* and *reality*, not an issue of mathematical logic. *Person* and *reality* must be recognized as "regulative concepts," as opposed to "use concepts," where regulative concepts actively regulate thought and action, while use concepts are more strictly representational. Thus a *person* becomes "someone who has obligations, duties, etc., to us, and towards whom we, likewise, have obligations, duties, etc." (p. 251). Similarly, "reality" is no longer "that which is independent of thought, desire, will, etc., but becomes that which makes legitimate demands on us to think, speak and behave in certain ways" (p. 251). And the concept of "truth" has the same regulative quality, in the sense of something that "agrees with reality." Further, a *person* (human, individual, actor) is defined in terms of reason and language, not in terms of physiology:

> A *person* is not merely a man or woman (its semantic sense), but a man
> or woman who is conceived as being an autonomous, rational agent,
> who is required to behave and to be treated by others in accordance
> with rational due process. Hence, *person*, like *reality*, is not a use-
> concept. (p. 241)

Understood in this way, these concepts are mutually referring: *reality* makes necessary demands for appropriate actions on persons, and *persons* necessarily respond to reality in appropriate ways. This means that *reality* (the world) must be conceptualized as substantively independent but formally responsive. Language makes it necessary for persons to understand their world as independent, and so also makes it difficult for them to understand their formal, conceptual relationship with that world.

> "To take a concept to be real" . . . is to act in a characteristic manner
> which is regulated by the concept. This is not to deny that the sense of
> "reality" is an object of thought, speech, and action which, in important
> respects, is independent of human thought, speech, and action. It is one
> of the ultimate subtleties of human thought that it creates a concept of
> that which is independent of itself as a way of coping with and ordering
> experience, and then goes on to invent procedures which shall determine
> when the concept may be properly invoked and shall safeguard it from
> subjectivization. (p. 216)

Thus we tend to understand ourselves and our world as though we were outside of language, rather than inside of it, and so "we tend to reify, to objectify the *person* concept and speak as if persons have the same categorical status as chairs and tables" (p. 251). Also we tend to reify and objectify *reality*, and so we tend to make reason an issue of some sacred truth, rather than an issue of language.

But if we begin to look at language "holistically," as Wavell suggests, rather than "piecemeal," as he characterizes scientific philosophy and linguistics, then we can begin to understand these terms as regulative, and reason as linguistic. Then we will understand that these are the concepts that regulate and bracket all human thought and action, and that define reason as interactional and reflexive, rather than as mathematical and objective.

> It would be difficult to exaggerate the importance of this fact for an understanding of the nature of reason. In the first place, it means that *reality* and *person* feature in the vast majority of rational motives and so are basic to rationality. Secondly, it makes these concepts different in kind from almost all other concepts. (p. 251)

For Wavell, mathematics is simply a technical, logical aspect of language, not a separate, a priori, and privileged reference for reason. Mathematics formalizes relationships of comparison, number, and form that are inherent in language, but this means that mathematical rationality is not independent of language and social life. Science has reified mathematics into a nonsocial, technical idea of reason, but this is a mistake about mathematics, and it leads to mistakes about knowledge, reason, and social legitimation. Mathematics is indeed a technical form of reasoning, but only within the context of linguistic, reflexive reason, in the same sense that medical techniques are rational only within the context of health. Thus if mathematical techniques are to be rational they must be constrained by the formal conditions of linguistic reason, the reflexive conditions that make reason possible. And this analysis of mathematics is shared by George Lakoff (1987), who argues that

> mathematics need not be construed as transcendentally true, true independent of the understanding of any beings. Instead, it can be construed as growing out of the nature of human rationality. . . . Mathematics . . . is the study of the structures that we use to understand and reason about our experience. (pp. 354-55)

Both Wavell and Lakoff suggest that language both reflects and structures human experience, and thus that knowledge and reason must be issues of language, issues that refer to the necessary formal conditions for human life. And Wavell takes this suggestion further, arguing that language imposes formal conceptual constraints on our fundamental ideas of individuals and nature, of persons and reality. He finds "rational motives" to be implicit in language, and he develops an analysis of these linguistic motives in terms of the formal validity, soundness, and sincerity criteria that structure the use of language, criteria characterizing language as rationality, rather than as syntax or semantics or magical access. But he never takes this analysis into a discussion of social theory and social legitimation, nor does Lakoff, even though both recommend new, less objectivist notions of reason and knowledge. Both recognize that reason and knowledge are legitimating terms, but both stop short of social analysis, primarily, it would seem, because they want to maintain their scientific detachment if not their scientific concepts. Both continue to analyze language as though it were detached from politics and institutions, even though Wavell provides impetus to a new social theory through his idea that the *person* concept involves actions on the world, and is linguistic and regulative, rather than objective and factual.

More than this is necessary, however, and in particular some institutional conception of linguistic motives must be derived from the analysis of language, motives that would show how human beings must be institutionally structured to act, formally, if social life is to be able to sustain its own possibility. Language formally motivates people to act in sustainable ways, but institutions may not, and so our social institutions must begin to be legitimated in accordance with these formal sustainable motives. And this can be achieved only on the basis of a social and interactional analysis of linguistic motives, something that Wavell seems to imply but does not provide.

Rhetorical Appeal and Pure Persuasion: Kenneth Burke

What is needed is the idea that language strives to sustain itself by imposing some formal interactional requirements—motives—on its human users, as they act socially to know, organize, and sustain social life. In this way the formal goal of language could be seen as imposing conceptual and institutional conditions on human actions, the conditions of being able to achieve effective, organized actions on an independent but responsive world. These conditions could be either misunderstood, through linguistic magic, or recognized, through linguistic reason, and if they are recognized then they can be used for institutional legitimation, in the name of sustainability. So we need an analysis of language as it affects human actors from the inside, rather than only human reasoners. In particular, we need an analysis of language as it affects individual inter-actions with others, since the crucial linguistic issue is the organization of effective social actions, through ideas of reason and knowledge. Such an analysis has been provided by Kenneth Burke (1969) in his book *The Rhetoric of Motives*. Burke's perspective is literary, rather than linguistic or philosophic, and so he is interested in explaining social actions, rather than reason or language as a separate phenomenon. Accordingly, he does not take a detached, external perspective but rather looks at language in terms of how it must affect, formally, the beings-who-use-language, the beings who act and communicate and organize in terms of the formal constraints imposed by language. This is what it means to analyze lan-guage from the inside, and from this perspective Burke can suggest a reinterpretation of both natural explanations and social theory. When this analysis is combined with the analyses of Wavell, Lakoff, and others, who seek to redefine the legitimating notions of reason and knowledge in terms of language, then we can begin to develop a linguistic social theory, as well as the criteria for linguistic, and thus ecological, social legitimation.

Burke sees language as a structure of symbolic differences, and he ap-proaches the analysis of language in terms of what it must mean, at the formal level of linguistic motives, to use language to act and communi-cate from within that structure of differences. For Burke, human beings are defined by the use of language, where language is a structure of sym-bols that divides the world into different kinds of things:

> Man, as a symbol–using animal, experiences a difference between *this* being and *that* being as a difference between *this kind of* being and *that kind of* being. . . . Here, implicit in our attitudes toward things, is a principle of *classification*. And classification in this linguistic, or formal sense is all-inclusive, "prior" to classification in the exclusively social sense. (p. 282)

These symbolic differences are necessarily structured, in the sense of classificatory order: the concepts of "tables" and "chairs" are included in and transcended by the concept of "furniture," which in turn is tran-scended by the concept of "matter," and so on. Language imposes a structure of symbolic differences, and one of the necessary differences imposed by language is the difference between beings-who-use-language and other kinds of things. The former—human beings, individuals—

necessarily experience a world of symbolic differences from within those differences, and thus they necessarily use language to act and communicate within this context of differences, to order these differences, through knowledge, as a basis for successful action.

In particular, individuals use language to interact with other individuals, who are themselves experienced as symbolically different *kinds* of beings. John will experience Mary as a woman, as having another nationality, as having a different religion, as being younger, and so on, and this myriad potential range of symbolic differences will be available to distinguish all individuals from all other individuals along various dimensions. Language will be used to communicate across these symbolic differences, and it is here that Burke finds the formal linguistic motives, the motives of rhetorical appeal. Language creates a necessary *mystery* between different kinds of language-using beings: the other individual is inherently *mysterious* to the degree that he or she is symbolically different. And so language creates the formal ground for the necessity of continuous rhetorical appeal across the mystery of symbolic differences. The mystery makes communication—interaction, coordination—inherently problematic, and the rhetorical appeal is a formal, linguistic effort to transcend the mystery and establish a common ground for interaction, a ground that could be love, mutual interests, mutual values, or other shared concerns. "For rhetoric . . . is rooted in an essential function of language itself, . . . the use of language as a symbolic means of inducing cooperation in beings that by nature respond to symbols" (p. 43). These are the formal motives of rhetorical appeal, and they underlie all specific individual acts of communication and persuasion. "The linguistic motive eventually involves kinds of persuasion guided not by appeal to any one local audience, but by the *logic of appeal in general*" (p. 129).

In order for this appeal to have the possibility of success, however, there must be the (formal) possibility of a shared basis of identification, a shared identity—man, attorney, Hispanic, American—that enables a rhetorical appeal to bridge the mystery of difference. Thus the logic of linguistic communication (linguistic motives) involves both the formal necessity of the mystery of difference and the formal necessity of a common ground that bridges that difference and on which an appeal can be based. Language structures both the necessity of difference and the necessity of transcending difference through communicative appeal. But if the latter succeeds absolutely, then there is no longer any mystery of difference, and thus the logic of language is both to create the necessity of rhetorical identification and to prevent its complete success. The logic of language is to maintain its own possibility, which means to maintain both the mystery of difference and the possibility of transcendent identification. This means that there is also an inherent linguistic motive to self-interfere with the success of rhetorical identification, to inhibit complete identification for the sake of maintaining the possibility of communication, of rhetorical appeal.

Burke calls this the logic of *pure persuasion*, where " 'pure persuasion' is an absolute, logically prior to any specific persuasive act. It is of the essence of language" (p. 252). In pure persuasion the true goal of appeal is to maintain the possibility of appeal, and thus communicating beings must maintain a degree of "standoffishness": "In its essence communication involves the use of verbal symbols for the purposes of appeal. . . . And 'standoffishness' is necessary to the form, because without it the appeal could not be maintained" (p. 271). Thus language use has a dual structure and involves a necessary tension: it must make possible the transcending of mystery and at the same time perpetuate that mystery. All communication, no matter how apparently grasping and acquisitive, must contain an element of pure persuasion; all individuals must try to maintain their own unique sense of identity (the mystery of symbolic difference) through a formal effort to *interfere* with whatever rhetorical appeals for power, property, or love they may be making. The rhetorical plea must remain unanswered.

> When the plea is answered, you have gone from persuasion to
> something else. Where you had previously been trying to get in, you
> may now have to try getting out. . . . This is what we mean by the
> technical or formal need of "self-interference" as a motive in persuasion.
> (p. 274)

And this formal motive in linguistic persuasion would appear in various cultural guises, such as the rituals of deference and demeanor, or the taboos of sexual courtship.

> Where an anthropologist or sociologist might derive sexual tabus from
> institutional sources, we would not deny his evidence. We would only
> say that, over and above all such derivations, there is, *implicit in language
> itself*, the act of persuasion; and *implicit in the perpetuating of persuasion* (in
> persuasion made universal, pure, hence paradigmatic or formal) *there is
> the need of "interference."* For a persuasion that succeeds, dies. To go on
> eternally (as a form does) it could not be directed merely towards
> attainable advantages. And insofar as the advantages are obtainable, that

particular object of persuasion could be maintained as such only by interference. Here, we are suggesting, would be the ultimate rhetorical grounds for the tabus of courtship, the conditions of "standoffishness." (p. 274)

Burke completes his analysis with a discussion of the formal basis for the possibility of rhetorical identification across differences. Language involves a formal structured *order* of symbolic *differences*, and thus any particular experience of difference (mystery) always takes place in the context of a particular experience of *ordered* differences. The idea of difference implies the idea of order, and vice versa, so that any particular experience of difference can always be potentially bridged through an appeal to the transcendent order that connects and coordinates those differences. Men and women can establish identity across difference through an appeal to the transcendent order of sex and courtship, while business associates can establish a communicative identity through an appeal to market interests, and so on. This transcendent order is always provided culturally and institutionally, through tradition, religion, values, law, and the like, but the *form* of such an order is a structural necessity of language, the structure of a formal order that organizes relations between symbolically different kinds of things. Thus language includes the formal necessity of *ordered differences*, and in the context of this necessity language-using beings (individuals) always act through the formal linguistic motives of pure persuasion. We formally appeal to the conception of a transcending order as the basis for shared identification and communication—and we always formally inhibit the completion of that identification in order to maintain the uniqueness of individual identity, the mystery of difference.

In all specific efforts at communication, the particular conception of order is provided by a cultural image of appropriate social interaction between particular, recognized differences—men and women, young and old, workers and owners, warriors and farmers. This cultural image of order—traditional relations, market relations, and so on—provides an established, accepted array of appropriate differences (kinds of beings) interconnected through a general organizing principle of social order. This is where we get such particular cultural rituals as those of courtship, family, production, employment, education. The formal linguistic *principle of order* is always institutionally embodied in a cultural ordering of social positions, an ordering of power and privilege, an ordering that is always hierarchical. But it is the formal *principle of order* that is linguistically important, not any particular hierarchical version of it. There must always be a hierarchical cultural order as the basis for individual communicative appeals across symbolic differences, but no particular hierarchical order can ever be linguistically privileged. Language imposes the necessity of order, but not the necessity of any particular order, so that any particular cultural hierarchy is always subject to disruption in the name of a competing version of order. Specifically, at the formal level of *principle* the conceptual reversal of hierarchical privilege makes as much sense as the institutional practice legitimating that privilege, a conceptual reversal to which both Christian theology ("the last shall be first") and Marxist theory ("the dictatorship of the proletariat") have appealed.

Thus the structure of language requires a legitimate institutional ordering of differences, but it also requires a fundamental formal commitment to the legitimacy and maintenance of symbolic differences. Any particular institutional order will organize sets of differences, but only in terms of certain recognized kinds of people—heterosexuals, medical doctors, taxpayers—and only in an accepted hierarchical order of power and privilege. Other possible kinds of people—homosexuals, midwives, tax refusers—will necessarily be excluded by that particular institutional order. This means that the formal linguistic commitment to difference will always provide a ground for the criticism and replacement of any particular order in the name of other, equally valid differences, differences whose recognition would require another institutional order.

Thus Burke finds an inherent tension in the enabling structure of language, a tension between the *principle of order*, embodied as hierarchical institutions, and the *principle of difference*, embodied as a necessary resistance (self-interference) by individuals to a full identification and acceptance of the privileged categories and ranks imposed by a particular hierarchy. In order to be human (language users), individuals need to be involved in an institutional order, so that an appeal to the principle of order can be used to establish communication and cooperation. From the perspective of language, then, individuals cannot be thought of as "natural" and a priori, since they can be coherently conceptualized only in the organized (social) context of one another, just as the words in a language must be understood in terms of one another. But individuals, as language users, need the *principle of order*—social order as such—not any particular "true" or "natural" social order, and indeed the necessity of the principle of order can always be used to assert the legitimacy of alternative and disruptive social orders. In the context of language, individuals must see themselves as belonging to established social groups, but they must also be able to assert their distance and independence from all those groups. As language users, individuals will always maintain some sense of their own uniqueness, their own problematic relationship with others, and thus the need for rhetorical appeal. And it is in the formal, linguistic defense of this uniqueness—self-interference, standoffishness—that individuals will be able to be, and will inherently be, subversive to any established order. An established order will always deny the value of certain kinds of differences, and yet those differences will be linguistically available to individuals as the basis for formulating an alternative, equally legitimate order.

As Burke points out, but only in passing, there is an issue of equality here. As a formal *principle* the necessity of order is a necessity of equality. It is an ordering of terms into a coherent whole, where each term has a particular, important, and necessary place with respect to the others, and with respect to the formal order that constitutes them as "terms." With respect to this formal order, each place is equally valuable, and each term shares in the structure equally. The structure creates the value of each term, and each term is equally valuable to the structure. There may be a hierarchy of terms, such as "furniture" being "superior to" (more general than) "table" or "chair," but this is not a hierarchy of worth and privilege, only a hierarchy of order. The *principle of order* is always institutionally embodied, however, and as an institutional structure it is always a hierarchy of power and privilege, a hierarchy of exclusion and inequality. The principle of order organizes differences, where each shares in the order equally, but an institutional order always simplifies and denies many differences, making social order and social action possible through a structure of unequal power and access.

Thus the linguistic tension between *order* and *difference* becomes a social tension between *hierarchy* and *equality*. The structure of language encourages a formal experience of individual equality, as Habermas argues and analyzes. But this structure does not support some kind of "natural" equality, where individuals are "naturally" equal in terms of some kind of inherent motivation or need, and where only the proper, "natural" institutions can finally achieve equality. Nor is it some kind of ideal equality of power, a lack of institutional hierarchy, as Habermas seems to suggest with his notion of the "ideal speech situation." Rather, it is exactly the formal sense of an enabling, constitutive order, where the existence of a formal, organizing hierarchy is not only compatible with but necessary for a sense of equality of value and worth. This is a formal

equality of access, rather than a substantive equality of institutional position or power. The structure of language encourages a formal equality
of access to the enabling principle of order, where all positions in the formal hierarchy are equally important, equally valuable, and equally deserving of protection, equally necessary for the whole. In this sense all
individuals clearly will not have, and cannot have, equal institutional
power and privilege, but they can all expect, and demand, an equality of
value and significance, an equal security of place, uniqueness, and worth.
As Burke comments, "Though *hierarchy* is exclusive, the *principle* of hierarchy is not; all ranks can 'share in it alike' " (p. 141).

This is the kind of equality that language formally requires, an equality of an order of *differences*, not of some kind of "natural" similarities. It
is a formal equality of different kinds of beings, different places, different
values, different attitudes, different cultures. These different people will
all be at different positions in an organized structure, but with respect to
the *principle* of the organization, they will all be equal, all have an equal
sense of access and security. But it is also the kind of equality that particular institutional arrangements will always begin to deny, as formal hierarchical rank is turned into "sacred" or "rational" power and privilege.

> Hence, to say that hierarchy is inevitable is not to argue categorically
> against a new order on the grounds that it would but replace under one
> label what had been removed under another. It is merely to say that, in
> any order, there will be the mysteries of hierarchy, since such a principle
> is grounded in the very nature of language. (p. 179)

Language requires particular institutional arrangements, as the basis for
concrete social actions, but it also encourages the disruption of those particular arrangements, in the name of the formal legitimacy of difference
and a formal commitment to equality of access. "To say that hierarchy is
inevitable is not to say that any particular hierarchy is inevitable; the
crumbling of hierarchies is as true a fact about them as their formation"
(p. 141).

A Social Theory of Differences

Through his idea of pure persuasion, Burke develops the notion of a linguistic tension between *order* and *difference*, a formal tension that is manifested as an institutional tension between *hierarchy* and *equality*. In
essence, Burke outlines a linguistic social theory, a theory based on the

idea that language strives to sustain itself through formal constraints on social interaction. Burke uses this theory to analyze various textual conceptions of individual interactions, seeing individuals as utilizing *pure persuasion*—the formal mysteries of hierarchy—in order to maintain individual identity and interactional coherence. But the theory can be expanded to analyze the necessary structure of social institutions, particularly if we recognize that the legitimating notions of reason and knowledge must be based on language, not mathematics or nature. Then we can see that institutions must be structured around a formal social version of pure persuasion in order to be rational and coherent, that is, in order to sustain the formal possibility of social life. This would be a legitimating idea of pure persuasion, where the identifying appeal to hierarchical order would be to a rational or ecological order, and the necessity of self-interference would take the form of legitimated critical access to the established hierarchical order, in the name of reason. Social life would be seen as having a formal linguistic structure, a structure in which the organizing, coordinating need for a legitimate hierarchical order would always be accompanied by a disruptive need for criticism against that order. This criticism would be directly justified through various social versions of reason, such as justice, freedom, and equality, but these ideas would be understood linguistically and thus would be derived from the formal linguistic pressure toward sustainability. This would be the social form of pure persuasion, where no particular version of social legitimation (institutional order) could be identified with "truth" or "reason" since the structure of language would require the critical reshaping of that order in the name of the excluded differences, as a way of sustaining the formal linguistic structure of differences.

As a social theory, then, this analysis of language would point toward a necessary, formal tension between the need for social *legitimation* and the need for social *criticism*. This would be the institutional form of the social tension between *hierarchy* and *equality*, a tension imposed by the formal, linguistic tension between *order* and *difference*. As we have seen, scientific social theory imposes a conceptual focus on a postulated tension between the individual and society, a tension derived from the foundational scientific conception of the autonomous, "natural" individual. In terms of this analytic tension, social theory must try to find the "proper" social order to go with the "natural" individual, where the final legitimating reference is to "nature"—the "natural" characteristics of the individual—rather than to sustainability. But through a reference to language the analytic tension of social theory becomes the linguistic tension between order and difference, rather than the magical tension between mind and nature, between social choices and natural laws. This formal linguistic tension cannot be "properly" resolved through a uniquely "rational" set of institutions. Rather, it must be seen as an intrinsic necessity of social organization, of social-natural relations, a necessity imposed by the structure of language, as that structure formally organizes social life and social actions around the inherent goal of sustaining its own possibility.

In this way social life becomes an analytic issue of sustainability, rather than an analytic issue of "truth" or "nature," or "reality." And in particular social life becomes an analytic issue of the necessary, reciprocal tension between legitimation and criticism, between the formal linguistic need for institutional order, as a basis for social actions, and the formal linguistic need for disruptive criticism, in defiance of the institutional denial of particular differences, and thus in support of the formal *principle* of difference. From the scientific perspective social theory becomes primarily an issue of social *order*, an issue of "rationally"—legitimately— *ordering* "natural" individual motivations. From the perspective of language, however, social theory becomes primarily an issue of the tension between *order* and *difference*, between *legitimation* and *criticism*, and thus in the context of science this perspective throws analytic attention on the neglected issue of *criticism*. Society is seen as requiring legitimation in order to generate social actions, social organization, and coordination, but it is also seen as requiring criticism, as constantly generating the grounds for criticism and disruption, in order to sustain its own formal possibility.

This is an ecological possibility, a social-natural possibility. Social life depends upon the legitimation of specific social practices, but it also depends upon the possibility of criticizing those practices in the name of ecological sustainability. The formal reference to language, as the basis for valid knowledge, creates the legitimating reference to sustainability, as a basis for rational criticism. And the reference to sustainability requires a formal conception of social-natural interaction, the kind of conception that is denied by both the traditional vision of religion and the technical vision of science. As a formal structure, language mediates between actions and the world, between social life and natural processes, and if this structure is to sustain its own possibility, then it must generate and legitimate actions that will successfully sustain this mediation. In order to sustain itself, language must generate practices that are ecologically coherent, which means that if knowledge is referred to language then the

formal criteria for knowledge must include a reference to ecological coherence, to sustainability. This is the reference that scientific knowledge
cannot make, and thus that scientific technology can technically disregard. Scientific knowledge cannot legitimate the criticism of its own conception of truth and reality in the name of ecological coherence. It must
rather legitimate certain kinds of "natural" institutions regardless of their
ecological consequences.

Through a reference to language, knowledge must not only legitimate
specific institutions in the name of sustainability (social benefit, freedom,
justice), it must also legitimate the criticism of those same institutions in
the name of sustainability. It is this necessary critical commitment that
both science and religion have missed, because of a conceptual commitment to "true reality," but it has always been there, since any set of
"proper" or "sacred" institutions can be criticized in the name of ecological coherence, sustainability, survival. Language has always created this
critical possibility, among individual members of a social order, but the
legitimacy of disruptive criticism has never been built into the legitimation of particular practices, since these practices have always been legitimated in terms of a final "truth." From the perspective of language,
however, the only legitimate institutions would be those that would
legitimate disruptive criticism against themselves, in the name of ecological coherence. The ideas of "truth" and "reason" would refer to a reflexive notion of sustainability, rather than to a categorical notion of absolute
reality, and in this way specific practices would be seen as necessarily disrupting the conditions of their own legitimacy, through their social-
natural effects.

But this would not involve the legitimating of criticism as such, for its
own sake, so that not all criticism against the established institutions
would necessarily be legitimate. Legitimate criticism, like legitimate institutions, would have to be based on the ecological idea of sustainability,
which would mean, among other things, on the idea of legitimate ecological criticism. This would prevent critical debate from degenerating
into incompatible assertions of "truth," because there would always be a
shared, ecological reference for reason and truth, the reference to language. Thus under certain historical conditions certain practices would
have to be seen as rational, and certain criticisms would have to be seen as
mistaken. Criticism would have to be evaluated for its rationality, since it
might be derived from self-interest or frustration, rather than reflexive
analysis, but it would always have legitimate access, in the sense of being

deserving of evaluation. Particular criticisms would not be institutionally validated simply as criticisms, although the *principle* of criticism would necessarily be validated as such. The reference for all issues of legitimacy would be sustainability, and thus the only legitimate criticisms would be those that could argue for or demonstrate ecological failures on the part of the established practices, where such ecological failure would include the institutional denial of legitimate critical access.

Thus criticisms that are not valid at one time may indeed be valid at a later time, and so forth. If the reference for rationality is ecological coherence, then what is rational at one time may not be, and probably will not be, rational at another time. At any given time there must be an accepted, legitimate version of ecological rationality, an institutional order. But the notion of rationality must be institutionally encouraged to remain conceptually free from those particular institutions; it must be encouraged to remain ecologically "wild." The institutional tendency, of course, will be to identify the legitimating notion of rationality with those particular institutions, with that particular hierarchy of power and privilege, in the name of an ultimate "truth," a sacred "reality." It is this tendency that both the scientific and the religious versions of knowledge encourage and validate, and it is this tendency that the legitimating reference to language, to sustainability, must counteract. And in the context of an established institutional order, and a legitimate version of rationality, this tendency can be structurally counteracted only through an explicit social commitment to the formal linguistic *principle of difference*.

In any particular institutional order, certain kinds of differences between people will necessarily be denied, and indeed should be denied for the sake of an enabling order. These differences will still be available linguistically, symbolically, but they will be denied as part of a rational order, with respect to acceptable kinds of behaviors, roles, interactions. In particular, certain specific positions within the institutional order will be seen as the repositories of legitimate rationality, and the particular kinds of people in those positions — scientists, intellectuals, scholars, experts — will be seen as the official arbiters of legitimate rationality. These are the people who will maintain and adjust the social order in accordance with its legitimating references: prosperity, freedom, equality, survival. Their formal commitment will be to rationality, but their practical commitment will tend to be to maintaining a version of rationality that protects their privileged institutional place, their position as the arbiters of reason. This means that whatever disruptive criticisms of these particular practices become ecologically necessary, ecologically rational, they will probably not be developed and asserted by these official arbiters of rationality. Rather, these official arbiters will more likely tend to deny and ridicule any such criticism, in the name of their own official rationality and their own privileged positions.

Thus if a disruptive, critical rationality is to be presented, as it must be in the context of changing social-natural conditions, then it will tend to be presented from another position within the established order, a position that is not particularly privileged by the rationality of that order. Indeed, it will tend to be presented by individuals or groups that are not specifically a part of that order, not in terms of the institutionally legitimated differences between people. In modern society certain relevant examples would be the emergence of criticisms of the medical profession by women, or the emergence of criticisms of manufacturers by workers and consumers, or the emergence of criticisms of food processing by nutritionists. In each of these cases the emergence of rational criticisms validated a particular kind of group, a kind of difference, that had not previously been recognized as institutionally relevant to that particular issue. In each case the issues of health and access (sustainability) validated a critical version of rationality, and a new kind of significant difference, against the institutional version of rationality. In principle the developing, reflexive flaws in the established system of rationality will be seen best by people who are somewhat excluded from that system, by people who have little or nothing to lose by using the available formal linguistic resources to step outside that system and criticize it. A given institutional order will generally try to perpetuate itself, whatever the ecological cost, and thus its official arbiters of rationality will at some point stop being ecologically rational.

This means that a critical rationality will tend to come from people on the periphery of the established order, from people who can see the sustainable rationality of a new, disruptive version of hierarchical order. Such people are always part of any established order, but usually their legitimacy is absolutely denied in the name of the "rational truth" that legitimates that hierarchy. However, if the idea of rationality were understood linguistically, as a reflexive idea, then these kinds of people would always be seen as having a potentially legitimate voice, since the legitimating commitment would be to the *principle* of difference, not to a particular set of "true" and "rational" differences. Every particular hierarchy would be seen as necessarily creating the conditions for its own irrationality, and the rational criticism would have to emerge from people who were not fully incorporated into the institutional benefits of that hierarchy. Thus the established order, as a legitimate, sustainable social order, with its rationality referred to language rather than to nature, would have to encourage the legitimacy of social differences as a matter of principle, on the recognition that reflexive rationality is an issue of legitimate differences, of viable differences in position and perspective within any given order. The social commitment could not be to a "true" set of specific *kinds* of people: property owners, market competitors, workers, and so on. Rather, the social commitment must be to legitimating the *principle* of difference, to encouraging and multiplying different kinds of people and positions and values for their own sake, within the bounds of social order, because it would be through the legitimacy of difference that new and necessary forms of rationality would emerge.

Something like this is already being suggested in the social context of the new modes of work and organization that are being developed under the influence of computers, automation, and the need for worker learning and flexibility. Analysts such as Larry Hirschhorn and Shoshana Zuboff have shown that these new industrial possibilities will require, or at least enable, less rigid bureaucratic categories and more openness to innovation and redirection from within the organizational hierarchy. Their argument is that the organization will be more efficient and effective if it encourages this openness to learning, criticism, and comprehension among its members, whatever their hierarchical position. Zuboff (1988), for example, calls this an "informed organization" with a learning environment:

> An informed organization is structured to promote the possibility of useful learning among all members and thus presupposes relations of equality. However, this does not mean that all members are assumed to be identical in their orientations, proclivities, and capacities; rather, the organization legitimates each member's right to learn as much as his or her temperament and talent will allow. . . .
>
> The relationships that characterize a learning environment thus can be thought of as posthierarchical. This does not imply that differentials of knowledge, responsibility, and power no longer exist; rather they can no longer be assumed. Instead they shift and flow and develop their character in relation to the situation, the task, and the actors at hand. (pp. 394, 401-2)

This is the idea of legitimating critical and effective access throughout the organization, and it is seen as serving the necessary, inherent goals of the organization. Similarly, I am arguing that the social order must be seen, formally, as an organization, or metaorganization, with its own inherent, formal goal, and that legitimating critical access is the only organizational strategy that is rational and ecological.

This is the institutional payoff of a reflexive, ecological rationality. The institutional commitment must be to the viability, in principle, of social differences — differences in attitude, values, interests, culture, and so on. Social differences would be encouraged for their own sake, for the sake of their diversity of perspective, because it would be this diversity that would encourage and maximize social flexibility with respect to social-natural conditions. This diversity would maximize the possibility of reflexivity, the possibility of rational criticism against established practices. And this commitment to social differences would have to be absolute, built into the legitimating ideas of knowledge and reason, since the established institutional pressures would tend to minimize the significance of certain kinds of disruptive differences. This means that the fundamental social commitment for legitimacy, more fundamental than any particular version of rationality, or ecological "truth," would have to be to the legitimacy and viability of social differences, to encouraging and protecting the multiplication of myriad differences between people. This would be a society of differences, of "wildness" and "weirdness," where people would be encouraged to enjoy one another's differences rather than suspect them. And these differences would be protected in the sense that people could claim a legitimate "right" to their particular commitments of interests and values and culture, as long as these commitments were not willfully disruptive of the social order. People could claim a "right" to a particular place within the social order, a place of their own, with their own identity and uniqueness, a place safe from arbitrary institutional invasion in the name of a final "truth," such as either a "rational" or a "sacred" "reality."

This would be the institutional commitment to a reflexive rationality, and clearly it would be complicated to put into practice. Such institutions would have to be able to legitimate disruptive ecological criticism but not all disruptive criticism, which would mean they would have to work out ways to distinguish rational (ecological) criticisms from pseudorational criticisms, criticisms that were simply self-interested or willful. In practice none of this would be easy, and it may often break down. (And, indeed, scientific rationality has brought us to the edge of such a critical, "wild" rationality, and it does often break down.) But the validity of the reflexive conception, and of the institutional effort, does not depend upon the ease of its practical success. Rather, it depends upon the need for a formal reflexive commitment, a commitment to ecological coherence, and upon the recognition that no other version of knowledge can be made coherent. In the context of science—and scientific technology and environmental disasters—we must make an effort to incorporate an ecological reference into our legitimating notion of knowledge, to extend the idea of health to cover the construction of all technology and practices rather than simply medical technology and practices. In this context the institutional effort must be made, regardless of its potential confusions and failures, and the institutional effort can be made only in the context of a coherent and articulate conceptual effort, an effort that develops the necessary and reflexive resources of language, with its formal structure of individual motives and institutional commitments.

Linguistic Knowledge and Reflexive Criticism

In outline this is what a social theory based on language would look like. Obviously the outline is sketchy, with many theoretical ramifications that cannot be developed here. As a social theory the basic theoretical commitment is to see social life as inherently *organized*, in the sense of having an inherent, formal goal, the goal that structures organizational strategy. Social life would be seen as organized in the same sense that language is organized, in terms of a reflexive goal, rather than as "naturally" structured by individualized motivations, in the sense of naturally interacting atoms. If social life is conceptualized in terms of a formal goal, and in terms of the necessary linguistic motives associated with that goal, then social theory will begin to look at individuals, social action, and nature differently. In particular, social theory will become social-natural theory, in the sense that the conception of nature will become an intrinsic part of the domain of social theory, as a legitimating and organizing reference. The idea of nature will be seen as having inherent social implications, and thus as being subject to legitimate social evaluation and criticism. And the idea of rationality will be seen as having an ecological reference, rather than strictly a natural or traditional reference.

In these terms productive technology would be developed in accordance with a formal reference to sustainability, on the model of the formal medical reference to health. Such a formal reference would enable the progressive technical commitments of scientific technology, but only in the sense of scientific medicine, only in the sense of always enabling the legitimate social inhibition of such technology in the name of health. This would mean that the scientific idea of nature would have to change. The idea of nature would have to be conceptualized as including an inherent reference to social life, just as the idea of the human body includes such a reference. And this would involve a critique of physics, a critique expanding on the one I have begun, a critique that would center on how to conceptualize natural processes as though they were not independent of our ability to conceptualize them.

Natural process would be conceptualized as having a formally necessary but substantively contingent relationship to social actions, with formal necessity being an issue of the structure of language. In this way language would become a conceptual aspect of nature—a part of the basic structure of nature, like gravity or the weak force. Thus such notions as electrons, or spin, or charge, would necessarily refer, as part of their theoretical meaning, to their conceptual location in language, and thus to their conceptual location in the reflexive knowledge and organizational actions that are part of a social-natural world. Nature would be understood as linguistic, rather than as categorically detached, and the development of technology would reflect this reflexive and reorienting conception of knowledge. The knowledge of nature, as the generator of technology, would accept its own constitutive involvement with the structure of language, with all the complex social concomitants that this structure implies. Already the conceptual dilemmas (incoherences) of physics have forced it to include, as a fundamental aspect of nature, the social idea of *consciousness*, thus indicating internal scientific pressure toward a social and reflexive idea of rationality. But neither physics nor its technology has recognized the rational necessity of a reference to sustaining social life, and such a recognition is possible only if knowledge is referred to language, rather than to mathematics and nature. The world must be recognized as independent and manipulable—thus legitimating technology—but at the same time as conceptually involved with our knowledge and social actions—thus legitimating only a certain kind of reflexive and participatory technology.

In particular, the legitimacy of technology would be evaluated in terms of its organizational support and encouragement for reflexive participation and criticism, rather than in terms of its purely technical achievements. Rational technology would become an issue of encouraging, rather than of inhibiting, effective critical access and involvement by all participating individuals. Rational technology would have both a technical and a social dimension, with both technical efficiency *and* a participatory, critical structure being necessary for rationality, as is currently more or less the case with medical technology. In these terms the issue of rational technology is well illustrated by the current debate surrounding the new computer and robotic technology in the workplace, the debate over whether this technology will be used to further control and degrade workers (deskilling) or to support and enhance their specifically human abilities and capacities (flexibility). From the perspective of language this is a debate not only about the market, profit, and social justice, but also about critical access, rationality, and ecological legitimation, a debate that should be recast and reformulated in the context of a linguistic and ecological social theory.

These are the kinds of conceptual implications that a reflexive rationality has for natural theory. For social theory such a rationality will direct conceptual attention toward the legitimation of social differences, as an issue of reflexive criticism and ecological coherence, rather than toward the legitimation of particular social positions, as an issue of "true reality." Individuals will be understood in terms of their differences from one another, differences that enable new and critical perspectives, rather than in terms of their "natural" similarities. And the idea of equality, as a normative reference for social legitimation, will be understood in terms of an ordering of differences, rather than in terms of an ordering of similarities. The idea of equality is clearly the inherent social commitment of scientific knowledge, and scientific social theory has routinely interpreted it in terms of the basic similarities of "natural" individuals, with simply different legitimating versions of what those "natural" motivations might be—property accumulation, control of the product, irrational instincts, or whatever. But from the perspective of language this scientific idea of "natural" individual equality can be seen as having two conceptually distinct aspects, aspects that are only contingently related. One is the *critical* aspect, the idea of legitimating the principle of equal critical access against all established versions of "truth," in the name of a "wild" reference for knowledge, a reference that can never be "tamed" and identified with a particular social tradition. This was the basic assertion of Galileo, as he used a formal idea of reason to defy established authority, and it is an assertion that undermines all sacred versions of social authority. The other is the *natural* aspect, the idea that "nature" is the true reference for knowledge, and thus the only possible location for such a critical reference. This is the idea that requires the detached, autonomous mind, together with a magical notion of mathematics, as linguistic access. When these two ideas are combined, as in scientific knowledge, then the critical individual must also be the "natural" individual, and social theory must be committed to both the idea of equality and the idea of "natural" individual similarities, similarities that can be directly (magically) known.

If these ideas are conceptually detached, however, as in a linguistic knowledge, then the commitment to an equality of critical access can be separated from a commitment to "objective" institutions for "natural" individuals. In this way the idea of equality can legitimate flexibility, diversity, and reflexivity, rather than a specific institutional commitment to the "natural" order, where vast inequalities of power and privilege can be justified in the name of "objective" equality. Thus a formal commitment to equality can be made compatible with the practical necessity of organizational hierarchy only insofar as all members of the hierarchy would have the right of legitimate critical access against it in the name of a "wild," ecological rationality. In effect, the idea of equality would require an absolute institutional commitment to the legitimacy of social differences, within the limits of a viable, organized social order. All individuals would be guaranteed the "right" to choose and maintain their own social location within the order, their own particular values and perspectives. In this conception, society is understood as inherently *organized*, like a language, which means that individuals are inherently compatible with some kind of institutional authority and hierarchy, not inherently resistant to it as a result of "natural" individual similarities. But what they are not compatible with is an institutional defiance of the structure of language, which means an institutional denial of equal critical access against established authority, an institutional identification of "rationality" with hierarchical authority.

In this conception individuals are defined by participation in an order, not by "natural" interests, so that they are not necessarily oppressed or exploited because they have less institutional power than others. Indeed, they may choose to have less power, in order to escape necessary duties and be free to pursue others interests and values. Also, they may achieve meaning and purpose through participation in an organized system, so that following orders becomes a rational commitment, not a surrender of equality. But they would necessarily be incompatible with, and oppressed by, an institutional order that denied their ability to create an identity and find a security of place within that order, as long as that place was compatible with ecological rationality. In this conception the idea of equality refers to an institutional guarantee, in the name of rationality, that all individuals can maintain effective local control over their chosen lives, and that any disruption of that local control must be legitimated in the name of a shared ecological rationality. More generally this idea of equality refers to an institutional guarantee of legitimate critical access against all established authority in the name of a "wild," ecological rationality, a guarantee based on the reflexive necessity of legitimating critical *differences* of identity, values, and perspectives. Thus the idea of equality is ultimately referred to the idea of sustainability, to ecological coherence, and this is the final conceptual payoff of a linguistic conception of knowledge. The commitment to equality becomes a negative, critical commitment to a "wild" rationality, a rationality that is always external to any established institutional order and thus that is always legitimately available to criticize and disrupt that order.

This means that the legitimating reference to ecology is also, and necessarily, a reference to a powerful set of normative institutional commitments, commitments concerning equality, critical access, security of place, participation, rationality, freedom from arbitrary invasion, and so on. The issue of ecological coherence is not separate from the traditional concerns of social theory, but rather suggests a new conceptual perspective on the understanding of those traditional social concerns. The issue of ecological coherence has always *seemed* to be separate from such social issues as justice, equality, and freedom, because the issue of ecology had to do with natural processes, and social theory routinely accepted the categorical scientific separation of nature from society. From the scientific perspective social-natural relations are very difficult to conceptualize, and they are virtually impossible to conceptualize reflexively. But if the scientific separation of nature from society is seen as an issue of legitimation, rather than as an issue of "truth" or "reality," then social-natural relations can begin to be conceptualized directly, in which case they must be conceptualized reflexively, since they are central to the very possibility of conceptualization. And in this case they must be conceptualized in the context of the formal goal of social-natural sustainability, a goal that imposes formal structural conditions—equality, critical access—on the kinds of social practices that can be legitimated as rational.

Social-natural relations must be conceptualized directly, in terms of a *necessary but formal* relationship between social actions and natural processes, and such a relationship must be understood in terms of the formal, reflexive structure of language. Thus an ecological rationality must be based on a formal understanding of language, an understanding of inherent linguistic motives structured into regulative terms such as *reality* and *person*. This is the direction that social theory must take, the direction of exploring the conceptual conditions of knowledge and social life, rather than of exploring the "natural" characteristics of individuals. In this direction knowledge must look at itself from the inside, rather than at "reality" from the outside, and so knowledge must become an issue of reflexive sustainability rather than of magical access. Accordingly, social theory, as social-natural theory, must begin to take its place as the central conceptual domain in the quest for knowledge and legitimation, rather than simply accepting the conceptual formulations of natural theory. In particular, social theory must begin to explore the formal social-natural structure of language, for it is only through a reference to language that the idea of knowledge can be made coherent and that knowledge can become fully "wild," fully critical. And it is only through a commitment to a truly "wild" knowledge that sustainable social institutions can be legitimated.

References

Works Cited

Bacon, Francis. 1960. *New Organon and Related Writings* (ed. Fulton H. Anderson). Indianapolis: Bobbs-Merrill. (Original work published 1620)

Balikci, Asen. 1967. "Shamanistic Behavior among the Netsilik Eskimos," in John Middleton, ed., *Magic, Witchcraft, and Curing* (191-210). Garden City, N.Y.: Natural History Press.

Beattie, John. 1967. "Divination in Bunyoro, Uganda," in John Middleton, ed., *Magic, Witchcraft, and Curing* (211-32). Garden City, N.Y.: Natural History Press.

Becker, Carl. 1932. *The Heavenly City of the Eighteenth Century Philosophers*. New Haven, Conn.: Yale University Press.

Berger, Peter. 1969. *The Sacred Canopy*. Garden City, N.Y.: Anchor.

Bernal, J. D. 1971. *Science in History, Volume 2: The Scientific and Industrial Revolutions*. Cambridge: MIT Press.

Bickerton, Derek. 1990. *Language and Species*. Chicago: University of Chicago Press.

Boyd, Richard. 1984. "The Current Status of Scientific Realism," in Jarrett Leplin, ed., *Scientific Realism* (41-82). Berkeley: University of California Press.

Bridgeman, P. W. 1964. *The Nature of Physical Theory*. Princeton, N.J.: Princeton University Press.

Burke, Kenneth. 1969. *A Rhetoric of Motives*. Berkeley: University of California Press. (Original work published 1950)

Burtt, E. A. 1954. *The Metaphysical Foundations of Modern Science*. Garden City, N.Y.: Anchor.

Campbell, Jeremy. 1989. *The Improbable Machine: What the New Upheaval in Artificial Intelligence Reveals about How the Mind Really Works*. New York: Simon & Schuster.

Descartes, René. 1965. *The Discourse on the Method, Optics, Geometry, and Meteorology* (trans. Paul J. Olscamp). Indianapolis: Bobbs-Merrill. (Original work published 1637)

———. 1983. *Principles of Philosophy* (trans. V. R. Miller and R. P. Miller). Dordrecht: Reidel. (Original work published 1644)

Douglas, Mary. 1966. *Purity and Danger*. London: Routledge.

Dummett, Michael. 1979. "Common Sense and Physics," in G. F. MacDonald, ed., *Perception and Identity* (1-40). Ithaca, N.Y.: Cornell University Press.

Durkheim, Emile. 1951. *Suicide: A Study in Sociology* (trans. John A. Spaulding and George Simpson). New York: Free Press. (Original work published 1897)

———. 1967. *The Elementary Forms of the Religious Life* (trans. Joseph Ward Swain). New York: Free Press. (Original work published 1915)

Easlea, Brian. 1980. *Witch Hunting, Magic, and the New Philosophy: An Introduction to the Debates of the Scientific Revolution 1450-1750*. Atlantic Highlands, N.J.: Humanities.

Einstein, Albert. 1945. *Ideas and Opinions by Albert Einstein* (ed. Carl Seelig). New York: Crown.

———. 1983. *Sidelights on Relativity*. New York: Dover.

Evans-Pritchard, E. E. 1967a. "The Morphology and Function of Magic: A Comparative Study of Trobriand and Zande Ritual and Spells," in John Middleton, ed., *Magic, Witchcraft, and Curing* (1-22). Garden City, N.Y.: Natural History Press.

———. 1967b. "Some Features of Nuer Religion," in John Middleton, ed., *Gods and Rituals* (133-58). Garden City, N.Y.: Natural History Press.

———. 1970. "Witchcraft among the Azande," in Max Marwick, ed., *Witchcraft and Sorcery* (27-37). Baltimore: Penguin.

Feynman, Richard. 1964. "The Value of Science," in A. B. Arons and A. M. Bork, eds., *Science and Ideas* (3-9). Englewood Cliffs, N.J.: Prentice-Hall.

———. 1967. *The Character of Physical Law*. Cambridge: MIT Press.

Fine, Arthur. 1984. "The Natural Ontological Attitude," in Jarrett Leplin, ed., *Scientific Realism* (83-107). Berkeley: University of California Press.

Firth, Raymond. 1970. "Reason and Unreason in Human Belief," in Max Marwick, ed., *Witchcraft and Sorcery* (38-40). Baltimore: Penguin.

Freud, Sigmund. 1961. *Civilization and Its Discontents* (trans. James Strachey). New York: W. W. Norton. (Original work published 1930)

Galilei, Galileo. 1957. "The Assayer," in *Discoveries and Opinions of Galileo* (trans. Stillman Drake). Garden City, N.Y.: Anchor. (Original work published 1623)

———. 1967. *Dialogue Concerning the Two Chief World Systems* (trans. Stillman Drake). Berkeley: University of California Press. (Original work published 1632)

Gaukroger, Stephen. 1978. *Explanatory Structures*. Sussex: Harvester.

Geertz, Clifford. 1966. "Religion as a Cultural System," in Michael Banton, ed., *Anthropological Approaches to the Study of Religion* (1-46). London: Tavistock.

Gellner, Ernest. 1974. *Legitimation of Belief*. Cambridge: Cambridge University Press.

Golinski, Jan. 1988. "The Secret Life of an Alchemist," in John Fauvel, Raymond Flood, Michael Shortland, and Robin Wilson, eds., *Let Newton Be!* (147-67). New York: Oxford University Press.

Gregory, Bruce. 1990. *Inventing Reality: Physics as Language*. New York: John Wiley.

Guthrie, Stewart. 1980. "A Cognitive Theory of Religion," *Current Anthropology*, 21, 2: 181-203.

Habermas, Jürgen. 1970. *Toward a Rational Society*. Boston: Beacon.

———. 1984. *The Theory of Communicative Action, Volume 1: Reason and the Rationalization of Society* (trans. Thomas McCarthy). Boston: Beacon.

Hacking, Ian. 1983. *Representing and Intervening*. Cambridge: Cambridge University Press.

Halévy, Elie. 1955. *The Growth of Philosophic Radicalism* (trans. Mary Morris). Boston: Beacon.

Heisenberg, Werner. 1958. *Physics and Philosophy: The Revolution in Modern Physics*. New York: Harper Torchbooks.

Hobbes, Thomas. 1958. *Leviathan: Parts I and II*. Indianapolis: Bobbs-Merrill. (Original work published 1651)

Hogbin, H. Ian. 1967. "Pagan Religion in a New Guinea Village," in John Middleton, ed., *Gods and Rituals* (41-76). Garden City, N.Y.: Natural History Press.

Horton, Robin. 1967. "African Traditional Thought and Western Science" (Parts 1 and 2), *Africa* 37, 1: 50-71; 37, 2: 155-87.

_____. 1982. "Tradition and Modernity Revisited," in Martin Hollis and Steven Lukes, eds., *Rationality and Relativism* (201-60). Cambridge: MIT Press.

Jacob, Margaret. 1976. *The Newtonians and the English Revolution*. Ithaca, N.Y.: Cornell University Press.

Jeans, Sir James. 1930. *The Mysterious Universe*. New York: Macmillan.

Kline, Morris. 1980. *Mathematics and the Loss of Certainty*. Oxford: Oxford University Press.

_____. 1985. *Mathematics and the Search for Knowledge*. Oxford: Oxford University Press.

Kluckhohn, Clyde. 1970. "Navaho Witchcraft," in Max Marwick, ed., *Witchcraft and Sorcery* (217-36). Baltimore: Penguin.

Lakoff, George. 1987. *Women, Fire, and Dangerous Things: What Categories Reveal about the Mind*. Chicago: University of Chicago Press.

Lévi-Strauss, Claude. 1966. *The Savage Mind*. Chicago: University of Chicago Press.

Macpherson, C. B. 1973. *Democratic Theory: Essays in Retrieval*. Oxford: Oxford University Press.

Meyer, John W. 1986. "Myths of Socialization and Personality," in Thomas C. Heller, Morton Sosna, and David E. Wellbery, eds., *Reconstructing Individualism: Autonomy, Individuality, and the Self in Western Thought* (208-21). Stanford, Calif.: Stanford University Press.

Meyer, Philip. 1970. "Witches," in Max Marwick, ed., *Witchcraft and Sorcery* (45-64). Baltimore: Penguin.

Mill, John Stuart, and Jeremy Bentham. 1961. *The Utilitarians: Bentham and Mill*. Garden City, N.Y.: Doubleday.

Monod, Jacques. 1971. *Chance and Necessity*. New York: Vintage.

Nadel, S. F. 1970. "Witchcraft in Four African Societies," in Max Marwick, ed., *Witchcraft and Sorcery* (264-79). Baltimore: Penguin.

Newton-Smith, W. H. 1981. *The Rationality of Science*. London: Routledge.

Putnam, Hilary. 1981. *Reason, Truth, and History*. Cambridge: Cambridge University Press.

Randall, John Herman. 1940. *The Making of the Modern Mind*. Cambridge, Mass.: Houghton-Mifflin.

Reiss, Timothy J. 1982. *The Discourse of Modernism*. Ithaca, N.Y.: Cornell University Press.

Rorty, Richard. 1979. *Philosophy and the Mirror of Nature*. Princeton, N.J.: Princeton University Press.

Russell, Bertrand. 1957. *Mysticism and Logic*. Garden City, N.Y.: Anchor. (Original work published 1917)

Skorupski, John. 1976. *Symbol and Theory*. Cambridge: Cambridge University Press.

Smith, Adam. 1909. *An Inquiry into the Causes and Consequences of the Wealth of Nations*. New York: Collier. (Original work published 1776)

Spiro, Melford E. 1966. "Religion: Problems of Definition and Explanation," in Michael Banton, ed., *Anthropological Approaches to the Study of Religion* (85-126). London: Tavistock.

Trigg, Roger. 1980. *Reality at Risk: A Defense of Realism in Philosophy and the Sciences*. Sussex: Harvester.

Turner, Victor. 1968. *The Drums of Affliction*. Oxford: Clarendon.

van Fraassen, C. Bas. 1984. "To Save the Phenomena," in Jarrett Leplin, ed., *Scientific Realism* (250–60). Berkeley: University of California Press.

von Weizsäcker, C. F. 1973. "Physics and Philosophy," in Jagdish Mehra, ed., *The Physicist's Conception of Nature*. Dordrecht: Reidel.

Wavell, Bruce. 1986. *Language and Reason*. Berlin: Mouton de Gruyter.

Weber, Max. 1958. *From Max Weber* (eds. H. H. Gerth and C. Wright Mills). New York: Oxford University Press.

Weinberg, Stephen. 1977. *The First Three Minutes*. New York: Basic Books.

Wigner, Eugene. 1967. *Symmetries and Reflections*. Bloomington: Indiana University Press.

Zuboff, Shoshana. 1988. *In the Age of the Smart Machine: The Future of Work and Power*. New York: Basic Books.

General Bibliography

Adorno, Theodor W. 1976. "Cultural Criticism and Society," in Paul Connerton, ed., *Critical Sociology* (258–76). New York: Penguin.

Alford, Robert R., and Roger Friedland. 1985. *Powers of Theory*. Cambridge: Cambridge University Press.

Allman, William F. 1989. *Apprentices of Wonder: Reinventing the Mind*. New York: Bantam.

Ambrose, Alice. 1967. "Linguistic Approaches to Philosophical Problems," in Richard Rorty, ed., *The Linguistic Turn: Recent Essays in Philosophical Method* (147–55). Chicago: University of Chicago Press.

Aribib, Michael A. 1985. *In Search of the Person: Philosophical Explorations in Cognitive Science*. Amherst: University of Massachusetts Press.

Aristotle. 1947. *Introduction to Aristotle* (ed. Richard McKeon). New York: Modern Library.

Aronowitz, Stanley. 1988. *Science as Power*. Minneapolis: University of Minnesota Press.

Austin, J. L. 1965. *How to Do Things with Words* (ed. J. O. Urmson). New York: Oxford University Press.

Baker, Keith Michael. 1975. *Condorcet: From Natural Philosophy to Social Mathematics*. Chicago: University of Chicago Press.

Baldamus, W. 1984. "Epistemology and Mathematics," in Nico Stehr and Volker Meja, eds., *Society and Knowledge: Contemporary Perspective in the Sociology of Knowledge* (349–64). New Brunswick, N.J.: Transaction.

Barnes, Barry. 1975. *Scientific Knowledge and Sociological Theory*. London: Routledge.

_____. 1985. *About Science*. Oxford: Basil Blackwell.

Berman, Morris. 1981. *The Reenchantment of the World*. Ithaca, N.Y.: Cornell University Press.

Blackstone, William T., ed. 1974. *Philosophy and Environmental Crisis*. Athens: University of Georgia Press.

Bloor, David. 1976. *Knowledge and Social Imagery*. London: Routledge.

_____. 1983. *Wittgenstein: A Social Theory of Knowledge*. London: Macmillan.

Bohm, David. 1980. *Wholeness and the Implicate Order*. Boston: Routledge.

Bolter, J. David. 1984. *Turing's Man: Western Culture in the Computer Age*. Chapel Hill: University of North Carolina Press.

Bookchin, Murray. 1982. *The Ecology of Freedom*. Palo Alto, Calif.: Cheshire.

_____. 1990. *Remaking Society: Pathways to a Green Future*. Boston: South End.

Bos, H. J. M. 1980. "Mathematics and Rational Mechanics," in G. S. Rousseau and Roy Porter, eds., *The Ferment of Knowledge: Studies in the Historiography of Eighteenth Century Science* (327–56). Cambridge: Cambridge University Press.

Brodbeck, May. 1968. "Meaning and Action," in P. H. Nidditch, ed., *The Philosophy of Science* (97-120). London: Oxford University Press.

Burke, Kenneth. 1945. *A Grammar of Motives*. Berkeley: University of California Press.

Butterfield, Herbert. 1965. *The Origins of Modern Science*. New York: Free Press.

Carnap, Rudolf. 1967. "On the Character of Philosophical Problems" in Richard Rorty, ed., *The Linguistic Turn: Recent Essays in Philosophical Method* (54-62). Chicago: University of Chicago Press.

Carrithers, Michael, Steven Collins, and Steven Lukes, eds. 1985. *The Category of the Person: Anthropology, Philosophy, History*. Cambridge: Cambridge University Press.

Casti, John L. 1989. *Paradigms Lost: Images of Man in the Mirror of Science*. New York: Morrow.

Chomsky, Noam. 1965. *Aspects of the Theory of Syntax*. Cambridge: MIT Press.

Churchland, Paul M. 1979. *Scientific Realism and the Plasticity of Mind*. Cambridge: Cambridge University Press.

Clagett, Marshall, ed. 1969. *Critical Problems in the History of Science*. Madison: University of Wisconsin Press.

Clark, Mary E. 1989. *Ariadne's Thread: The Search for New Modes of Thinking*. New York: St. Martin's.

Collingwood, R. G. 1945. *The Idea of Nature*. London: Oxford University Press.

Commoner, Barry. 1971. *The Closing Circle*. New York: Bantam.

_____. 1990. *Making Peace with the Planet*. New York: Pantheon.

Connerton, Paul, ed. 1976. *Critical Sociology*. New York: Penguin.

Cornman, James W. 1975. *Perception, Common Sense, and Science*. New Haven, Conn.: Yale University Press.

Corradi, Juan E. 1984. "On Culture and Power: The Modern Husbandry of Knowledge," in Nico Stehr and Volker Meja, eds., *Society and Knowledge: Contemporary Perspective in the Sociology of Knowledge* (293-310). New Brunswick, N.J.: Transaction.

Crozier, Michel. 1964. *The Bureaucratic Phenomenon*. Chicago: University of Chicago Press.

Danto, Arthur, and Sidney Morgenbesser, eds. 1960. *Philosophy of Science*. New York: New American Library.

Davies, Paul. 1980. *Other Worlds*. New York: Simon & Schuster.

Dearden, R. F., P. H. Hirst, and R. S. Peters. 1972. *Reason: Part 2 of Education and the Development of Reason*. Boston: Routledge.

Debus, Allen G. 1978. *Man and Nature in the Renaissance*. Cambridge: Cambridge University Press.

Deloria, Vine, Jr. 1979. *The Metaphysics of Modern Existence*. San Francisco: Harper & Row.

_____. 1973. *God Is Red*. New York: Dell.

Dennett, Daniel. 1976. "Conditions of Personhood," in Amelie Oksenberg Rorty, ed., *The Identities of Persons* (175-96). Berkeley: University of California Press.

Devall, Bill, and George Sessions. 1985. *Deep Ecology: Living as if Nature Mattered*. Salt Lake City: Peregrine Smith.

Dijksterhuis, E. J. 1969. "The Origins of Classical Mechanics from Aristotle to Newton," in Marshall Clagett, ed., *Critical Problems in the History of Science* (163-84). Madison: University of Wisconsin Press.

Dryzek, John S. 1987. *Rational Ecology: Environment and Political Economy*. Oxford: Basil Blackwell.

Dumont, Louis. 1985. "A Modified View of Our Origins: the Christian Beginnings of Modern Individualism," in Michael Carrithers, Steven Collins, and Steven Lukes, eds., *The Category of the Person: Anthropology, Philosophy, History* (93-122). Cambridge: Cambridge University Press.

Durkheim, Emile. 1966. *The Rules of the Sociological Method* (trans. Sarah A. Solovay and John H. Mueller; ed. George G. Catlin). New York: Free Press. (Original work published 1938)

Einstein, Albert, and Leopold Infeld. 1951. *The Evolution of Physics.* New York: Simon & Schuster.

Ellul, Jacques. 1964. *The Technological Society* (trans. John Wilkinson). New York: Knopf.

Elvee, Richard Q. 1982. *Mind in Nature.* San Francisco: Harper & Row.

Etzioni, Amitai. 1961. *A Comparative Analysis of Complex Organizations.* New York: Free Press.

Farrington, Benjamin. 1944. *Greek Science.* Baltimore: Penguin.

Feyerband, Paul. 1975. *Against Method.* London: NLB.

———. 1978. *Science in a Free Society.* London: NLB.

Flew, Andrew, ed. 1965. *Logic and Language* (1st and 2nd series). Garden City, N.Y.: Anchor.

Fodor, Jerry. 1979. *Language and Thought.* Cambridge, Mass.: Harvard University Press.

Foucault, Michel. 1970. *The Order of Things: An Archaeology of the Human Sciences.* New York: Vintage.

———. 1972. *The Archeology of Knowledge and the Discourse on Language* (trans. A. M. Sheridan Smith). New York: Pantheon.

———. 1978. *The History of Sexuality, Volume 1: An Introduction* (trans. Robert Hurley). New York: Vintage.

Freudenthal, Gideon. 1986. *Atom and Individual in the Age of Newton: On the Genesis of the Mechanistic World View.* Dordrecht: Reidel.

Gadamer, Hans-Georg. 1976. "The Historicity of Understanding," in Paul Connerton, ed., *Critical Sociology* (117-33). New York: Penguin.

Gasking, Douglas. 1965. "Mathematics and the World," in Andrew Flew, *Logic and Language* (427-45). Garden City, N.Y.: Anchor.

Geertz, Clifford. 1973. *The Interpretation of Cultures.* New York: Basic Books.

Geymonat, Ludovico. 1965. *Galileo Galilei.* New York: McGraw-Hill.

Glacken, Clarence J. 1967. *Traces on the Rhodian Shore.* Berkeley: University of California Press.

Goldsmith, M. M. 1966. *Hobbes's Science of Politics.* New York: Columbia University Press.

Gorz, André. 1980. *Ecology as Politics* (trans. Patsy Vigderman and Jonathan Cloud). Boston: South End.

Greene, Marjorie. 1974. *The Knower and the Known.* Berkeley: University of California Press.

Gribben, John. 1984. *In Search of Schrodinger's Cat: Quantum Physics and Reality.* New York: Bantam.

Griffiths, A. Phillips, ed. 1967. *Knowledge and Belief.* London: Oxford University Press.

Habermas, Jürgen. 1970. *Toward a Rational Society: Student Protest, Science, and Politics* (trans. Jeremy J. Shapiro). Boston: Beacon.

———. 1970. "On Systematically Distorted Communication," *Inquiry,* 13: 205-18.

———. 1970. "Towards a Theory of Communicative Competence," *Inquiry,* 13: 360-75.

———. 1979. *Communication and the Evolution of Society.* Boston: Beacon.

Hall, John A. 1985. *Powers and Liberties: The Causes and Consequences of the Rise of the West.* Berkeley: University of California Press.

Hammersley, J. M. 1974. "The Technology of Thought," in Jerzy Neyman ed., *The Heritage of Copernicus: Theories "More Pleasing to the Mind"* (394-415). Cambridge: MIT Press.

Hampshire, Stuart. 1967. "The Interpretation of Language: Words and Concepts," in Richard Rorty, ed., *The Linguistic Turn: Recent Essays in Philosophical Method* (261-68). Chicago: University of Chicago Press.

Hanson, Norwood Russell. 1960. "The Copenhagen Interpretation of Quantum Theory," in Arthur Danto and Sidney Morgenbesser, eds., *Philosophy of Science* (450-70). New York: New American Library.

————. 1961. *Patterns of Discovery: An Inquiry into the Conceptual Foundations of Science.* Cambridge: Cambridge University Press.

Harding, Sandra. 1986. *The Science Question in Feminism.* Ithaca, N.Y.: Cornell University Press.

Hare, R. M. 1985. "Liberty and Equality: How Politics Masquerades as Philosophy," in Ellen Frankel Paul, Fred D. Miller, and Jeffery Paul, eds., *Liberty and Equality* (1-11). Oxford: Basil Blackwell.

Harre, Rom. 1980. "Knowledge," in G. S. Rousseau and Roy Porter, eds., *The Ferment of Knowledge: Studies in the Historiography of Eighteenth-Century Science.* Cambridge: Cambridge University Press.

Hattiangadi, J. N. 1987. *How Is Language Possible? Philosophical Reflections on the Evolution of Language and Knowledge.* La Salle, Ill.: Open Court.

Heisenberg, Werner. 1971. *Physics and Beyond: Encounters and Conversations* (trans. Arnold J. Pomerans). New York: Harper Torchbooks.

Held, David. 1980. *Introduction to Critical Theory: Horkheimer to Habermas.* Berkeley: University of California Press.

Hempel, Carl G. 1956. "On the Nature of Mathematical Truth," in James R. Newman, ed., *The World of Mathematics* (1619-34). New York: Simon & Schuster.

Hessen, Bernard. 1974. "The Social and Economic Roots of Newton's 'Principia,' " in Willis H. Truitt and T. W. Graham Solomons, eds., *Science, Technology, and Freedom* (89-99). Boston: Houghton Mifflin.

Hirschhorn, Larry. 1984. *Beyond Mechanization: Work and Technology in a Postindustrial Age.* Cambridge: MIT Press.

Hirschman, Albert O. 1977. *The Passions and the Interests: Political Arguments for Capitalism before Its Triumph.* Princeton, N.J.: Princeton University Press.

Hoffmann, Banesh. 1947. *The Strange Story of the Quantum.* New York: Dover.

Hofstadter, Douglas R. 1979. *Godel, Escher, Bach: An Eternal Golden Braid.* New York: Basic Books.

Horkheimer, Max. 1974. *Eclipse of Reason.* New York: Seabury. (Original work published 1947)

Hubner, Kurt. 1983. *Critique of Scientific Reason* (trans. Paul R. Dixon, Jr., and Hollis M. Dixon). Chicago: University of Chicago Press.

Hughes, H. Stuart. 1958. *Consciousness and Society.* New York: Vintage.

Jacob, François. 1973. *The Logic of Life: A History of Heredity* (trans. Betty E. Spillman). New York: Vintage.

Jacob, Margaret C. 1988. *The Cultural Meaning of the Scientific Revolution.* New York: Knopf.

Jahn, Robert G., and Brenda J. Dunne, eds. 1984. *On the Quantum Mechanics of Consciousness with Application to Anomalous Phenomena* (rev. ed.). Princeton, N.J.: Princeton Engineering Anomalies Research Laboratory.

Johnson, Michael L. 1988. *Mind, Language, and Machine: Artificial Intelligence in the Poststructuralist Age.* New York: St. Martin's.

Jones, Robert Allen, and Henrika Kuklick, eds. 1981. *Knowledge and Society: Studies in the Sociology of Culture Past and Present* (Vol. 3). Greenwich, Conn.: JAI.

Katz, Jerrold J. 1967. "The Philosophical Relevance of Linguistic Theory," in Richard Rorty, ed., *The Linguistic Turn: Recent Essays in Philosophical Method* (340-55). Chicago: University of Chicago Press.

_____. 1981. *Language and Other Abstract Objects*. Lanham, Md.: Rowman.

_____. 1986. *Cogitations: A Study of the Cogito in Relation to the Philosophy of Logic and Language, and a Study of Their Relation to the Cogito*. Oxford: Oxford University Press.

Kearney, Hugh F. 1964. *Origins of the Scientific Revolution*. New York: Barnes & Noble.

Keller, Evelyn Fox. 1979. "Cognitive Repression in Contemporary Physics," *American Journal of Physics*, 47, 8: 718-21.

_____. 1980. "Baconian Science: A Hermaphroditic Birth," *Philosophical Forum*, 11, 3: 299-308.

_____. 1985. *Reflections on Gender and Science*. New Haven, Conn.: Yale University Press.

Klaaren, Eugene M. 1977. *Religious Origins of Modern Science: Belief in Creation in Seventeenth Century Thought*. Grand Rapids, Mich.: Eerdmans.

Kripke, Saul. 1977. "Identity and Necessity," in Stephen P. Schwartz, ed., *Naming, Necessity, and Natural Kinds* (66-101). Ithaca, N.Y.: Cornell University Press.

Kristol, William. 1985. "Liberty, Equality, Honor," in Ellen Frankel Paul, Fred D. Miller, and Jeffery Paul, eds., *Liberty and Equality* (125-40). Oxford: Basil Blackwell.

Kuhn, Thomas S. 1970. *The Structure of Scientific Revolutions* (2nd ed.). Chicago: University of Chicago Press.

_____. 1977. *The Essential Tension: Selected Studies in Scientific Tradition and Change*. Chicago: University of Chicago Press.

La Fontaine, J. S. 1985. "Person and Individual: Some Anthropological Reflections," in Michael Carrithers, Steven Collins, and Steven Lukes, eds., *The Category of the Person: Anthropology, Philosophy, History* (123-40). Cambridge: Cambridge University Press.

Lakatos, Imre, and Alan Musgrave. 1970. *Criticism and the Growth of Knowledge*. Cambridge: Cambridge University Press.

Lakoff, George. 1980. *Metaphors We Live By*. Chicago: University of Chicago Press.

Langford, Jerome J. 1966. *Galileo, Science, and the Church* (rev. ed.). Ann Arbor: University of Michigan Press.

Lehrer, Keith. 1974. *Knowledge*. London: Oxford University Press.

Leiss, William. 1972. *The Domination of Nature*. Boston: Beacon.

Lenski, Gerhard. 1966. *Power and Privilege: A Theory of Social Stratification*. New York: McGraw-Hill.

Lentricchia, Frank. 1983. *Criticism and Social Change*. Chicago: University of Chicago Press.

Lévi-Strauss, Claude. 1963. *Structural Anthropology* (trans. Claire Jacobson and Brooke Grundfest Schoepf). Garden City, N.Y.: Anchor.

Llobera, Joseph R. 1981. "The Enlightenment and Adam Smith's Conception of Science," in Robert Allen Jones and Henrika Kuklick, eds., *Knowledge and Society: Studies in the Sociology of Culture Past and Present* (Vol. 3) (109-36). Greenwich, Conn.: JAI.

Lovejoy, Arthur O. 1960. *The Great Chain of Being: A Study in the History of an Idea*. New York: Harper & Row.

Lovins, Amory. 1977. *Soft Energy Paths: Toward a Durable Peace*. New York: Harper Colophon.

Luhmann, Niklas. 1989. *Ecological Communication* (trans. John Bednarz, Jr.). Chicago: University of Chicago Press.

Lukes, Steven. 1970. "Some Problems about Rationality," in Bryan R. Wilson, ed., *Rationality* (194-213). New York: Harper & Row.

_____. 1973. *Individualism*. New York: Harper & Row.

Luria, S. E. 1973. *Life: The Unfinished Experiment*. New York: Scribner's.

Lyotard, Jean-François. 1984. *The Postmodern Condition: A Report on Knowledge* (trans. Geoff Bennington and Brian Massumi). Minneapolis: University of Minnesota Press.

MacIntyre, Alasdair. 1966. *A Short History of Ethics*. New York: Macmillan.

———. 1970. "The Idea of a Social Science," in Bryan R. Wilson, ed., *Rationality* (112-30). New York: Harper & Row.

———. 1981. *After Virtue*. Notre Dame, Ind.: University of Notre Dame Press.

MacLane, Saunders. 1981. "Mathematical Models: A Sketch for the Philosophy of Mathematics," *American Mathematical Monthly* (August-September): 462-72.

Macpherson, C. B. 1962. *The Political Theory of Possessive Individualism: Hobbes to Locke*. London: Oxford University Press.

Malcolm, Norman. 1967. "Knowledge and Belief," in A. Phillips Griffiths, ed., *Knowledge and Belief* (69-81). London: Oxford University Press.

Marcuse, Herbert. 1964. *One-Dimensional Man: Studies in the Ideology of Advanced Industrial Society*. Boston: Beacon.

———. 1969. *An Essay on Liberation*. London: Penguin.

Margolis, Joseph. 1978. *Persons and Minds: The Prospects of Nonreductive Materialism*. Dordrecht: Reidel.

Maturana, Humberto R., and Francisco J. Varela. 1980. *Autopoiesis and Cognition: The Realization of the Living*. Dordrecht: Reidel.

Mauss, Marcel. 1985. "A Category of the Human Mind: The Notion of Person; the Notion of Self" (trans. W. D. Hollis), in Michael Carrithers, Steven Collins, and Steven Lukes, eds., *The Category of the Person: Anthropology, Philosophy, History* (1-25). Cambridge: Cambridge University Press.

McCarthy, T. A. 1976. "A Theory of Communicative Competence," in Paul Connerton, ed., *Critical Sociology* (470-97). New York: Penguin.

———. 1982. "Rationality and Relativism: Habermas's 'Overcoming' of Hermeneutics," in John B. Thompson and David Held, eds., *Habermas: The Critical Debates* (57-78). Cambridge: MIT Press.

McMullin, Ernan. 1978. *Newton on Matter and Activity*. Notre Dame, Ind.: University of Notre Dame Press.

Mead, George H. 1962. *Mind, Self, and Society* (ed. Charles W. Morris). Chicago: University of Chicago Press. (Original work published 1934)

Mehra, Jagdish. 1974. *The Quantum Principle: Its Interpretation and Epistemology*. Dordrecht: Reidel.

Merton, Robert. 1970. *Science, Technology, and Society in Seventeenth Century England*. New York: Harper & Row.

Monan, J. Donald. 1968. *Moral Knowledge and Its Methodology in Aristotle*. London: Oxford University Press.

Mulkay, Michael. 1979. *Science and the Sociology of Knowledge*. London: Allen & Unwin.

Nagel, Ernest. 1968. "The Structure of Teleological Explanations," in P. H. Nidditch, ed., *The Philosophy of Science* (80-96). London: Oxford University Press.

Newman, James R., ed. 1956. *The World of Mathematics*. New York: Simon & Schuster.

Neyman, Jerzy, ed. 1974. *The Heritage of Copernicus: Theories "More Pleasing to the Mind."* Cambridge: MIT Press.

Nidditch, P. H., ed. 1968. *The Philosophy of Science*. London: Oxford University Press.

Noble, David. 1977. *America by Design*. New York: Knopf.

O'Briant, Walter H. 1974. "Man, Nature, and the History of Philosophy," in William T. Blackstone, ed., *Philosophy and Environmental Crisis* (79-89). Atlanta: University of Georgia Press.

Ophuls, William. 1977. *Ecology and the Politics of Scarcity*. San Francisco: Freeman.

Pacey, Arnold. 1983. *The Culture of Technology*. Cambridge: MIT Press.

Pagels, Heinz R. 1982. *The Cosmic Code*. New York: Simon & Schuster.

Papineau, David. 1979. *Theory and Meaning*. Oxford: Oxford University Press.

Paul, Ellen Frankel, Fred D. Miller, and Jeffery Paul, eds. 1985. *Liberty and Equality*. Oxford: Basil Blackwell.

Perrolle, Judith. 1987. *Computers and Social Change: Information, Property, and Power*. Belmont, Calif.: Wadsworth.

Perrow, Charles. 1972. *Complex Organizations: A Critical Essay*. New York: Random House.

Petersen, Aage. 1968. *Quantum Physics and the Philosophical Tradition*. Cambridge: MIT Press.

Pickering, Andrew. 1984. *Constructing Quarks*. Chicago: University of Chicago Press.

Piore, Michael J., and Charles F. Sabel. 1984. *The Second Industrial Divide*. New York: Basic Books.

Pitkin, Hanna Fenichel. 1972. *Wittgenstein and Justice*. Berkeley: University of California Press.

Polanyi, Karl. 1957. *The Great Transformation: The Political and Economic Origins of Our Time*. Boston: Beacon. (Original work published 1944)

Porritt, Jonathon. 1985. *Seeing Green: The Politics of Ecology Explained*. Oxford: Basil Blackwell.

Powers, Jonathan. 1982. *Philosophy and the New Physics*. New York: Metheun.

Price, Derek J. de S. 1969. "Contra-Copernicus: A Critical Re-estimation of the Mathematical Planetary Theory of Ptolemy, Copernicus, and Kepler," in Marshall Clagett, ed., *Critical Problems in the History of Science* (197-218). Madison: University of Wisconsin Press.

Prichard, H. A. 1967. "Knowing and Believing," in A. Phillips Griffiths, ed., *Knowledge and Belief* (60-68). London: Oxford University Press.

Putnam, Hilary. 1978. *Meaning and the Moral Sciences*. Boston: Routledge.

Quine, Willard V. O. 1960. *Word and Object*. Cambridge: MIT Press.

————. 1981. *Theories and Things*. Cambridge, Mass.: Harvard University Press.

Reed, Michael. 1985. *Redirections in Organizational Analysis*. London: Tavistock.

Rescher, Nicholas. 1974. "The Environmental Crisis and the Quality of Life," in William T. Blackstone, ed., *Philosophy and Environmental Crisis* (90-104). Atlanta: University of Georgia Press.

Rorty, Amelie Oksenberg, ed., 1976. *The Identities of Persons*. Berkeley: University of California Press.

Rorty, Richard, ed. 1967. *The Linguistic Turn: Recent Essays in Philosophical Method*. Chicago: University of Chicago Press.

Rousseau, G. S., and Roy Porter, eds. 1980. *The Ferment of Knowledge: Studies in the Historiography of Eighteenth-Century Science*. Cambridge: Cambridge University Press.

Rumelhart, David E., James L. McClelland, and the PDP Research Group. 1986. *Parallel Distributed Processing: Explorations in the Microstructure of Cognition* (2 vols.). Cambridge: MIT Press.

Ruse, Michael. 1979. *The Darwinian Revolution: Science Red in Tooth and Claw*. Chicago: University of Chicago Press.

Russell, Bertrand. 1945. *A History of Western Philosophy*. New York: Simon & Schuster.

Ryle, Gilbert. 1949. *The Concept of Mind*. New York: Barnes & Noble.

Sahlins, Marshall. 1976. *Culture and Practical Reason*. Chicago: University of Chicago Press.

Sandel, Michael J. 1982. *Liberalism and the Limits of Justice*. Cambridge: Cambridge University Press.

Scheffler, Israel. 1967. *Science and Subjectivity*. Indianapolis: Bobbs-Merrill.

Schmidt, Alfred. 1971. *The Concept of Nature in Marx*. London: NLB.

Schnaiberg, Allan. 1980. *The Environment: From Surplus to Scarcity*. New York: Oxford University Press.

Schwartz, Barry. 1986. *The Battle for Human Nature: Science, Morality, and Modern Life*. New York: Norton.

Schwartz, Stephen P., ed. 1977. *Naming, Necessity, and Natural Kinds*. Ithaca, N.Y.: Cornell University Press.

Searle, John. 1969. *Speech Acts: An Essay in the Philosophy of Language*. Cambridge: Cambridge University Press.

Shapere, Dudley. 1974. *Galileo: A Philosophical Study*. Chicago: University of Chicago Press.

Shoemaker, Sydney. 1976. "Embodiment and Behavior," in Amelie Oksenberg Rorty, ed., *The Identities of Persons* (109-38). Berkeley: University of California Press.

Stanley, Manfred. 1978. *The Technological Conscience: Survival and Dignity in an Age of Expertise*. Chicago: University of Chicago Press.

Stapp, Henry P. 1985. "Consciousness and Values in the Quantum Universe," *Foundations of Physics*, 15, 1: 35-47.

Stehr, Nico, and Volker Meja, eds. 1984. *Society and Knowledge: Contemporary Perspective in the Sociology of Knowledge*. New Brunswick, N.J.: Transaction.

Stent, Gunther. 1969. *The Coming of the Golden Age*. New York: Museum of Natural History.

———. 1978. *Paradoxes of Progress*. San Francisco: Freeman.

Stone, Christopher D. 1987. *Earth and Other Ethics: The Case for Moral Pluralism*. New York: Harper & Row.

Stout, Jeffery. 1981. *The Flight from Authority: Religion, Authority, and the Quest for Autonomy*. Notre Dame, Ind.: University of Notre Dame Press.

Strawson, P. F. 1959. *Individuals: An Essay in Descriptive Metaphysics*. Garden City, N.Y.: Anchor.

Stretton, Hugh. 1976. *Capitalism, Socialism, and the Environment*. Cambridge: Cambridge University Press.

Suppe, Frederick, ed. 1977. *The Structure of Scientific Theories* (2nd ed.). Urbana: University of Illinois Press.

Swanson, Guy E. 1960. *The Birth of the Gods: The Origin of Primitive Beliefs*. Ann Arbor: University of Michigan Press.

Taylor, A. E. 1955. *Aristotle*. New York: Dover.

Taylor, Charles. 1985. "The Person," in Michael Carrithers, Steven Collins, and Steven Lukes, eds., *The Category of the Person: Anthropology, Philosophy, History* (257-81). Cambridge: Cambridge University Press.

Thompson, John B. 1982. "Universal Pragmatics," in John B. Thompson and David Held, eds., *Habermas: The Critical Debates* (116-33). Cambridge: MIT Press.

———, and David Held, eds. 1982. *Habermas: The Critical Debates*. Cambridge: MIT Press.

Tocqueville, Alexis de. 1945. *Democracy in America* (2 vols.). New York: Vintage.

Todd, Alexandra Dundas. 1989. *Intimate Adversaries*. Philadelphia: University of Pennsylvania Press.

Truitt, Willis H., and T. W. Graham Solomons, eds. 1974. *Science, Technology, and Freedom*. Boston: Houghton Mifflin.

Turnbull, Colin M. 1983. *The Human Cycle*. New York: Simon & Schuster.

Turner, Bryan. 1986. *Equality*. London: Tavistock.

Viner, Jacob. 1972. *The Role of Providence in the Social Order: An Essay in Intellectual History*. Princeton, N.J.: Princeton University Press.

Volti, Rudi. 1988. *Society and Technological Change*. New York: St. Martin's.

von Mises, Richard. 1956. "Mathematical Postulates and Human Understanding," in James R. Newman, ed., *The World of Mathematics* (1723-55). New York: Simon & Schuster.

Vygotsky, Lev S. 1962. *Thought and Language* (trans. Eugenia Hanfmann and Gertrude Vakar). Cambridge: MIT Press.

Wartofsky, Marx W. 1974. "Is Science Rational?" in Willis H. Truitt and T. W. Graham Solomons, eds., *Science, Technology, and Freedom* (202-9). Boston: Houghton Mifflin.

Watson, James D. 1968. *The Double Helix*. New York: New American Library.

Weber, Max. 1958. *The Protestant Ethic and the Spirit of Capitalism*. New York: Scribner's.

Westfall, Richard. 1958. *Science and Religion in Seventeenth Century England*. Ann Arbor: University of Michigan Press.

_____. 1977. *The Construction of Modern Physics: Mechanisms and Mechanics*. Cambridge: Cambridge University Press.

Weyl, Hermann. 1956. "The Mathematical Way of Thinking," in James R. Newman, ed., *The World of Mathematics* (1832-51). New York: Simon & Schuster.

White, Leslie. 1956. "The Locus of Mathematical Reality: An Anthropological Footnote," in James R. Newman, ed., *The World of Mathematics* (2348-65). New York: Simon & Schuster.

Whitehead, Alfred North. 1925. *Science and the Modern World*. New York: Mentor.

Whorf, Benjamin L. 1956. *Language, Thought, and Reality: Selected Writings of Benjamin Lee Whorf* (ed. John B. Carroll). Cambridge: MIT Press.

Wiggins, David. 1976. "Locke, Butler, and the Stream of Consciousness: And Men as Natural Kinds," in Amelie Oksenberg Rorty, ed., *The Identities of Persons* (139-74). Berkeley: University of California Press.

Williams, L. Pearce. 1969. "The Politics of Science in the French Revolution," in Marshall Clagett, ed., *Critical Problems in the History of Science* (291-308). Madison: University of Wisconsin Press.

Wilson, Bryan R., ed. 1970. *Rationality*. New York: Harper & Row.

Winch, Peter. 1958. *The Idea of a Social Science*. London: Routledge.

_____. 1970. "Understanding a Primitive Society," in Bryan R. Wilson, ed., *Rationality* (78-111). New York: Harper & Row.

Winner, Langdon. 1977. *Autonomous Technology*. Cambridge: MIT Press.

Wisdom, John. 1965. "Gods," in Andrew Flew, ed., *Logic and Language* (194-216). Garden City, N.Y.: Anchor.

Wittgenstein, Ludwig. 1958. *Philosophical Investigations*. New York: Macmillan.

Wolff, Robert Paul. 1968. *The Poverty of Liberalism*. Boston: Beacon.

Wolgast, Elizabeth H. 1987. *The Grammar of Justice*. Ithaca, N.Y.: Cornell University Press.

Wright, Will. 1975. *Sixguns and Society: A Structural Study of the Western*. Berkeley: University of California Press.

_____. 1982. *The Social Logic of Health*. New Brunswick, N.J.: Rutgers University Press.

Index

Will Wright is associate professor of sociology at the University of Southern Colorado. He holds an M.A. in mathematics and a Ph.D. in sociology from the University of California at Berkeley and is the author of *Sixguns and Society: A Structural Study of the Western* (1975) and *The Social Logic of Health* (1982).